THE GREEK GIFT

THE GREEK GIFT:
politics in a
Cypriot village

by
PETER LOIZOS

Lecturer in Social Anthropology, London School of
Economics and Political Science, University of London

ST. MARTIN'S PRESS · NEW YORK

© Peter Loizos 1975

AFFILIATED PUBLISHERS: Macmillan Limited, London
also at Bombay, Calcutta, Madras and Melbourne

12-19-78

to the unfortunate people of Cyprus

Contents

Tables

Figures

Appendices

Plates

Acknowledgements

Debts can be diffuse or specific; I owe a lot to early teachers:
Dave Alman, C. D. Baggley, Jack Borland, J. A. Crook, Donald
Davie, H. S. Davies, A. A. J. Foster, Pat Hazard, G. C. Homans,
Laurie Jagger, David McClelland, Robert N. Rapaport, Gilbert
Seldes, Philip Vellacott.

More specific thanks are due to Sir Raymond Firth for strong
early encouragement, to my supervisor Anthony Forge for
criticism always welcome and incisive, to Mike Attalides for
many valuable discussions and endless generosity in Cyprus, to
Edward Hammonds for an education in politics, to Peter Hellier
for generosity with hard-earned knowledge, to Lionel Caplan for
helpful comments, to J. K. Campbell, J. Davis and F. G. Bailey
for thorough criticisms, to Delilah and Menachem Amir and to
Maria Inez Ribeiro da Fonseca for their friendship, to Herb
Gans whose scepticism was bracing, and to Caroline Moller
for patience, affection and much more while this was being
written.

I have an intellectual debt to three writers whose books made
my own work much easier if inevitably derivative—F. G. Bailey,
J. K. Campbell and J. A. Pitt-Rivers. If their work is cited less
often than their influence merits this is to avoid repetition, not to
conceal priority.

My thanks to the four ladies who have typed various drafts:
Mrs. Margery Alfandary, Mrs. Pat Blair, Mrs. Hilda Jarrett, Mrs.
Joan Wells; and to staff of the Drawing Office and the Photo-
graphic Unit at the L.S.E. My thanks also to Carla Wartenberg
for reading a German source.

Before, during and after the major fieldwork on which this
book is based I was supported most generously by the Social
Science Research Council. For two shorter subsequent trips to
Cyprus I am grateful to the Nuffield Foundation.

My family, friends and co-villagers from 'Kalo' must be thanked
collectively and anonymously, which they may or may not regret
but they know that to name one is to name all. I hope nothing in
this book causes them to regret helping and encouraging me. All
errors or inadequacies are, of course, entirely my own.

Author's Note

Throughout this book I write of 'villagers' and to Greek-speaking readers a word of explanation is needed. *The Oxford Dictionary of Modern Greek* renders the word *choriádis* as 'peasant, countryman, (fig.) boor'. In Cyprus the dialect version of this word, *chorgkádis* is often used by townsmen and countrymen to suggest the last meaning. But when I write in English of 'villagers' I mean the word to have no such overtones but merely to mean someone who lives in a village, for which the Demotic Greek word might be *chorikós*.

I have opted for no particular system of rendering Greek words. One characteristic of Cypriot Greek dialect is that stress occurs in many words at a different position from that of mainland Greek. I have usually spelled words to get close to Kalo village dialect; nor have I been concerned to distinguish accent marks for orthographic reasons. In this book where stress marks are used they are as a guide to pronunciation only.

Since the village is 'Kalo', then a member of the village will be a Kalo*tis*, and members of it will be Kalo*tes*. For some other villages -itis (sing.) and -ites (plural) are used.

This book is a shortened, revised version of a thesis I wrote for the Ph.D. in the University of London, 1972, called *Social Organisation and Political Change in a Cypriot Village*. In particular much material on social organization has been left out of chapters 2–5.

At the time of my fieldwork the Cypriot £ was exchanged at par with £ sterling. Throughout this book when *donum* is used, this is the government *donum*, about one-third of an acre, or roughly one seventh of a hectare.

This book deals with events up to summer 1970, and the final draft was written during 1972–3. It does not take account of the anti-Makarios coup, led by Greek army officers, in July 1974, nor of the subsequent Turkish invasion. In September 1974, the people of Kalo were refugees, facing a desperately uncertain future.

Dramatis Personae

1. *Sklyros*

Age 46; 4 children, 30 *donums*, left, on village AKEL committee (p. 110) and many other leadership posts. One child studying in U.S.S.R. Related to (2)–(6) below.

2. *Vourros*

Age 43; 3 children; over 70 *donums*; unaligned. Nicosia resident, with very large land holdings in Kalo. Born in Kammari, his wife the only child of a wealthy Kalo farmer. Has English university degree, teaches in a private school. Continuously active in Kalo affairs, and often chosen to represent the village in external matters. Believes in rationality, progress, science, fair play, rule of law. His wife is first cousin to (1) and (4) and second cousin to (5) and (6).

3. *Patris*

Age about 47; 7 children, well over 100 *donums* (see Appendix 4). Moderate right-wing leader, village PEK representative; for many years the village leader most likely to oppose Sklyros. His oldest daughter is married to:

4. *D. Fanos*

Age 34; 2 children, 15 *donums*; formerly with left-wing nationalist leader Lyssarides (12), but in recent years has re-aligned himself with right-nationalist leader Azinas (10), and the PF party. His wife's father (3) has no sons, and D. Fanos is very close to him. A secondary school graduate, he now has a middle-range civil service post in the Co-operative Department. A rising young man in the village.

5. *Dhaskalos*

Age 33; 1 child, 31 *donums*; right-nationalist school teacher whose exact alignment with national leaders remains unknown. Was once believed to support extreme pro-Grivas elements, now probably much closer to centre-right. A man feared in the village

because of his extremely aloof character, whose younger brothers
have been active in various right-wing groups. Dhaskalos follows
village politics very closely, but rarely shows his hand. Second
cousin to (1), (4), (5) and (6). Affine of (2) and (3).

6. *Y. Tangos*

Age 40; 4 children, 28 *donums*; oldest of the Tangos brothers and
the only leftist among them, although he is married to daughter
of wealthy right-nationalist farmer. Y. Tangos is physically tough,
on village AKEL central committee, ideologically firm, has visited
U.S.S.R., and is certainly among the most influential men in
Kalo. He is second cousin to (1), (4) and (5) and also to the wives
of (2) and (3).

7. *Moustachas*

Age 50; several children, 36 *donums*; the former EOKA leader in
Kalo; strongly right-nationalist. A small, part-time, government
manual job supplements his farming income. Little education but
until recently enjoyed considerable power in Kalo because of his
EOKA record.

8. *Vasilakis*

Age about 35; no children; at least 10 *donums*; sister's son to (7);
Army officer, extreme right-wing. Feared rather than admired.
Regarded as 'fanatic' in politics.

9. *Aglas*

Age about 45; lawyer; born to wealthy Kalo farming family, but
now resident in Nicosia. Large land holdings in Kalo, which he
often visits. Candidate for right-wing PF party in 1970. First
cousin to (3) and friendly with (4), through common political
links outside village.

10. *Andreas Azinas*

(Real name) Commissioner of Co-operatives, a senior civil servant
of quasi-ministerial powers. Formerly active in EOKA, was also

once prominent in PEK, the right-wing farmers' association, and informally a man of influence in Nicosia political circles.

11. *Nikos Sampson*

(Real name) Right-nationalist politician and newspaper proprietor. Distinguished EOKA militant, who has never held ministerial office, but continued to be influential through his newspaper. Attracts disgruntled former EOKA militants, but has never taken up an anti-Makarios position. 1970 became joint leader of PF party.

12. *Vassos Lyssarides*

(Real name) Makarios' personal physician, a social democrat who manages to remain classified as a 'nationalist'. 1970 ran his own party, EDEK. A bitter opponent of:

13. *Polykarpos Yorgadjis*

(Real name) EOKA militant who became Minister of the Interior; by appointing his supporters to the police force, and as village *múktars*, he built up a large intelligence network and patronage powers. This was at first thought to be in the service of President Makarios, with whom he quarrelled in 1969 and was forced to resign his ministry. Later there was an attempt to kill Makarios; Yorgadjis was killed very soon after. Prior to this had founded the United Party, with:

14. *Glafkos Clerides*

(Real name) English-trained barrister: Makarios' chief negotiator in intercommunal talks with Turkish leaders, A sophisticated parliamentarian, is well liked by Nicosia bourgeoisie and merchant class. Defended EOKA suspects, 1955–59.

Note

Figures for land are for irrigated land in Kalo village area only. For political parties, see p. 239.

Introduction

This book is concerned with politics in a mainly Greek village
in Cyprus, from the time the island achieved Independence in
1960 to the national elections of 1970. The analysis of parish-
pump politics is in itself worthwhile if somewhat limited, but
this book has broader aims. It seeks to show by example how an
intensive study of a small unit, a traditional task of social anthropology, can help understanding of the larger society and its
politics, a traditional task of political science. Of course a village
is not the state writ small; among other things it lacks the complexity, the range of institutions and the political authority of the
state, and there can be no good argument that to study a small
community is like looking at the larger society through the
wrong end of a telescope. But the understanding of a small unit
may nevertheless be essential for the full comprehension of the
larger society.

One reason for this is that modern states tend to develop in
ways which eventually involve rural people. Whether the political system at the centre represses or permits rural representation
in the nation's political life, the power holders in the capital are
unlikely nowadays completely to ignore their rural subjects. The
extent to which rural people are conscious or unconscious of this
interest is itself something which will influence the nature of their
relation to the capital. In its cruder form, the key question here
is whether the system has granted them any rights, and if so, how
far are they able to use them? If it has not granted them any
rights, do they propose to seek them?

A reason more specific to Cyprus, but possibly relevant elsewhere too, is that men of humble rural origins enter the urban
elite and continue in certain ways to represent the interests of
the communities in which they were born. This does not mean
that in most things they go on behaving just like their rural
fathers. Far from it. Just how far their values will in fact be
different will depend on the circumstances of the particular
society, but even when they are trying very hard to stress how
different they are from the men in the villages they have left

their attempts cannot make much sense without understanding what they are reacting *against*. That is to say, any part of an elite which has recently come in from the countryside will need to be understood in terms of that countryside. If this emergent segment of the elite is also involved in the political representation of that countryside, its analytic yield to an understanding of national politics will be much increased.

This is by no means a common situation. In many societies modern politics or independence from foreign rule have not let many rural people into the political elite, simply because an exclusive traditional elite has deftly filled the power vacuum. This seems particularly likely where *latifundia* exist, or where there has been a firmly entrenched traditional feudal aristocracy. Portuguese rural society as analysed by Cutileiro (1971) showed no tendency to admit low-born villagers to political power; my reading of Indian village studies suggests that this kind of mobility is as rare on that subcontinent as it is in Portugal, and much of Latin America could be added to this list.

In some societies the elite has not been so exclusive. Late nineteenth-century Cyprus had a small mercantile elite, but lacked a landed aristocracy; many villagers owned the land they worked, and mass education, along with economic development allowed village-born people to enter the expanding urban elite. Something similar seems to have happened among the Ibo people of Eastern Nigeria, and among the Tolai of New Britain.[1] In all three cases the traditional authority system allowed a relatively open competition for power and prestige, and such elites as existed were unable to bar the entry of more humble persons into their ranks. In societies like these the understanding of rural political and social organization will play an important part in understanding national leadership.

THE VILLAGE AND MODERN POLITICS: AMBIGUOUS
BENEFITS

My argument so far is that an anthropological study of a small community may prove a valuable complement to the nation-centred studies of the political scientist. It need hardly be said that the reverse will also apply when the anthropologist tries to understand how the larger society affects the smaller unit. Much of this book is concerned with the impact of modern politics, as well as more general factors of social change, on a particular village. What happens to village social relations when modern politics penetrate them? Do modern politics bring new benefits to the villagers? If so, at what price? Do political ideologies (which formally require the opposition of their adherents) set men more fiercely at each other's throats than in the old days? If so, how do villagers deal with the ambiguous gifts of modern politics? What strategies do they adopt to get the greatest benefits at the least social cost? Or are they simply thrown into confusion, apathy, and alienation by the arrival of politics?

By modern politics I mean the activities of politicians, or party agents, and the entry of political ideologies into the village. It is widely reported that when these things begin in rural communities the local elders start to recall an Arcadian state, 'before politics came and spoiled things'.[2] They are of course trying to trick their listeners into the belief that in the good old days they never fought and all got along cosily together. While this was hardly ever the case, the elders are not being entirely deceitful; out of their complaints one can abstract several themes. Before modern politics in such societies, men understood and fought over things which were largely within their own local control— women, land boundaries, prestige, material rights of all kinds. After modern politics, they fight over things beyond their control, sometimes without clearly knowing why.

To enlarge on the elder's complaint, it can be said that when modern politics involve developed ideologies with opposed ways of seeing the world, they do alter the nature of political competition. In the case of the right- and left-wing ideologies described in this book, the actual labels are defined by their apparently non-negotiable hostility *to each other*. At the same time the very novelty of the labels and what goes with them in a rapidly changing world means that traditional rules for controlling political conflict may not be adequate to deal with the new contests. Perhaps new rules will emerge, but as yet only some people in the society understand that this is happening. In such situations, half the participants are used to a world in which the rules were understood and everyone played the same game; the other half may be involved in more dangerous activities, with no consensus about rules, and little experience in handling a situation which lacks consensus. Such is the situation described for one Cypriot village.

But the benefits of modern politics are ambiguous not only because of these new confusions, and the altered nature of political competition. They are ambiguous because the actual benefits offered are both essential and uncertain. In Cyprus since 1960 the political alignment of a villager may determine whether he or his dependants get certain benefits—jobs, scholarships, import licences, interventions in administrative or judicial procedures, cheap medical care, cheap travel, and so forth. Support for a political position may bring these benefits, but support for the wrong position may bring—as a punishment—the denial of the benefits. Villagers believe that their alignments are recorded on lists, and put in files, by the various political leaders; perhaps, they think, if the power structure changes, those who are rewarded today may be punished tomorrow. Although I have not seen the lists and files, I share the villagers' beliefs in their existence, although with more reservations about the efficiency of those who maintain them.

The benefits and penalties just mentioned are not in the control of villagers. They are all in the hands of powerful outsiders, usually men in the capital. A villager who aligns himself with such powerful outsiders is employing a new and dangerous resource in his personal competition for prestige, and such use of new resources is a highly charged issue in village life.[3] Villagers would like to secure the desired benefits but they usually do not wish to incur great hostility from other villagers who may be aligned with other opposed political groups. Yet why should they not simply throw in their lot with those powerful outsiders?

At this point the argument focuses still closer upon the highly particular nature of Kalo village itself. It is in several ways successful and prosperous. For the last seventy years it has grown steadily and yet managed to support most of its children within its confines: there has been no large-scale emigration. It is economically successful in the sense that things have been getting markedly better for most of the villagers as long as they can remember. Land is profitable and most families have some. Those who do not have enough can take advantage of the small scale of the island, the nearness of the village to the capital, and the new roads and new jobs, to supplement their land holdings by work in or outside the village. These factors allow the villagers to see most of their children marry other village children; land, wealth, and marriage partners are all things which villagers like to see kept within the control of the village.

The success of the village underpins a key value which the villagers invoke when political competition threatens the course of village social relations. The value is that of village solidarity, which has a number of aspects, discernible in different contexts. First, it involves stressing the superiority and basic homogeneity of the village in contrast to other villages, and its unity in the face of outside threats. It also involves attempting to settle disputes between villagers peacefully where possible. It involves limiting the scope of conflict between politically corporate groups, and limiting the definition of politics, so that as much of village life as possible is defined as 'out of politics'; that is, by such definitions, villagers insist that outside political alignments should not be allowed to influence day-to-day village life. The social and economic success of the village underpins the values and actions which express the analytic notion 'village solidarity', and the villagers have good material and conceptual reasons for conducting their lives in their chosen way. But this is a continuously changing situation, not one in which all the villagers, all of the time agree about what is happening or what should happen. To value solidarity is not to live without dispute, and to exclude a great deal from the definition is not to live without politics.

Here some thoughts of Frederick Barth are helpful.[4] He has described situations in which people see themselves as prospering *together* by the term 'relations of incorporation'. He has in mind a range from the lineage (or other forms of extended kin group) in simple societies, to the joint stock company and other organizations in complex societies. He contrasts such relations of incorporation, with another kind which he calls 'transactional relations' in which people try to increase their benefits by themselves, acting alone, in competition with others rather than in co-operation. Barth suggests that the balance between these two kinds of social action will be of crucial interest in analysing social relations within collectivities.

In my analysis the norm of village solidarity is invoked when people seek for whatever reason to extend the scope in village life of relations of incorporation. To invoke the norm of village solidarity is to try to make others restrain the lonely and naked pursuit of self-interest; it is to try to persuade them that they have more to gain by co-operation with co-villagers than by going it alone. Yet men in making such appeals may be seeking to further their own short-term self-interest, while appearing to speak for the long-term good of the village. I take the view that norms are weapons in political debates (rather than simple determinants of actions). The key debates of politics in the village are

debates about how far self-interest should be or can be subordinated to public interest. In these debates the actors struggle to
define their terms in ways advantageous to themselves. Such
debates are not always conducted clear-headedly or conclu-
sively—one must not over-emphasize the calculation or rationality
of the matter. But because they resemble those of more complex
social units, I find myself in dispute with Crick[5] when he tries to
deny some small-scale communities—he does not name names—
the dignity of Politics with a capital P. That is why I try to avoid
the term 'village politics' which in Crick's mouth would imply
small-minded back-scratching, and instead use 'politics in the
village' which implies something more akin to national politics. I
hope by the end of the book the reader will not think this
distinction picayune.

The first chapter begins with a sketch of the island's history from
the arrival of the British in 1878, to the elections of 1970. This
account is not comprehensive, but selects those events and issues
which will be reflected and refracted in the villagers' lives. The
rise of left- and right-wing groupings is stressed, and the struggle
of the right-nationalist organization EOKA to oust the British and
achieve *Enosis*—union with mainland Greece—take the reader to
Independence in 1960. This is followed by the intercommunal
violence of 1963 between the island's Turkish minority and Greek
majority and the *de facto* secession of the Turks, in armed enclaves, which continues to the time of writing. During the period
1878–1970 it is clear that the rural population has enjoyed continually increasing prosperity, but that its experience of participation in national or representative politics has been extremely
uneven: in fact, villagers are inexperienced in national politics,
and what experience they have, in face of major upheavals, and
sporadic violence, has taught them extreme caution.

The second chapter introduces the village of Kalo, and provides essential facts about its recent past, and present setting.
Since the turn of the century the village has been marked by
continuous population growth, as well as a shift from traditional
dry-farming based on oxen, livestock husbandry and cereal cultivation to an irrigated, capital intensive cash-cropping of vegetables and citrus fruits. Better communications, literacy and the
growth of political agencies in village life have marked the other

profound change: once, the village was a moral community, in which competition was chiefly for honour, land and other factors within villagers' control. Now, these forms of competition continue, but are subordinated to struggles over resources which are controlled outside the village, by men who seek political loyalty under a variety of ideological labels.

The third chapter starts by comparing four categories of villagers in terms of their class, status and power positions, to anticipate the discussion of degrees of freedom in political action, and the social bases for leadership roles. In descending order of political power the four categories are (i) the 10 per cent who are educated men; (ii) the 40 per cent who are full-time farmers; (iii) the 30 per cent who are skilled workers with some land, and (iv) the 20 per cent who are unskilled labourers, with little or no land. From here the analysis continues with the fundamental importance of the size of land holdings, of supplementary occupations, and of status factors in work, including education. There is a brief discussion of the recent shift to citrus cultivation which permits educated men to pursue profitable 'white-collar' farming, in addition to holding salaried and prestigious jobs. The chief economic constraints on political activity are thus made clear.

The fourth chapter is concerned with kinship and marriage. The central fact here is that a man is judged both by himself and by others in terms of his ability to provide for his dependants. This family-centred value is the first guide to a man's actions. In addition, the particular nature of the developmental cycle of the domestic group requires that each child receive a portion of its parents' property at its own marriage. Marriage, then, places a continual burden of provision and responsibility on household heads, while providing for the marrying child in particular a new set of important relatives and allies. The arrangement of marriage is a critical test of prestige in the village, for a man's standing is partly measured by the desirability of his sons and daughters as marriage partners within the village. This chapter also explores the relation between kinship solidarity, and individual freedom of choice in political alignment. Kinship is usually defined by villagers as something too important to permit of political dispute, but a man in his role as independent household head may seek any political alliances he chooses; only he must not allow such alliances to weaken the proper solidarity between kinsmen, and between affines.

Chapter five examines other bases for association in social

relations. Particularly ritual godparenthood (*koumpariá*), friendship, and relations based on age, neighbourhood and work, may all
be used either to intensify relations between men of equal prestige
and power, or those whose power is unequal, in which case, the
notion of patron-client relations becomes relevant. Common
membership in the village is then discussed, to show how far
this involves opposition to other villages, and how far it is reflected in the refusal of villagers to share village gossip with outsiders. The extent to which the norm of village solidarity is used
to prevent violence between villagers is analysed, and this is
followed by discussion of the practical benefits of this norm. The
way villagers succeed in controlling land, cash, and marriageable
children is a measure of the villagers' dependence on each other
both economically, and in their local prestige system.

Chapter six narrows the inquiry to politics in the village. The
range of formal offices available through the day-to-day administration of the village is described, and the recruitment of office
holders, who are usually full-time farmers, persuasive speakers
and men with a general reputation for reliability. The discussion
then turns to a more general analysis of leadership and power,
with wealth, education, force, and contacts with powerful outsiders being the main contributing factors. The ideologies of left
and right wings are then explored, as are the costs and benefits to
individuals of alignment with one group or the other. This leads
to a discussion of the ways in which political cleavage between
formally opposed groups has been restricted in Kalo. Lastly, the
omádha, a usually clandestine political support group is described, and its divisive potential in village social life.

Chapter seven presents in detail six case histories taken from
the period 1963–70 in which political processes threatened or
tested the peace of the village. The first case shows an educated
wealthy man attempting to found a club for educated men in the
village, and being thwarted by the resistance of the former
EOKA underground leader; the club would have symbolized certain key social cleavages in the village, and it was suppressed in
the name of 'keeping politics out of village life'. The second case
shows the same two men in opposition, only this time the occasion is an attempt by the educated men to exercise a measure
of bureaucratic control over the village militia, itself formed in
response to disturbances in the wider society. This case suggests
how the villagers attempt to diminish cleavage by creating *ad
hoc* village-wide committees, which symbolize unity even when

it is patently lacking. The third case brings the threat of open violence nearer to the surface of village life, when the supporters of two rival national leaders are brought into open opposition. It suggests how great can be the gap between intentions in the capital, and consequences in the village, and highlights the deployment of new resources in village-level politics.

The fourth case shows right and left groups contesting a key administrative committee, and once again outside agencies are decisive resources; the case shows how hostile groups accommodate to each other in periods when national politics are conducive to co-operation, but also stresses that, even in situations where such accommodation is enjoined, there can still be ample room for political manoeuvre. The fifth case analyses another administrative election, and argues that beneath the apparent right/left opposition were a number of more personal animosities which better explain the actions of the principals. It also reveals the characteristic political culture of village activists, the style and idiom of their calculations. The sixth case shows the conflict between public and private interests which arose when an administrative post was at issue, and village leaders found themselves under fire for possible dereliction of duty.

Chapter eight has three main themes. Firstly, it is about villagers attempting to speed up the construction of a dam by the central government, and the difficulties encountered when the local Market Town opposes the scheme. It is, then, concerned with local conflicts of interest, and shows the villagers as temporarily united to pursue a single aim. Secondly, it concerns the difficulties experienced by villagers when they deal with central government and argues that as yet most villagers display marked dependence on men in power, rather than attempts to control them through representative politics. Thus even the major demonstration which men of five villages brought to the capital was better understood as a plea for attention, than a show of strength. Thirdly, chapter eight raises the issue of who leads the village in external relations; certain village-born men, who through education and wealth, now live in the capital, and are part of the urban elite. These men have landholdings in the village, and maintain strong social relations with village kin and friends. The dam campaign shows them as the men to whom villagers allocate key roles of representation in the dangerously uncertain world of external relations, and the need for pressure on central government.

Chapter nine continues this theme, as well as adding an extra dimension to the rivalry between the village, and Market Town. For here the issue is the proper administration of the citrus retail sales co-operative which is dominated by a Market Town committee, but which also services the surrounding villages. Once again, local particularisms feature prominently, and once again, educated villagers make all the political running. The outcome for the village is increased representation in the administration of the citrus co-operative; and for the man who organizes the campaign, a better control of his own affairs, and enhanced authority in the eyes of his fellow villagers. But the understanding of this issue between village and Market Town, deepens the understanding of the dam campaign as well, for it involves the same major parties, at the same period of time.

Chapter ten concerns the 1970 elections to the Legislative Assembly. These were the first in ten years, and one of the relatively rare occasions for villagers to exercise the vote in national elections. The analysis focuses on the interweaving of local and national issues. I seek to explain, for example, the reasons which lay behind the particular voting pattern of Kalo village, which was completely at variance with the national district returns, and this leads to a detailed discussion of relations between village clients, and patrons who are national politicians. In showing why a populist leader on the nationalist right enjoyed strong support in the village, I am forced to consider two issues: how certain villagers used his election campaign as a substitute for blood-revenge of a murdered kinsman; and how this issue neatly dovetailed into the populist leader's claim to speak for militants who had participated in the EOKA independence struggle, yet had felt they had been denied their just rewards.

The 1970 election brings the solidarity of the village to a critical point, for village leaders find the campaign divides friends, kinsmen, and other villagers in an almost unmanageable way. National issues are stated with an intensity which threatens to swamp the village-made control devices. A number of disputes which arise out of the campaign are discussed in detail, and in particular how norms of village solidarity clash with the use of external resources, and the notion of party loyalty. In the event, the villagers manage to contain the cleavages intensified by the election, and I argue that given the active tradition that village solidarity must be maintained, the 1970 elections in retrospect have increased the authority of the norm, and made more probable the containment of future conflicts.

NOTES

1. For the Ibo, see for example, Henderson (1972); for the Tolai, see Epstein (1969).
2. See, for example, Cohen, A. (1965: 104) and Ruel (1969: xx).
3. See Bailey (1969: 144–82).
4. Barth (1966).
5. Crick (1962: 13–33).

1
Island

INTRODUCTION

Cyprus, an island of 3,572 square miles in the Eastern Mediterranean, has recently enjoyed a greater share of international
attention than its smallness might seem to warrant, but since most
of this book is concerned with the politics of a single village in
Cyprus, the recent history of the island must inevitably be
sketched in.[1] This will be done in a highly selective manner in
which the reader will be offered a number of themes, persons
and issues which bear continuously on the village of Kalo. In
this chapter, then, I shall concentrate on the following themes:
first, how the British, who gained control of the island in 1878
were induced to grant it independence in 1960; this will involve
discussing the meanings of *Enosis* (union with Greece), which
dominated the period and served as a rallying-cry during the
period of armed struggle by EOKA, 1955–9. The second theme
is how an organized left-wing party, AKEL, emerged and how it
came to be opposed by right-wing nationalists. Thirdly I shall
show how Turkish opposition to *Enosis* contributed in 1963 to
the breakdown of the infant republic of Cyprus, and led to the
arrival of a UN Peace-keeping Force. Fourthly the continuing antagonism between the two key Greek Cypriot leaders, Archbishop
Makarios, and General Grivas will be described, for the conflict
between their supporters lies at the root of the political unrest
during the first ten years of Cypriot Independence, 1960–70.

1878–1959: ENOSIS, AKEL, EOKA

Cyprus was occupied by many rulers throughout her history. The
Ottoman Turks held the island from 1573 to 1878, whereupon the
British acquired it. At this time the ethnic composition was
roughly 75 per cent Greek Cypriots and 23 per cent Turkish
Cypriots, who had arrived on the island during Turkey's period of
rule and some of whom were probably converts from Christianity.

Under the Ottoman Turks the leaders of the autocephalous Greek Orthodox Church in the island were also the Greek majorities' political spokesmen, and from the first days of British occupation until 1931 made regular requests for the political union (*Enosis*) of Cyprus with Greece. Turkish community leaders with equal and complementary regularity voiced their opposition to this. The British Government took no notice of requests for *Enosis* until the 1914–18 war, and Greece never pressed the point. Occasionally British politicians made sympathetic mention of the Greek Cypriots' claim, and the Greek Representatives in the Legislative Assembly continually tried to pressure the Governor in the 1910–30 period by threatened or actual non-co-operation over budgetary matters. Usually the British, in alliance with the Turkish representatives, could get around these obstructions.

It has been suggested[2] that the intensity of the Church's support for *Enosis* resulted partly from the threat to its power created by the arrival of the British, who weakened its previous position as sole spokesman for the Greek majority. Taxation and administration were partly organized through Church officials. After the British came, this relationship changed. The new government refused to allow its officials to help the church collect ecclesiastical taxes. It approved a Legislative Assembly with popularly elected secular representatives. It supported popular education and, after a trial period, relieved the Church of direct responsibility for the appointment of teachers. Finally, in the 1920s, the British allowed (but did not encourage) the rise of left-inspired trade unions.

I have discussed at length elsewhere[3] the different meanings that *Enosis* had for different sections of the population at different times. It was a slogan which asserted that Greek Cypriots were linked to the Greeks of the mainland, 500 miles away. It served to tell the island's Turkish minority, who could on a clear day see the coast of mainland Turkey (a potential 'big brother'), that the Greek majority of Cyprus also could call on outside support, mainland Greece. It served to tell the British rulers, that the Greek Cypriots were related to those distant figures of classical antiquity whom the British so admired. It served to rally all the anti-leftists' forces in the island, since the leftists were more concerned with organizing the island's population on *class* lines, and were inclined to look to the Soviet Union as a moral touchstone. However, leftists could usually be induced to sign petitions requesting that the British grant *Enosis* because as time, and Greek education went on, in many people's minds 'wanting *Enosis*' probably became indistinguishable from 'being Greek'; so to refuse to sign a petition would have seemed like renouncing being Greek. Given the presence of the Muslim Turkish minority, on one hand, and the British on the other, most Greek-speaking Christians probably felt that they were Greek first, and anything else, like a trade unionist, second.[4]

In 1931 there was a short and apparently spontaneous outbreak of violence by Greek Cypriots in favour of *Enosis*, which was firmly put down. From then on until 1945 the Legislative Assembly was suspended, the Governor ruling by decree, and village headman being appointed, not elected.

In 1924 a Communist Party was formed which attracted some teachers, and began trade union organization. It seems to have played little part in the events of 1931, but was nevertheless banned in 1933. It re-formed in 1941 when parties were again allowed, and in 1946 won municipal elections in four out of the island's six major towns. At the same time the Church and other right-wing nationalist elements began to back the formation of nationalist, anti-communist trade unions and farmers' associations. There were at this time a number of other national and Orthodox Christian political associations, such as OHEN, which were to prove an important focus for later militancy.

AKEL, as the reformed communist party was named, was in the early 1940s probably at the height of its strength in the island. But when on the mainland of Greece a civil war raged in three rounds between 1945 and 1949, AKEL, unwilling to commit itself to *Enosis* while the future of the left in Greece was in the balance, demanded instead independence and self-government. There was a moment in May 1948 when the British Government, through the proposed Winster Constitution, came close to getting the left representatives to co-operate in a limited measure of self-government, but the moment passed, the left switched from a line demanding self-government, to join with the right in demanding *Enosis*. However, this vacillation about *Enosis* did the Cypriot left a great deal of harm for it allowed the right to portray them as opportunists, and insincere in their stand on *Enosis*.

Fresh from organising an anti-communist militia in Greece, a village-born Cypriot called George Grivas started to form EOKA in the early 1950s; he carefully excluded all leftists. On 1 April 1955 he opened a new campaign for *Enosis* by armed struggle; from then until February 1959, with several truces as punctuation,

B

Grivas waged a hit-and-run war against the British which culminated not in the desired *Enosis* but in the Zurich Agreements,
whereby the island became an independent republic, guaranteed
by Greece, Turkey and Britain, with 70 per cent of civil service
jobs going to the Greeks and 30 per cent to the Turks, in an overall unitary structure. During the Emergency of 1955–9 the Turks
had been encouraged by their fears as well as by British diplo-
macy to voice their opposition to *Enosis* more and more energetically, and finally bloody clashes took place between the Greeks
and Turks of the island; but leaders of both communities
attempted to rally their followers to enter upon independence in
a spirit of restraint and compromise.[5]

EOKA is important for understanding Greek Cypriot politics at
both local and national levels, because former membership in it
is the basis for many relationships which create political support.
Also, national political factions between former EOKA leaders
are reflected in village groupings. Finally, EOKA leaders still have
a near monopoly on that inexhaustible resource in Greek Cypriot
political encounters—the claim to be the only true fighters for
Enosis.

In its original organization, EOKA had a military side, under
Grivas, an experienced Army officer, and a political side, PEKA,
which seems to have been more closely linked to Makarios and
senior churchmen. It is probable that the military/political
division also reflected to some extent certain cleavages in Cypriot
society, between village and town, uneducated and educated,
but there is to my knowledge no systematic material to decide
this point. My own analysis of the backgrounds of eighty-six
official EOKA fighters killed in action or captivity shows only
six of them to have been urban-born, and only a handful to have
had characteristics which would have placed them in any
plausible elite. There is a useful sense in which EOKA was an
organization for people who had never belonged to an organization before, and perhaps the novelty and attraction of this
experience contributed something to the persistence of the organization after Independence, in the form of local and national 'ex-
fighters' associations.

After Independence, for obvious reasons, many people said
they had been members. On one level, the ideology of the independence struggle was 'we were all in the Organization', but
since those families who suffered hardship could later claim
important benefits—scholarships to Greece for their children,

medical assistance, jobs, etc., it became necessary to differentiate between those who had offered more or less. Grivas himself handed out a number of certificates, which stated that individuals had in fact served in or helped the Organization, and of course membership in the ex-fighters' association became an important indicator. The fact that Makarios included in his first cabinet four young men under thirty, who had all been prominent in one or another branch of EOKA, was a sign of its political importance in the new republic. At lower levels of organization, it appears that prominent EOKA men acted for the first two or three years of Independence as an informal duplicate civil service, overseeing and intervening in many administrative decisions, especially those related to job appointments, import licences, building and development permissions, and scholarships. This was a kind of EOKA honeymoon, during which people sought for themselves and their dependants rewards to which they saw themselves as eminently entitled. If it was sometimes objected in certain quarters that the EOKA people lacked formal qualifications for some of the benefits they sought, there was an immediate and morally compelling defence—these men had endangered their lives during the struggle, while others had from positions of security and privilege been pursuing for their own self-interest those very qualifications.

Since 1960 an important cleavage in Greek-Cypriot society has been between categories (and sometimes groups) of persons in which the main moral resources have been references to dedication and self-sacrifice during the 1954–9 and 1963–4 nationalist activities on the one hand, and the formal, legalistic, bureaucratic values of qualifications and technical competence on the other. To have served one's country in EOKA may, for a tough and courageous young village boy, have needed no academic ability, school fees, command of English or familiarity with city ways. However, as members of the urban elite never tire of pointing out, other qualities than the ability to use a gun are needed to run a modern state.

Inevitably, a reaction set in against the EOKA honeymoon, but even if it had not done so, so many people stepped forward to claim the rewards of service to the nation that many were bound to have been disappointed. A wealthy country could have passed a GI Bill of Rights and socially enfranchized all comers. A poor country must pick and choose. To do this is to create dissatisfaction.

INDEPENDENCE, 1960–70: TURKISH SECESSION AND GREEK DISUNITY

16 August 1960, marked the independence of the island, which had been preceded two weeks earlier by national elections to the House of Representatives, in which AKEL, the communist party under an electoral pact with Makarios, was returned unopposed in five out of the thirty-five Greek seats, the other thirty seats going to a loose nationalist coalition, called the Patriotic Front. Fifteen seats, and the post of Vice-President of the Republic with important veto powers, went to the Turkish National Party.

The next three years saw two important developments: first was open breach between Makarios and Grivas both over the issue of *Enosis* and relations within the Turkish community. This inevitably involved their supporters. The second development was a struggle between the Greeks and Turks over the implementation of the constitution. Many Greeks were dissatisfied with the notion that the Turkish 18 per cent of the island should be guaranteed 30 per cent of civil service jobs, to be applied in every grade, and other benefits. These tensions came to a head in a constitutional crisis over budget approvals, and in December 1963 the first fighting broke out between the two ethnic communities.

In 1964 sporadic fighting continued at different points in the island. Among the Greeks volunteer militias formed in many villages, often based on experienced EOKA members, including Kalo. It is not clear what was the legal status of these militias, or how much clandestine support from Greek political figures had prepared the way for their formation. Grivas, who, owing to his differences with Makarios, had 'retired' to the Greek mainland, returned to Cyprus in June 1964, expressly to form a disciplined National Guard to replace the volunteer militias. This step seems to have been most necessary, since irregular units, owing to problems of poor discipline and communication, had created serious political difficulties for the Makarios government.

The return of Grivas, and the formation of the National Guard, were not only moves by the Greek Cypriots to further their ends against the Turks. Several writers agree that they had implications both for the difficult relations between the Greek government and Makarios at this time, and also for Makarios's personal position. Campbell, for example (Campbell and Sherrard, 1968: 270), suggests that the Americans persuaded the Greek government to allow Grivas to return to Cyprus in June 1964 as a move to control the increasingly independent policies of Makarios. Legg seems to confirm this, for he writes (Legg, 1969: 223) of subsequent developments in 1965:

> Archbishop Makarios, who differed from General Grivas over the future course of Cyprus towards union with Greece, found that control of the Cypriot armed forces rested not with his government, but with Grivas. In an effort to counter this, Makarios was attempting to build up the gendarmerie as an alternative force. Supposedly, the Aspida plot, at first intended only to undermine Grivas, began with a visit of Andreas Papandreou to Makarios.

This would appear to be the origins of the fierce disputes between Yorgadjis, Minister of the Interior and responsible for the police (which Legg calls the gendarmerie) and Grivas, as Commander of the newly formed National Guard.

One consequence of this period of fighting and militia formation seems to have been that rivalries between Greek political leaders became more open. Since a number of different individuals formed their own militias, small centres of power arose which also had different political colourings. (These groups, *omádhes*, will be discussed at length in chapter 6.) There appear to have been at least the following groupings from the 1964–5 period: (i) a Grivas grouping, of strong right-wing anti-communists, also bent on fierce opposition to the Turks; (ii) a group following the former EOKA fighter Nikos Sampson, a man who had been somewhat fluid in his political opinions but who remained nominally both a supporter of Makarios and a critic of the Zurich–London Agreements. He led a group in the Nicosia fighting of 1963–4; (iii) Vassos Lyssarides, Makarios's personal physician, a nationalist, but far and away the most left-wing political leader in the nationalist camp. He also formed a volunteer militia group in this period, which so distinguished itself in an assault on St. Hilarion that Lyssarides managed to disarm much nationalist mistrust of his left-wing views. He also acted as Makarios's Hermes to the Third World, and was the man responsible for bringing in weapons from various socialist countries, during the early part of the crisis; (iv) the Makarios group, which originally included a number of ministers and politicians, but particularly Clerides, Yorgadjis and Papadopoulos; according to a series of articles published in April 1966 in the extreme nationalist *Patris* newspaper, these men had overall responsibility for a military organization to be ready in the event of difficulties with the Turkish community, and which would carry out necessary measures to achieve *Enosis*.

The period of 1964–5 was one of continual unrest, rumours of planned coups against Makarios, and growing rivalry among nationalist politicians. The communists continued to support Makarios, and avoid provoking (and thus uniting) the nationalists. In March 1964 the first UN contingents came to Cyprus, and they are still there at the time of writing. Since 1964 there has been occasional limited fighting between the Greek and Turkish communities, with a period in winter 1967 when the mainland Turkish army came very close to invading the island, following the death of some Turkish Cypriots in Kophinou village. During the last five years, constitutional talks have gone on between Glafkos Clerides for the Greeks, and Raouf Denktash for the Turks. Thus, since December 1963, there has been virtual stalemate in intercommunal relations, with a *de facto* patchwork partition of the island.

In March 1968 Archbishop Makarios was overwhelmingly re-elected President of the Republic by the Greek community. Since then the two most important events were the political impetus he gave to the formation of political parties among the Greeks, in February 1969, and the successful completion of elections in the Greek community, May–June 1970. These elections for the Legislative Assembly were the first to be held for ten years, but for the two years immediately preceding them, in the climate of unrest it sometimes looked doubtful if they would be held at all.

This was because of the violent birth of a new political organization in the island, the *Éthnikon Metópon*, or National Front. This was an underground organization, which apparently had units all over the island, which first made its presence felt by distributing leaflets attacking various government ministers for corruption, betrayal of the national interest, and a general failure to prosecute the cause of *Enosis* more vigorously. In 1969 and early 1970 there were a number of violent attacks on high officials, usually involving shootings, or the bombing of homes. Arms and explosives were seized from police stations and mining camps. There was a general atmosphere of tension, the newspapers were again full of stories of coups being planned, and when I returned to the village for three weeks in December 1969, I was immediately warned by villagers not to ask questions about the *Éthnikon Metópon*.

In March 1970 there was an assassination attempt on President Makarios, and a few days later former Interior Minister Yorgadjis was shot to death outside Nicosia by persons unknown. Yorgadjis had resigned his ministry a year earlier after rumour had implicated him in an assassination attempt on Colonel Papadopoulos, the leader of the mainland Greek junta. At the time Yorgadjis and Makarios were said to have quarrelled bitterly, and Makarios to have forced Yorgadjis's resignation. When Yorgadjis was killed, popular opinion was that he had been behind the attempt on Makarios's life, and this was supported by the identity of some of the men arrested for that attempt, and later tried and imprisoned.

In May 1970, the island had not recovered from these incidents when some seventy armed men took over the central police station in Limassol, the second largest town of the island, held it for an hour, and made off with a large haul of weapons. They were soon caught and identified as the *Iéros Lóchos*, Holy Brigade, an offshoot of the *Éthnikon Metópon*. They claimed to have expected their action to be supported all over the island and the proclamation of *Enosis* to follow immediately. Their arrest was followed by major purges and reorganizations of the police force, and a lengthy public trial of some twenty of those caught; many others were pardoned, others published declarations of loyalty to President Makarios. Those tried were in the main artisans and junior white-collar workers.

These incidents (particularly the assumed involvement of Yorgadjis in the attempt on Makarios's life) caused great unease in the island, particularly since Yorgadjis, as minister over the police, had been responsible for giving to many people the jobs they held. The man who had in February 1969 founded the United Party with Yorgadjis, Glafkos Clerides, was left with the unenviable political legacy of his association with the dead man; his problem was effectively to dissociate himself and his party from the mud flung readily from all sides at Yorgadjis's name, but aimed with equal violence at the survivors.

Once again, Cypriot politics became the scene of attempts on all sides to monopolize the legitimacy of Archbishop Makarios, who was—if popular accounts are to be believed—giving tacit support to all parties from AKEL through to the more respectable

right-nationalist groups. Only Evdokas and the Grivas faction
failed to claim secret Presidential favour.

This particular kind of material has been selected from the
independence period because it supports and clarifies the material
later considered from the village fieldwork. If I have appeared
to dwell unduly on instability, rivalry, tension and the naked
exercise of power, this perhaps reflects the view of my predominantly village informants. But although the stridency of the
Cypriot press often lends the magnifying and distorting qualities
of an echo chamber to the smallest political messages, I believe
that an impartial and well-informed observer in the capital would
have produced similar observations and emphases. A full account
of the government programmes of the period would have to review the considerable social and economic progress made by the
Greek community, and a number of achievements in the areas of
social welfare and agricultural development. Such progress was
not nearly so marked for the Turkish community, restricted by
their own retreat within enclaves of usually infertile land, and
hampered by their leaders' policy of separate development.

CONCLUSION

One of the more striking facts to emerge from this discussion has
been the discontinuity of political representation over the last
forty years. Before 1931 villagers were able to exercise some
choice in the selection of village *múktars*, and there was an
electoral system for the Members of the Legislative Assembly.
At the time of writing, *múktars* continue to be appointed by government. From 1931–59 there were no elections to the Legislative
Assembly, and politically most of this period was marked by
opposition—sometimes violent—to British rule. Elections to the
Assembly were held in 1959, postponed for 1964 due to the intercommunal unrest, and only held again in 1970.

Two other types of national elections were open to villagers
in this period—for Archbishop, and for President of the Republic
since 1959. Since 1945 there have in fact been two elections for
Archbishop and two for President, In all these cases there have
been two candidates each time, and each time the organized left
has been formally supporting one; however, it is worth noting too
that Archbishop Makarios III, the successful winner of the
second archiepiscopal election, has also been the favourite and
winner in both presidential elections.

Counting these electoral opportunities is prosaic, but it hints at the restrictions on representation implicit in them. Choice of two Archbishops, two Presidents, and two Legislative Assemblies (over forty years) does not amount to a great deal of electoral experience. When the predominance of Makarios in three of these elections, and the passivity of the left's electoral tactics in two of them are also considered, as well as the recent rash of contingencies and crises surrounding the electoral process which are the legacy of intercommunal strife, then the poverty of electoral experience is underlined. This is in sharp contrast to the continuity and relative progress in the economic and social sectors.

There are two other tendencies which must be noted. One is the obvious fact of transition from British to Cypriot rule. This has turned out to be ridden with difficulties. The second is a transition from an indigenous political process dominated entirely by elite leadership, trying to wrest benefits from a colonial government, to a situation where universal suffrage must lead to a responsiveness on the part of elected representatives to mass demands. In chapter 10 I shall describe how during the 1970 elections politicians of all parties wooed the wondering electorate with promises of social benefits—something of a novelty for their listeners. In this they were only carrying on the attempts of men like HajiPavlou, in the 1920s, to appeal on a populist platform to a suspicious peasantry. In this chapter the fact of a discontinuity between the days of HajiPavlou and the campaign speeches of May 1970 has been presented. This discontinuity meant that everything that was done for villagers for fifty years was done from above. The political instability of the period, contrasted with the parallel economic development may explain the villagers' ambivalence to representative politics, which in comparison with the fruits of personal labour, offer benefits more doubtful than certain.

NOTES

1. My main sources for the background material in this chapter have been Hill (1952), Stephens (1966), Alastos (1955), Campbell and Sherrard (1968), Tsoucalas (1969), Foley (1964), Harbottle (1970), Xydis (1972). However, there was little more substantial than newspaper articles to provide for the period from 1968 onwards, for obvious reasons. No definitive study of Greek Cypriot political history since 1931 exists, and most writers concentrate on intercommunal relations.

2. Kyriakos Markides, personal communication. At time of writing Markides is preparing his doctoral thesis for publication, but I have not been able to read it.
3. 'The progress of Greek nationalism in Cyprus, 1878–1970' in (ed.) Davis, J. (1974) *Choice and Change: essays in honour of Lucy Mair*, L.S.E. Monographs on Social Anthropology, no. 50, London: Athlone.
4. I do not think there had been a comparable movement among the Turkish minority. Anderson (1958) suggests that the spirit behind postwar legislative reform of Islamic law was one of intensified ethnic consciousness, in direct opposition to the Greeks. The Turkish minority began, under British stimulation, to counter demands for *Enosis* with their matching demand for *Taxim*, partition, in the late 1950s. More recently, the notion of *Double Enosis* has been widely discussed in both communities. By this is meant, partition of the island, with one section becoming part of the political community of Greece, and the other of Turkey.
5. For a useful analysis of the period, the Constitution and its breakdown, *see* Kyriakides (1968).

2
Village

Twenty miles west of Nicosia, the capital of Cyprus, lies a flat area of rich agricultural land, where a number of villages and a Market Town have recently concentrated on cultivating citrus fruit. Both land and people are markedly richer than land and people elsewhere in Cyprus, and this fact, taken with the closeness of the region to the capital, immediately rules out any claim that the villages are typical of Cyprus in general. Kalo village is just one of those which cluster around Market Town, indeed it is only three miles away from it and connected to it, as well as to the capital, by good asphalt roads.

In this chapter the recent past of Kalo will be sketched in, before concentration on the political history of the village from the turn of the century to independence in 1960. The most striking social changes have been the following: first, the change from a traditional agriculture based on subsistence dry farming, cereal cultivation and the keeping of livestock, to irrigated, mechanized mixed farming, with vegetables and citrus fruit as main cash crops. Secondly, the change from being a relatively isolated, inward-looking place where most men could not read or write, to one in which most men read a daily newspaper, and receive with it perspectives of a wider society. Thirdly, and here the emergence of politics is particularly involved, the change from a moral community, with established rules of social and political conduct, to one where values, identities and rules are increasingly influenced by external forces.

From the memories of the oldest men and women, combined with written sources it is possible to get an impression of the village in 1900. There were 122 houses, with a total of 452 persons in them (see Table I). About two-thirds of the householders described themselves as 'farmers' by which they meant they had enough land to keep them occupied and support their dependants. The remaining third were divided between unskilled labourers, who worked on the land of richer men, particularly as ox-ploughmen, and skilled manual workers, such as carpenters, builders and tailors. Since hardly anyone had access to water for summer crop irrigation, most agriculture involved cereal cultivation, which depended entirely on winter rainfall. To plough, oxen were favoured.

TABLE 1

Kalo Population, 1881–1969

	CHRISTIANS	MUSLIMS	TOTAL	HOUSES
1881	N/A	N/A	451	114
1891	329	116	445	121
1901	348	104	452	122
1911	423	97	520	130
1921	546	101	647	150
1931	598	68	666	166
1946	898	76	974	212
1960	1,219	72	1,291	287
1969 (authors' estimate)			1,431	318

Source: Cyprus Government Censuses.

Notes
1. There was no 1941 Census due to the 1939–45 World War.
2. At time of writing no more recent census has been carried out.
4. For a discussion of the Muslim population, see Appendix 2.
5. In 1969 I counted 318 houses in Kalo. Allowing an average of 4·5 persons per house, this gives 1,431 estimated population.

The wealthier families kept two; those families with one ox made arrangements with others in the same position, to form a team, or ploughed with the single ox. Some men with no ox paid others to plough their land, or used a donkey team. The other main agricultural activity was the herding of sheep and goats. Most families kept pigs and chickens in their large yards. Houses and animal quarters were alike built of mud-and-straw bricks, and were enclosed by high walls of the same substance.

In this period, an adequate supply of land was crucial and there is reason to think that the poorest families left the village to seek their fortunes in the towns.[1] The other options involved wage labour on the land of others, or developing some craft skill. Even men with land were frequently heavily encumbered by debt, and such calamities as illness or a drought year saw those in debt forced to sell their land. Several rich men in the village increased their landholdings by lending money to their poorer fellows, but in this they faced competition from money-lenders both in Market Town, and the capital.

The dry-farming period came to a close when in 1916 a group of twenty Kalotes, including several Turks, decided to form a company to bring up the underground water of the region by the chain-of-wells system. This technique had been tried over twenty years earlier by some of the Market Town farmers, and it is probable that when the Kalo company formed, it was following some demonstrated Market Town success.[2] The technique required a cash outlay since it involved substantial underground tunnelling by specialists, and it is probable that the men putting up the money would not in any case have wished to do such heavy manual work. The chain of wells was dug, starting from the east and running for several miles until it reached Kalo. The summer water thus brought up was divided among the share-holders in units of not less than three hours each according to the amount of capital they had put up. Water came to each member roughly every eight days, for as many units as he was entitled, and with this water he irrigated his summer crop.

The value of such a system was immediately apparent to the whole village and within a short time a second company had formed with some sixty members which proceeded to dig its own chain of wells parallel to those of the first company. There were vigorous protests from the members of the first company for they feared that the competing well system would encroach on their own water supply. Their fears proved justified so they retaliated by deepening their own well system until they had regained their water at the expense of the water of the second company. Informants say that the dispute split the village into two opposed factions, and that it divided kinsmen and friends. One informant claimed his mother and father were members of different companies, one by inheritance and the other by purchase.

After several attempts by each side to settle the matter by further deepening of the wells—each attempt costing more money—the two companies went to court.[3] Informants said that the court case went on for two years and cost the village £3,000, which taking the price of good land as an index would have been worth £150,000 by present-day prices. This seems a vast sum and informants were insistent that the dispute 'ruined the village' when the well-digging and legal fees were added to the bad feeling that resulted. In the event the court's judgement was interesting and may have provided, in view of the high costs of the conflict, a model to the village of how to conduct such matters in future. The ruling was that the two companies should merge. There were to be eighty members, each receiving his share of water every fifteen and a half days. The membership of the first company also had their share of water reduced, so the outcome for them seems to have been a loss of nearly half their volume of water. In the end about half of the households in the village had access to some quantity of summer water. The water company still exists in the village, and 81 out of the 318 households are members. Although it is probably only chance that has left the present number of owners so close to the original number, it seems from the current shares that relatively little subdivision has taken place.

The formation of water companies was the first step in the transformation of the traditional pattern. A number of other changes followed over the next thirty years. First, government support for the Agricultural Credit Bank allowed villagers to avoid falling into the hands of the moneylenders. Between 1923 and 1931, a hundred Kalotes joined the village branch of this society (see Table 2), and in this way agricultural debt became controlled and stabilized. New roads built by the government made the marketing of produce easier, and this, combined with the ever increasing availability of summer water gave the villagers new cash-cropping incentives. Tractors started to reach the village in the 1940s as well as diesel pumps to bring yet more underground water to the village's land. The Credit Co-operative encouraged the use of fertilizer, and in the 1950s both potatoes and carrots became profitable cash crops. They were joined by the planting of orange and grapefruit trees, a trend which was encouraged by very high world prices for citrus fruit which started to level out, and later to drop, in the 1960s. In spite of this, the planting of citrus trees became the dominant interest of village farmers, and although they continued mixed farming, by the time my fieldwork started in 1968 it was rare to find a man who did not have some land under trees, and common to find men who had so planted all their land.

The village in 1968 was then different in many ways from what

TABLE 2

*Membership of Kalo Agricultural
Credit Co-operative Society, 1923–40*

YEAR	MEMBERSHIP NUMBERS REGISTERED
1923	1–17
1926	18–43
1927	44–61
1928	62–75
1929	76–98
1931	99–100
1938	102–110
1939	111–152
1940	153–157

Source: Records of the Kalo Agricultural
Credit Co-operative Society.

Note: no member 101 was recorded by the secretary.

it had been in 1900. Only 40 per cent of the householders were living by farming alone (see Table 3). 10 per cent were white collar workers who left the village each day to work. 10 per cent operated trucks, cars or buses for a living. There were more labourers but fewer shepherds, as a proportion of the population. There were 318 houses, with a population of over 1,400. The old walled houses were giving way to houses made of bricks, without walls. The village was bigger and more complex than it had been, and its people were more involved in the world beyond the village.

Certain other changes, no less important, were less easily visible. Education is an example. The villagers claim that they had the first school in the immediate region, and even though village pride might be at work in such a claim, there is evidence of a kind to support it. In 1881 only 15 per cent of school age children in Cyprus went to school.[4] Kalo in 1881 had a primary school in which a certain Neophyttos Petrou received £16–13, raised by voluntary contributions, for teaching twenty Christian boys over one year. Twelve Muslim boys and three Muslim girls of Kalo were taught in this year by Mula Mustapha, who received a government payment of £10. In 1883 the number of Christian boys taught had risen to 59.[5]

Primary education in Cyprus received a great impetus between 1880 and 1930. Research in Kalo in 1968 suggested that numbers of men and women over fifty were illiterate, although many old men could read with great ease. Few men under fifty and few women under thirty were unable to read a newspaper. All village children now attend primary school, and most of them spend several years at secondary school. Numbers of young men and women have been to universities. In short, during this century, villagers have been increasing their children's education, and with it, their ability to absorb easily changes which reach them from the wider society. The days are gone when men of all ages rose to their feet in the coffee-shops to show respect for a primary schoolteacher. When most people can read and write, mere literacy loses its high status; today it takes a medical degree or a Ph.D. strongly to impress the younger villagers. One final but

TABLE 3

Changes of Occupation in Kalo

OCCUPATION	1923–35[1]	1968–9[2]
	%	%
Civil servants (police, teachers, firemen, clerks, etc.[3])	0	9·5
Full time farmers	58	41
Skilled manual workers (tailors, builders, carpenters, etc.)	15	8
Car owners/drivers	0	10
Others: coffee shop owners, retailers, etc.	3·5	11·5
Unskilled labourers	10	15
Shepherds	7·5	4·5
Muleteers	6	0

[1] Base number—81 non-repeated sequential entries in the *múktar's* register of births. There is reason to think that the large majority—though not all—births were registered in the village in this period. Those which were not would have been children of wealthier farmers.

[2] Base number—191 person census of male household heads.

[3] I learned from informants that at least two unmarried elementary school teachers were resident in the village in this period. One was from Kalo, one was not.

crucial change is reflected in how the villagers see the past: men who were starting work or already working in the 1930s told me *ítan phtóschia tóttes* (dialect), 'those were the days of poverty'. They added that then labourers worked 'from sunrise to sunset for just enough to buy bread, and we were hungry . . .' Since then things have been steadily better for most villagers. There are still poor men, but although they work hard they and their children do not to my knowledge go hungry. Actual living standards as measured by hours of work, food, clothing, health, life-expectancy and the use of labour-saving devices have risen greatly throughout this century. In Kalo deprivation is strictly relative, for by the standards of many other countries the Kalotes live lives of luxury and safety.

POLITICS IN KALO, 1920–31

The oldest men in the village described to me what they remembered of politics when they were young, and before enlarging on these fragments of memory, it is as well to give the general substance: they remembered having elections for the post of *múktar* (until the colonial government decided to appoint *múktars* in 1931) and they recalled campaigns for election by politicians who wished to be Members of the Legislative Assembly. They remembered a good deal of vote-buying and the calculated entertainment of potential supporters by the politicians; villagers supported powerful men in the hope of being helped by them later. The old men's accounts suggested that village animosities often decided how men voted in the national elections—that is, that local rivalries in the village prestige system often counted for more than the 'national' issues imported by the politicians. But nevertheless this early period was by no means lacking in ideological issues, for *Enosis* and peasant taxation were both lively topics of debate among villagers, stimulated by the politicians' speeches.

Although remote from the memories of even the oldest Kalotes, there had been formal opportunities for some villagers to vote in national politics since 1882, when a Legislative Assembly of twelve members was created, with a suffrage extended to all males aged eighteen upwards, who had paid the *verghi*, a tax on able-bodied male householders or bread-winners, collected by *múktars*. How such formal participation worked in practice it is hard to say, but in October 1906 little more than 20,000 people voted, although the island's population at this time was over

235,000.[6] Intimidation sometimes took place at elections: of the 106 registered voters of Rizokarpasso village who wished to vote for a certain candidate, only 20 voted at all, and of these only one for the man of his choice (Hill, 1952).

Kalo informants were able to remember two elections from the 1920s to the Legislative Assembly. They describe the 1926 election as if it were a contest between two men—Neoptolemos Paschalis, and a certain HajiPavlou. Paschalis they remember as a rich lawyer and money-lender, taking a pro-government position and vacillating on *Enosis*. HajiPavlou though also a lawyer was from a poor family and from the Paphos district, renowned for its poverty and backwardness. Apart from being a fervent *Enosist* he had populist leanings: he declared that he would abolish the *dekatia*, an agricultural tax which was a tithe on most produce. Paschalis said that if it was abolished it would only reappear in other forms so it was a pointless exercise. Haji-Pavlou riposted: there was no reason why only farmers should pay tax, and if the luxuries that city people used were taxed— here he mentioned lipstick and perfume—it would be fairer. He also suggested that church lands should be sold cheaply to farmers. Both these men made speeches in Kalo and in the case of HajiPavlou not only his ideas but the actual words he used are remembered by the older men. There is a reason for this: they emphasize that he was first and foremost an orator, even a demagogue, and among other methods by which he fired people up was with use of the demotic or popular language (as opposed to the more complex, remote and archaic form used in speeches by most educated people, *Katharevousa*, Purified Greek); he also seems to have produced in each village he spoke in, a simple rhyming tag to characterize that particular village as a lead-in to his speech. HajiPavlou won the 1926 election handsomely. Some of his tags were still remembered in 1970.

Informants of varied political persuasions now assert that Paschalis stood for the party of the rich and HajiPavlou of the poor. That HajiPavlou was a populist seems beyond doubt, but the situation was probably a little more complex. For although Paschalis like certain other Members was a money-lender, having both literally and metaphorically an interest in agricultural debt, he got strong support in Kalo, and not always from the richer villagers, for some of these voted for HajiPavlou. Not all the villagers with large landholdings indulged in money-lending, since some of them preferred to put all surplus cash straight into land,

and these men had no particular reasons to support Pachalis. Secondly, it must be remembered that even then the issue of *Enosis* had the effect of cutting across simple divisions of wealth. Furthermore from the earliest years of British rule right down to the 1950s there was a fundamental dispute among Greek Cypriot politicians over the issue of co-operation with the government or complete boycott in the cause of *Enosis.*[7] This helps to explain why Paschalis, who in the early 1920s had been an advocate of *Enosis*, could in a later period be seen by villagers as 'pro-government'—in the Legislative Assembly whoever voted in favour of any government policy ran the risk of being called a traitor if a period of nationalist agitation was starting up.

There was another reason for Paschalis's support in Kalo which once again is not a simple matter of rich and poor men's parties. Paschalis was the defence lawyer for certain Kalotes, the Andriadis family, several of whom were accused of murder in 1926. They got off. The Andriadis family were at the time a group of brothers, who were physically tough, and managed between them to retain control of the *múktar*ship for most of the period 1920–1955. Some of them had a good deal of land, some had little. Occasionally they quarrelled among themselves but often stood together in the face of any challenge by other villagers. In 1926 several members of this group of cognates and their affines had killed a poor man from a weak family in a drunken brawl. In spite of attempts by the murdered man's kin to get justice—which included appeals to high police officials, the police seem to have found it impossible to get any useful witnesses to the murder, although the whole village knew who had done it, and several bystanders had seen it happen. The murdered man's relatives told me that since the Andriadis family had had one of its members as *múktar*, it had built up good relations with police and other government officials, and had got the case dropped 'by feeding many people'. It seems probable that since the police did not get helpful testimony they would have had difficulty in securing a conviction in any case, but it is also probable that they were 'fed' (bribed). One result of the affair was that Paschalis, as lawyer for some of the Andriades, received extra support during the elections, and although he lost at the district level, in Kalo he received more votes than his rival.

The office of *múktar* was clearly important in the village. Informants say that in the old days *múktars* were always well-off because among other things they had to have the spare time for the paper work the job involved; and furthermore they had to be able to offer hospitality to visitors. Their duties included responsibility for reporting crime and calling in the police; co-operation with any visiting officials; the official registration of births, deaths and land transfers, and the collection of certain taxes. In Kalo there were elections for the post, and informants remember that there were two factions in continual opposition over it.[8] These factions had an essentially kinship core, they insist, although people could be attached by affinal, friendship or other links. Its seems membership was not completely stable, and people did sometimes switch factions without suffering any very severe sanctions.

However, some informants speak of this period as if there was a good deal of stability to the factions. The earlier issue of the two water companies has been mentioned. Apart from the post of *múktar*, and the elections for the Legislative Assembly, there was the church committee, and occasional elections for the post of archbishop which could have served as occasions for factional conflict. Some informants say, 'We always had two parties in those days, and if I was against you in one thing I was against you in all.' Once again, the situation was almost certainly not so simple. The fragments of evidence still available did not suggest that most men who supported a faction over one issue later usually remained together on a very different issue. The insistence on two stable 'parties' suggests that the village frequently divided into opposed groups, and that there were always two, as opposed to three or more. Also, it suggests that if a man had a personal grudge against another, he was likely to oppose him just for the sake of so doing, and regardless of the issue.

During this period people also remember that fights were common. They seem to have occurred after church on Sundays, when men drank wine and got drunk, and when young men went to the swings (a form of very mild courtship game in which young men could see the young women of the village). The other common occasion for fights was at weddings. There were several groups of tough brothers who got into fights with other groups. These groups too are sometimes described by the word *Kómma* which is also used for political or electoral parties. 'We were wild in those days' the old men say, and referring to the Andriadis brothers and their tendency both to control the post of *múktar* and to get tough with anyone they didn't like, they add 'The Andriades terrorized the village at that time.'

In 1929 there was a second election for the Legislative Assembly in which HajiPavlou again stood, while a man called Triandafillides stood in place of Paschalis. At first Triandafillides was declared the winner but later the Kalotes insist he was charged with electoral fraud, after witnesses had been found who said they had been bribed. In the end HajiPavlou was declared the winner. In Kalo at least one informant who had voted against HajiPavlou in 1926 now voted for him. The reason he gave me was dissatisfaction with the recent village *múktar* elections in which his candidate had failed. He normally voted with the Andriadis group, of which he was a member, but now he voted against them out of pique. Other informants are equally sure that at the national elections there were other cases of close kin voting for different candidates, and some describe the principle of choice and alignment as 'everybody did as he liked . . .'. Informants also remember being given sums of money to secure votes by agents of the candidates, and that large feasts were set up in the coffee-shops at which villagers caroused. They called out to the passers-by to join them, the clear implication being that to sit at the table meant to support the candidate. They add that different coffee-shops were, during the election period, the domains of the rival groups.

This period comes to a natural close in terms of the political issues under review when in 1931 the 'Uprising' started in the capital, during which the Governor's Mansion was burned. It does not seem to have been an organized attempt at insurrection on the part of the Greek community but more a demonstration which got out of hand.[9] Kalo's contribution to the event was that several villagers went and cut the telegraph wire linking Market Town to the capital. Government troops shot a few people in near-by villages, and the government sent people to find out who had cut the wire. The *múktar* was removed, as were many *múktars* all over Cyprus, because the government decided that many of them had been inadequately vigilant during the disturbances. From this time on *múktars* were essentially appointed. The next *múktar* knew perfectly well who had cut the wire but when asked said he did not think it was anyone from the village. He always adopted the tactic of dealing with thefts and petty crimes himself, without telling the police, because in this way his sources of information remained open and he avoided reprisals. His attitude exemplifies the ambiguity in the role of *múktar*. A little later he resigned for personal reasons, and the government

replaced him with a new man who was said to have given the
police the names of the wire-cutters. The police gave the wire-
cutters a beating up, but the new *múktar* himself did not avoid
reprisals from those he had informed on: for a number of years
he suffered repeated crop damage and stock theft.

After the 1931 Uprising, the Legislative Assembly was suspended and the Governor ruled by decree. At one stroke two issues
were removed which had been a magnet for village factions. The
fact that *múktars* were no longer elected meant that villagers
no longer could compete for control of the position most likely
to mediate their relations with the larger society. The fact that
urban politicians no longer made their periodic descents into the
village arena meant that, on the formal political level, there was
a pause in the incorporation of the village into the larger society.

LEFT AND RIGHT, 1931–60: IDEOLOGY TAKES ROOT IN
KALO

The 1930s are remembered in the village as days of extreme hardship. The island was hit by the economic depression which
affected the eastern Mediterranean as well as Europe, and Kalo
was no exception. Prices of produce and land fell, there was
much unemployment, and men travelled far from the village to
get any work they could. The 1939–45 war, for which some villagers volunteered, provided new work opportunities outside the
village building aerodromes; as the island's economy picked up,
there were other jobs to be had in the towns, and in service capa-
cities on the British bases. The new job opportunities were
accompanied by a more liberal political climate in which the
organization of trade unions was again permitted. In 1948 there
were thirty-four Greek Cypriot political 'parties', which included
twenty right-wing ones, and twelve of the left.[10]

In the previous chapter the emergence of a left-wing movement in the early 1920s was mentioned; leftish ideas reached
Kalo before the depression of the 1930s, for a prosperous and
well-read farmer had declared himself a Communist well before
the Uprising of 1931, and had also won to his views a young
primary school teacher, son to one of Kalo's two priests. The
school teacher, who under a pseudonym wrote short pieces for
HajiPavlou's newspaper *Laïki*, soon found himself in trouble
with the Church authorities, and was pressured into signing a
document which stated that he was not an atheist, in order to

be allowed to carry on teaching. He left the village and the island, not to return for forty years.

Old men recall how puzzled they were at the time to see that the two best-read men in the village were communists. This was chiefly because between the Church and the more outspoken left polemicists, the idea had been firmly established that leftists were atheists. This in itself was an alarming enough idea in a traditional society, but it also implied (to right-wing nationalists at least) that in rejecting God, the left also rejected being Greeks. I shall discuss these issues more fully in a later chapter. Here it is enough to suggest that in 1968 leftist ideas were still only grasped in parody by many older villagers.

In spite of the novelty of leftist ideas, they came in a time of great social change, and when the 1930s are included, in a time of great hardship. By the middle 1940s the left in Kalo had organized a number of supporters. The rightists recall that if they opened their mouths to argue in the coffee-shops they were always outnumbered. In those days, 1945–50, the leftists had a strong soccer team, while the right were organized in a religious association linked to the Church. Both of these associations primarily attracted men in their twenties.

The village now possessed the basis for political confrontations in the existence of groups consciously opposed to each other on the same lines as groups operating at the town level. National leaders were busily rejecting and boycotting the government's tentative offers of limited internal self-government. However, there were two rounds of archiepiscopal elections in 1947 and 1948 which gave the national parties a chance to test their organizations by backing opposed candidates for the job. Makarios II[11] was a strong anti-communist and eventually won. The left in Cyprus, and of course in Kalo, backed an opponent who was considered more 'progressive'. Although he lost in Cyprus, in Kalo his supporters could have mobilized more votes than did those for Makarios II and this fact is taken by both right and left-wing informants to prove that at that time the left was clearly stronger in sheer numbers. They also report that tempers ran higher in those days—'we were more fanatic then and we took it all very seriously'.

The fanaticism took an interesting form which stopped the matter being proven by the actual result of the ballot: for these ecclesiastical elections the electoral register was supervised by the village church committee, which sent the register to the

bishopric whence it returned with the names of certain villagers
scored through in red ink, as communists (and thus 'atheists') and
so ineligible to vote! It should be noted at this point that it was
the son of the church committee secretary who was leader of the
left group: in his account it was the committee members themselves who had supplied the information to the bishopric; however, his father, the secretary says that this did not occur but
readily agrees the information must have been supplied by
someone in the village.

The actual voting was to take place in the church. When the
leftists arrived they found the door barred to them and the
amended register produced as justification. 'We are Christians
too and entitled to vote,' they insisted, but this appeal failed. In
normal village usage the idea of being Greek and of being Christian is one and the same, and in telling the story the secretary of
the church committee did not find it odd that the leftists insisted
they were Christians: 'Surely no man would deny he is a Christian?' he said. The priest came outside to collect the proxy votes
of menstruating women (who were prohibited from entering the
church) and the leftists went away.

They decided to retaliate with a form of economic boycott. In
the Orthodox Church a worshipper normally buys a thin wax
taper on entrance for a few copper coins. Later in the service he
lights it and leaves it before an icon, whereupon after a few
minutes a church official extinguishes it. Later the church melts
down the tapers, makes new ones and resells them. The purchase
of a taper is thus in a sense analogous to a collection in some
other churches except it also involves an act of ritual participation
by the worshipper. The Kalo leftists decided to buy their own
tapers and bring them into church when they went, thus depriv-
ing the church of a form of revenue. In addition, they did not
hold a certain customary festival—*yiortí tou spitióu*—centring on
the ritual blessing of the house at which it is customary for the
priest and cantors to be feasted as well as paid a small fee for
ritual services. This boycott was kept up for several years and
only dropped when a local bishop was trying to muster possible
support against the archbishop and made peace with the left by
suggesting they might like to put up a candidate for the church
committee.

Kalo at this period had privately-owned retail stores selling a
wide range of essentials and run by villagers. Villagers felt that
such shops overcharged for many commodities, and the shop-

keepers were naturally forced to extend credit providing ample room for dispute in normal transactions, since among other things most villagers did not keep their own record of items purchased and were often incredulous at the amount they might have run up over several months. When the Kalo leftists—following a trend that had already started as a result of initiatives by leftist organizations—started collecting subscriptions for a co-operative retail shop, which would be non-profit and dividend-paying, they found a good deal of support in the village. The right, however, at first stayed out and tried to persuade the villagers it was a bad idea. When they realized that the idea was in fact quite popular they decided to co-operate and by an agreement with the left were allowed to put two representatives on the five-man committee which supervised the running of the shop. This readiness to accept compromise is similar in essentials to the solution to the two disputing water companies, since it involves dropping the intransigent position of all-or-nothing, and accepting that the unit as a whole will prosper more if this is done. It suggests an ability coolly to appraise the relative costs and benefits of different courses of action. In later chapters I shall show how this is a dominant theme of politics in the village for most of the villagers most of the time. When serious crises do threaten to break down the spirit of compromise, the long history of successful compromise is invoked, as a special character of Kalo village against other villages, and as proof that differences can be settled to the satisfaction of all. I shall also argue that this is likely only in a community where most people feel they have a real stake in things and see to some extent their individual prosperity and prestige as linked to relations within the community at large.

The superior strength of the left in Kalo did not last for very long, for in 1955 EOKA's campaign of insurrection against the British colonial presence broke out. This, it will be remembered, was a campaign which excluded the organized left, who in any case did not support it. In Kalo village a man called Moustachas, a farmer with substantial land who had for some years been an active member of a right-nationalist Christian youth organization, decided to form an EOKA group in the village. He attracted to the group a number of younger men, none of whom were leftists. This group obtained arms, and went out at night to harass or report on British troop movements. Although many villagers must have learned of the nocturnal comings and goings of the group, the villagers agree that there were no traitors. Leftists were

regarded with suspicion, and Moustachas's own brother, then a
member of a left trade union, was not allowed into the EOKA
leaders house; it would seem that during this period a number of
young men—possibly twenty or more—who had previously supported the left publicly now stopped doing so. In other parts of
Cyprus, leftists were attacked and sometimes killed by EOKA
members, who believed they had been betrayed, or merely because they believed the left were against them. In any event,
between 1955–9 it required more courage publicly to support the
left than it did before, or after, and naturally enough, a number
of Kalotes either changed their public positions, or simply kept
quiet.

The fact that EOKA's struggle culminated in Cyprus getting
independence from British rule had several effects on politics in
Kalo. First, it meant that the left was for the foreseeable future
upstaged by the right, since it had, the right insisted, contributed
nothing to the EOKA struggle. The left answered that they had
at the very least contributed cash to the frequent EOKA collections, had participated in many other ways, as far as they were
allowed. During the 1955–9 period, the village had a special co-
ordinating committee, which aimed to support the EOKA group,
and also to organize village affairs in such a way as to avoid recourse to British administrative agencies. The committee was a
form of boycott of the colonial government. The left were
excluded from this committee.

The upstaging of the left meant not only the loss of former
supporters, but that future supporters, young men being educated
or starting work, were less likely to be attracted to the left, since
in schools they were taught that the heroes of EOKA had brought
the country independence. A cult of the hero led to young men
feeling that it was the done thing to carry a gun; the fighting
between Greek Cypriots and Turks which started in 1963 only
added support to such ideas.

Finally, there was another legacy of Kalo's participation in
the EOKA struggle, and this was that certain men in the village
who were thought to have been active in it became informal
political leaders, and men whose words—no matter how softly
spoken—carried a good deal of weight in village affairs. In a later
chapter I shall describe how Moustachas was able to stop a club
forming merely by saying he thought it was a bad thing. If the
villagers allowed such men an authoritative voice it may have
been partly out of respect for the recent achievements of the

EOKA activists. But it was also partly out of that healthy respect for personal safety which the ordinary man extends to the man who carries a gun (or keeps one at home) and who has shown (or is thought to have shown) himself ready to use it. The EOKA struggle inevitably made the words of some men count for more than others in village affairs; and it meant that some men found themselves almost speechless on sensitive matters.

CONCLUSION

In this chapter fifty years of rapid change has been compressed to a minimum, to give essential background for later chapters. Any such compression does violence to the past, and the more distant that past the greater the violence. But the attempt must be made, for although the village has probably never been truly static, stable or isolated, yet the changes of the last half century have undoubtedly been of larger scale and of a different order from those previously. For the moment the village must be presented as if we could freeze it in time about the year 1900, so that what it has since become can more easily be grasped.

At the turn of the century the village was in the main an agricultural community, using the power of animals to break the soil and shift large loads. The pattern of subsistence agriculture meant that villagers needed cash only for paying taxes, or a few luxury goods, animals and heavy implements; most of their other needs could be satisfied by their own efforts, or by recourse to a village specialist. There were richer and poorer farmers, and men with little or no land who lived by labouring for others or by craft skills. There were undoubtedly related differences in consumption patterns, but among the Greek villagers[12] there were no strongly institutionalized differences. There was no aristocratic or feudal class; no class-controlled land, and few villagers could claim the distinction of literacy. Villagers shared a preoccupation with a common set of values involving notions of family honour and the superiority of some activities over others, land-owning over labouring for example. Kalo had the general characteristics of what Pitt-Rivers (1954: 14–33) has described as a morally unified community. Like the *pueblo* he describes, the village was a place where in spite of wealth or status differences, people cared more about the opinions of other villagers than about values or judgements from the wider society.

As time went on certain facts began to modify this picture.

The compromise which created a single water company out of two rivals was the first of a number of changes in agricultural technology, which was to include the use of machinery, fertilizers and a gradual switch from a peasantry based on cereal and livestock to capital-intensive cash-cropping. New roads, and government credit agencies also contributed to the changes in technology, and at the same time the growth of literacy helped such changes to be more easily digested by the younger villagers. The children of illiterate peasants grew up to be literate farmers. The traditional measure of a man's agricultural skills was no longer how well he ploughed with an ox-team, but how well he could handle a tractor.

It is much easier to build up a picture of traditional agriculture than of traditional politics. Perhaps the village in 1900 intellectually was already very different from what it had been in 1850. The evidence is not available. However, we know that early in this century villagers were involved in elections for their local *múktars*, and for the Legislative Assembly; and although their local preoccupations often influenced their behaviour in national politics, yet the early nationalist agitation was keenly remembered by the survivors of the period, and a few villagers had even been involved in the 1931 Uprising.

Fifteen years later national politics had taken a much firmer hold on village life. The opposed notions of right and left wings had become the dominant political identities of the activists, and two sides in the village were engaged in continual trials of strength. From these early trials the right-nationalists as represented by the EOKA activists emerged as the stronger by 1960, for they had pre-empted the armed struggle for independence. Yet throughout the years when the two opposed ideologies were gaining supporters, the villagers showed on a number of occasions that the lesson of the two water companies had been remembered: in politics as in economics, accommodation could be reached.

NOTES

1. This is suggested by analysis of genealogies. The few men who became educated also seem to have settled outside the village, sometimes abroad.
2. Jenness (1962), describes the actual technique, which is ancient. He also describes the efforts of Market Town to develop such wells in the late

nineteenth century. Chapters 8 and 9 will describe the village in competition with Market Town over the control of water, and of a citrus co-operative.

3. I have not been able to examine the court records, in this, and several other cases.

4. Christodoulou (1959: 59).

5. *Cyprus Gazette* CO 456 (1881) and (1883–4).

6. *Cyprus Blue Book* 1909–10.

7. Hill (1952: 488–568). Hill's bias against the *Enosis* movement is apparent; but his scholarship is unrivalled.

8. Surridge (1930), writing one year before the Uprising, makes it clear that although there were village elections for the post of *múktar*, the Governor chose the actual incumbent from a list of possibles initially chosen by village elections. After the 1931 Uprising, this system became simple appointment by the Governor. *Múktars* today are appointed by the Ministry of the Interior, although there are occasional suggestions from the government that one day elections will be restored. For further comments on the system see Shenis (1962).

9. Storrs (1939: 529–530).

10. Hill (1952: 560 note 5).

11. The present archbishop is His Beatitude Makarios III.

12. See Appendix 2 for the general position of the Kalo Turks in this study.

3
Work

In this chapter I shall examine the economic structure of Kalo village, chiefly to prepare the ground for the later analysis of political processes. The aim here is a traditional one—to distinguish the economic, status and power situations of different actors, in such a way as to identify key social categories. To run ahead of the argument, there are four major categories to be distinguished, which do not correspond to any clear distinctions maintained by the villagers (see Table 4).

Ten per cent of householders are educated men, mostly teachers and civil servants, with regular salaries, high status in the village through their education, and who are relatively independent in political behaviour within the village. They are often brokers between other villagers and powerful outsiders, and may be leaders in representing the village externally. They may be patrons to other villagers.

Forty per cent of householders are full-time farmers and by definition own sufficient land to be economically self-sufficient and self-employed. They may be wealthier than the educated men, but their lack of formal education keeps their status lower. They provide some village political leaders, for they tend to dominate a number of village committees and within the village to act independently, although outside the village they are more cautious. Within the village they may be patrons to weaker men, but will tend to be clients of powerful outsiders.

Thirty per cent of householders are skilled men, normally those who do not have enough land to be full-time farmers; they follow some trade or skilled work to supplement their land holdings. They lack the economic security of the first two groups, and are more reliant on the favour or custom of others. This does not exclude them from political leadership, but makes it less likely. In status they fall behind the educated men and full-time farmers, but they are also distinctly higher than the fourth group.

Twenty per cent of householders are the unskilled, mostly labourers and shepherds. They tend to own very little land, and to have no economic security, depending heavily on employment by others. They never supply leaders in village affairs, and are always clients. Politically they are passive, dependent, clients or spectators.

Having made these distinctions it is imperative to qualify them. First, the four categories do not so far lead to notions of group solidarity or identity among the villagers. There is a village distinction between educated and uneducated men, and there is a distinction between rich and poor men, but as will become clear, these distinctions sometimes cut across the four categories outlined, if only because many villagers have started to give their children higher education when they cannot give them enough land to be full-time farmers. Another such factor is that any individual may have close relatives in each of the other three categories. Solidarity with close kin is generally stronger than solidarity with unrelated persons in the same economic category.

In the following pages the distribution of land, status factors in work, education, and citrus growing will be discussed in turn. Each subject will be discussed to bring out the range of economic possibilities it involves for the individual, but I shall not systematically work through the four categories just introduced, for to do this would inevitably give the misleading impression that four discrete classes or strata exist in Kalo.

THE DISTRIBUTION OF LAND[1]

It is easy to see why land was highly valued when, as in the past, most villagers were peasant farmers. But it is still highly valued, even when men earn their livings in other ways, and this is chiefly because agricultural land is profitable in the region. As irrigation has increased, so have opportunities for continual cash cropping, both of legumes, and citrus fruit.

Land is by no means evenly distributed in the village—there are a few families with none, and a few with several hundred *donums*;[2] but it is *relatively* evenly distributed among the majority of families, and there is no large class of landless families. Nor are there large landowners who live without doing agricultural work, although there is now emerging a situation where the sons of peasant farmers are educated to the point that they will not undertake manual work, although they own land.

TABLE 4

The relations between economic situation, status and political power

MAIN JOB	%	ECONOMIC SITUATION	STATUS FACTORS	POLITICAL ROLE WITHIN VILLAGE	POLITICAL ROLE OUTSIDE VILLAGE	VILLAGE LABEL (LINKED TO NUMBER OF DEPENDENTS)
'Educated men' teachers, civil servants	10	Regular salaries not economically dependent on favour of other villagers. May employ labour; may own land but may come from poor family.	High status from education, contact with urban culture, from avoidance of manual work.	Influential and receive formal deference. Supply some leaders. Act as patrons or brokers for others. Never clients.	Often asked to represent village in external matters or to transact favours for fellow villagers. May be constrained by the alignments of their bureaucratic superiors in national politics.	'Rich' 'Doing all right'
'Full-time farmers' by definition men with more than 10 donums, and often more than 15 donums.	40	Land ownership gives security of basic capital. Normally economically independent.	Second to the educated but were the traditional elite of village. Higher status if their women do no paid work.	Dominate administrative committees and provide political leaders for national parties at village level. Rarely clients and sometimes patrons to poorer men.	Lack of education hampers them in dealing with urban elite, politicians or bureaucrats. Tend to be clients.	'Rich' 'Doing all right'

						'Doing all right' 'Middling' 'Poor'
C	'Skilled men' carpenters, builders etc. owners of tractors and trucks.	30	Mostly own useful amounts of land but not enough to meet needs. They rarely have a steady income from craft skill and depend on the custom of other villagers. But they have solid assets.	Lack the prestige of economic independence or education. Interact freely with farmers and aim to join them.	Occasionally reach leadership roles on committees but less frequently than full-time farmers. Rarely patrons but avoid being clients.	Usually clients.
	'Unskilled men' labourers, shepherds	20	Tend to own little or no land and must work every day to make ends meet. Wives and daughters take paid work.	Very low status.	Never leaders. Always clients. Never political activists.	Always clients. 'Poor'

Table 5 makes it clear that it is rare for households to start married life with no land at all, for less than two per cent do so; it also shows that over 70 per cent of the households have started with holdings falling between six and twenty-five *donums*. That is, 70 per cent of the households have started with holdings separated from each other by a factor of four. Some 20 per cent of the households have holdings which are really large, given the relative productivity of the land.

TABLE 5

Land received at marriage:[1] *191 households*

DONUMS	HOUSEHOLDS	PERCENTAGE
0	3	1·57
1–5	14	7·31
6–10	41	21·46
11–15	45	23·56
16–25	48	25·13
26–50	33	17·27
51 or more	7	3·66
	191	99·96

[1] The amount refers to *usufruct* and not to legal title only.

The villagers, of course, do not use percentages and tables to describe land or wealth. They use a few basic distinctions— *i phtoschí*, the poor; *i métrii*, middling people; *i kalí*, those who are doing all right, and finally *i ploúsii*, the rich or, interchangeably, *i árchontes*, people who run things. Such terms do not have sharp boundaries, and how they are used depends on who is speaking and his relation to the person being discussed. There would be wide agreement about extremes, but the use of the terms is often not a simple statement of fact; it is more a political act in miniature. When asked to explain why a particular family has been called 'middling', rather than 'rich', a speaker might point out that the family has many children, each of which can only expect on an 'equal shares' basis to receive a small parcel of land at marriage, so it would be wrong to think of them as 'rich'. No one would call a family with ten *donums* of land, and ten children anything but 'poor', since each child stands to get only a *donum* of land. A family with ten *donums* and two children might be called either 'middling' or 'doing all right', though not 'rich'.

Such remarks need a context. In 1968–9 agricultural land in Kalo fetched between £300 and £500 a *donum*. A house plot of half a *donum* was not less than £500. The lowest unskilled male labour, road work, was paid at £1 a day, while carpenters and builders were paid £2 or £3 a day, depending on the job. The profit to a farmer on one *donum* of mature orange trees would have varied from £50–£70 a year. To educate one child at secondary school costs in fees, fares, books etc, £65 a year, without counting loss of labour. To feed a family of six, giving them meat twice a week, and allowing for substantial domestic provision of staples like beans costs about £5. Agricultural land in sufficient quantities can be profitable in Kalo, but not every household either has enough to satisfy its ambitions, or enough to live on.

TABLE 6

Land Holdings at Maximum and Other Occupations

DONUMS AT MAXIMUM[1]	0–10	11–15	16–25	26–50	51 or more	
FULL-TIME FARMERS	—	4	27	31	14	= 76
MIXED OCCUPATIONS	30	32	33	18	3	= 116
						192

[1] It must be remembered that this sample includes young men, who married since 1960, and most of them have probably not reached their maximum holdings yet. Nor will the classification made here necessarily remain stable over time.

Table 6 illustrates the tautology that farmers must have land. It shows that over 90 per cent of those household heads with less than sixteen *donums* have another occupation as well as working the holding. In this situation, village categories have a close fit with sociological distinctions, for usually men only describe themselves as *gheorgós*, farmer, if they have a sizeable holding and no other job. It is a matter of pride for the older man at least to be what I call a full-time farmer, for the self-sufficiency implied by the word *gheorgós* (as opposed to the dependence implied in the word *ergátis*, labourer, for instance) is one of the strongest values of the village.

Table 6 then shows that men must supplement inadequate land holdings with other work. Since land holdings and circumstances fluctuate over time, it is not surprising that many men have done many different jobs at different times, according to need. A mason who late in life bought land may stop work as a mason, and work only on the land. A man with a good holding all under citrus trees finds himself with free time, so he opens a coffee-shop for extra income. It was common for men to reply to the question 'What do you do for a living?' by saying, 'I've done a bit of everything' and this often turned out to be no great exaggeration.

STATUS FACTORS IN WORK

When villagers talk about different kinds of work they are usually talking about a number of possible factors: is a man free to refuse work, or does his poverty leave him no choice? Do his women do paid work for other families? Does he have a regular income? Is his work manual? Does it require skill? Education? Is the work rural or urban?

Those men with little land, who earn their living by heavy labour for others, who cannot afford to refuse work, whose wives and daughters must also take paid labouring work are at the bottom of the village status scale. At the top are men who for one reason or another depend on no one for their prosperity, who employ labour, whose wives and daughters do nothing outside the house; these men have large land holdings, and they are fully occupied with them. Of equal status if not superior are the new elite of the village—teachers and civil servants who own land which yields them valuable extra income, but who do not do heavy manual work.

Between these extremes are a number of possibilities, each with slightly different status implications. A number of men own a moderate holding, which they supplement by earning money from ploughing the land of others by tractor. A new tractor costs £1,200, and there is roughly one tractor for every ten

Kalo households. The largest landowners are too busy with their own land, and too proud of their own independence, to plough other men's land for cash. So a specialist job exists, which needs a large capital investment, a high degree of skill, but offers perennial cash rewards, on a flexible schedule.

Men buy trucks, costing several thousand pounds, and use them on roughly the same lines. There are at least fifteen trucks in the village. Both trucks and tractors have the attractive feature that if a man is too busy or becomes too prosperous to want to drive the vehicle himself, he can rent it to another man, or offer him a wage to drive it. Using tractors and trucks in such ways is called by villagers *epichéirisis* 'business undertaking'. It suggests that a man has capital and freely decides whether to take work for a customer or not.

Carpenters, builders, mechanics and other men who have worked through apprenticeships are described as *technítis*, skilled worker. They earn two or three times as much per day as an unskilled labourer but like labourers, they do not usually have steady, secure work throughout the year but are hired on a day-to-day basis. They have strong trade unions, and when fully qualified, are addressed by the honorific '*mástore*', which is only used to skilled men. In Kalo today, very few young men under thirty-five work as unskilled labourers. Nearly all of those who have not completed secondary school, have become apprentices in the skilled trades. The labourers in the village are the older men.

Policemen, clerks, minor civil servants earn regular wages, they do not do manual work for their living, and to show this many of them allow the finger-nail on the smallest finger of the left hand to grow long. In addition, there is the extra fact that their work is, in the physical sense, removed from the village and rural activities, and associated with urbanity, administration and literacy. However, these men are usually unable to avoid a certain amount of occasional manual work in connection with their land holdings. They may try to avoid heavy work, such as irrigation, or specialist ploughing, and if as is usually the case, their land is under citrus trees, this leaves them little but pruning and the overseeing of fruit picking to do.

The village has produced in recent years two doctors, a dentist, a lawyer (none of whom live in the village), and a number of secondary school teachers, not to speak of primary school teachers and junior civil servants, who are usually village residents. In all cases these men and women are the children of peasant

farmers, most of whom were barely literate. Other young villagers are completing their studies in the professions. Villagers
have had to learn something about the relative merits of different
types of education.

All householders pay what is known as the School Tax, which in
1968 ranged from 10/- a year for the poorest household to £8
for the richest. The tax is paid regardless of whether the household has children at the village Primary School (*Demotikó*) or not.
Secondary education (*Gymnásio*) was paid for until 1970. It
ranged from £18 fees a year for the first year, to £30 a year for the
last of six years. On top of this there were books and the labour
lost when a child goes to school. It has been common since the
1930s for men to send their sons to gymnasium 'to see if they take
to learning' and if they didn't, to remove them from the school
after a year or two. The gymnasium at Market Town is so close
that there is little hardship in such experiments. Often a boy may
complete four or five years successfully and then fail the final
examinations two or three times. If a boy or girl obtains the
certificate of completion with good marks they become eligible
for a variety of white-collar jobs including minor civil service
grades. However, a popular choice at this point would be a
further two years' study at the Pedagogical Academy to qualify
for being a teacher in the primary school system on a starting
salary of about £40 a month. This offers certain advantages since
the teachers' trade union have a loan fund from which loans can
be raised for buying houses, or for aiding a younger sibling to
complete their education.

   Should the family decide to send a child to university in Greece
the cost moves up to a minimum of £30 a month for girls and a
little more for boys since they often smoke cigarettes and go out
on the town a little. Most university courses in Greece take four
or five years to complete, and more if the student does poorly in
examinations. However, on successful completion of a degree
course the rewards are commensurate: a student with a B.A.
degree from a Greek university may obtain employment as a
gymnasium teacher in Cyprus at a starting salary of £80 a
month. Medical, legal or scientific qualifications lead to a variety
of career possibilities. In addition, there are other educational
possibilities, such as a diploma or certificate in one of the trade

skills, in agriculture, business, hotel management and so forth.
All these choices have been taken in recent years by various
villagers, and usually after a great deal of investigation in the
form of questioning anyone who might know anything about the
situation, plus continuous discussion within the family.

However, no amount of investigation has enabled the villagers
to foresee certain changes in the national economy and their
effects. One example will suffice: until ten years ago a highly
desirable career for a young person was to become a teacher of
Philology in gymnasium, where over a third of the curriculum
hours are normally devoted to some aspect of the Greek language
and its literature. The prestige of Philology was also high because of its traditional association with Greek nationalism and
with the transmission of Greek cultural ideals. Furthermore, in
the minds of the older people, full fluent literacy was a great
achievement. Thus until the late 1950s the role of teacher carried
great status, and this was expressed in the custom whereby everyone, young and old alike, stood up when a teacher, even if a
young man, entered the village coffee-shop.

But in the last fifteen years the status of the teacher has been
somewhat lowered. First not all young people who are now
qualified teachers can find jobs as soon as they want them. At
the time of my fieldwork, the daughter of a prosperous farmer
had returned from five years' university studies in Greece with a
degree in Philology (Greek language and letters) but there were
not enough vacancies in the schools, and she remained unem-
ployed at home for a year, 'sitting' in the idiom of the village.
This caused intense concern among villagers who had chosen
Philology as a suitable career for their children. There were at
least two other girls studying the subject in Athens at the time,
both of poor families. While my fieldwork was going on,
Domestic Science joined Philology as a subject for which there
were few if any vacancies in the schools for teachers.

But the erosion of the teachers' status is not only a consequence
of this limited unemployment. Children of the village at university in Athens said to me, 'It doesn't mean a thing to be a gymnasium teacher in Cyprus today, let alone a primary school
teacher'. A proverb, probably of recent vintage, was often quoted
to me laughingly by farmers: 'Nowadays there are more school-
teachers around than there are donkeys in Asschia village'. The
fact that Asschia village is famous for having donkeys is part
of the joke; perhaps another part is the juxtaposition of teachers,

who should be clever, with donkeys, which are not. The joke compresses a number of changes in the last seventy years: the vast increase in popular education means that villages have ceased to be places where illiteracy is the norm, to places where—for people under fifty at any rate—illiteracy is a more or less shameful deviation. At the time of my fieldwork there were more than fifteen assorted teachers who were children of the village, and normally lived there, though teaching near by. Before 1930 there seems only to have been one or two at a time. Inevitably when nearly everyone can read and write, and when simultaneously, the number of teachers has greatly increased, the individual teacher can no longer command as much respect as before. It is rare today for men of any age to rise in the coffee-shop for a teacher, and it is usually an old, illiterate farmer who does so. If the old custom prevailed, with fifteen teachers in the village moving through the coffee-shops, the other villagers would be jumping to their feet every few minutes of the day.

These, then, are the factors which the villagers use to distinguish between different occupations; my intention so far has been to explore their status implications. When villagers are asked what they do, they answer the names of occupational roles, which in fact may simplify rather complex situations. 'I'm a farmer . . . a shepherd . . . a builder . . . a policeman . . . a clerk . . . a secondary school teacher.' Such answers convey to other villagers relatively precise implications about security of income, skill, arduousness of work, level of formal education and so forth, and it is these, rather than any absolute ranking between the roles, with which I have been concerned.

STATUS FACTORS IN WORK BY WOMEN

The ideal role structure of the village family is similar to that reported elsewhere in the Mediterranean—the male household head is the provider, the economic mainstay of the family. His wife has two key obligations—to maintain the sexual honour of the family intact, and to minister to the domestic needs of household members. This has been neatly expressed by Davis (1969) when he writes of South Italian family roles that the man's rights are sexual and his duties economic, while the woman's rights are economic, and her duties sexual. Men must support their families economically; women must nurture their families by housework; women must submit to the sexual demands of their husbands; and women must never by their actions give the community the slightest cause to doubt their sense of sexual shame.

The classic analysis of the honour-and-shame complex of values for Greek culture is that of Campbell (1964) and although in certain details the values and behaviour of Kalo people are different from those Campbell analysed, the essentials are similar. One strong component of the complex is the belief that a woman may properly have sexual contact with only one man during her life—her husband. Men believe that women are easily tempted (a natural consequence of male vanity) and so women must never be placed in situations where unrelated men can freely talk with them *à deux*. A man's social reputation is safest when his wife and daughters remain at home, or in the immediate neighbourhood occupied with housework; if they leave the home it should be in the company of kin where possible. Any situation in which an unmarried girl or married woman works for unrelated people is potentially hazardous and reflects badly on the man's role performance as provider.

In the main, the need for women to accept paid work, that is, work outside the home, and for non-related persons, is much greater in households that start marriage with little land. Eighty-two householders married between 1931 and 1950 were questioned about whether their wives or daughters did paid work. Of twenty-seven who had started marriage with less than ten *donums* of land, sixteen had women who did such work; of those with eleven to fifteen *donums*, nine out of the seventeen had women who did paid work. The proportion dropped among those who started marriage with sixteen to twenty-five *donums*: only six out of the eighteen having women who work; of those starting marriage with more than twenty-five *donums* only three out of twenty householders had women who worked for money.

These figures help put the notion of paid work by women into perspective. The fact that thirty-four householders out of the eighty-two have wives or daughters who must sometimes accept paid work means that in these houses the status of the man is slightly diminished. It does not mean that his honour (*timé*) is affected, unless that is, one of his women misbehaves sexually.[3] All things being equal, men prefer that their womenfolk do not need to take paid work. For then, village gossip has that much less to work on. In traditional times, all village women did both housework and agricultural work on their own land, no matter how rich they were. But recently, in the last twenty years, some village women who have married teachers or civil servants have been able to avoid all but the lightest agricultural labour. For the family land has been put under citrus trees, and to assert family status, husbands with regular salaries sometime prefer to pay other women to weed around the trees and pick the ripe fruit. This leaves nothing for their wives to do; and so daughters may sit at home embroidering or sewing, while their mothers work in the fields. Since the daughters have nowadays often spent some years at secondary school (their mothers usually only have been to primary school) they may also glance at newspapers, or more commonly read various women's magazines, the more frivolous of which are known as *romantiká*.

ECONOMIC AND STATUS FACTORS IN CITRUS CULTIVATION

Over the last fifteen years citrus cultivation has played a dominant part in the interests of the villagers. The problems, imagery and benefits of citrus cultivation are constant topics of conversation. This is partly to be explained, as I shall show, by the potential for high profit which citrus trees afford; but also, citrus cultivation differs in certain ways from other common agricultural activities. It seems likely, though this is difficult to show convincingly, that villagers over-estimate the profits to be had from citrus, and that owning trees has come to have symbolic meaning in its own right, a meaning which suggests prosperity and success. Two possible signs of this are, first, that poor men for whom the ownership of a few trees is not obviously a wise use of scarce resources, often nevertheless put part of their tiny holdings under trees; and secondly that it is becoming almost a formal element in a girl's dowry that she will have a small piece of land planted with saplings, in addition to her house.

The symbolic and status elements in citrus ownership are further suggested by the tendency for some men to reply to the question 'What do you do?' '*I me pervoláris*' 'I am an orchard owner'. The Greek word literally suggests 'someone associated with orchards' and does not specify actual ownership; but it is now used to stress ownership. More important, perhaps, it is used to differentiate the speaker from the more general category of farmer. In comparison with many other jobs, the care of trees is relatively unexacting physically, and relies more for success on skill and judgement than on the sheer drudgery of carrot or potato cultivation. Unlike many other crops, the standing trees are almost permanent, having a lifetime of thirty or forty years. The farmer is an all-rounder, trying crop after crop from season to season, and using above all his labour to make a profit. The citrus cultivator can be seen as a specialist, handling a long-term investment, and avoiding much heavy labour.

Most of the citrus trees in Kalo fields have been planted since 1955. But a small number of men, not more than twenty, had already planted citrus in the 1920s and 1930s, following the example of the people of Market Town. The first planting of citrus in Kalo for which I have data was in 1926, when one of the largest landowners in the village planted three hundred trees. Seven years later he dug them up again because he was not able to sell fruit profitably. Other pioneer citrus growers found that their water supplies failed, or the depression in citrus prices during the 1939–45 war was enough to discourage them. Some dug up their trees, and others merely failed to look after them, and planted other crops among them. But in 1968 there were several orchards over thirty years old, producing fruit and income. Those who had kept their trees have not had cause to regret it.

Between 1941 and 1954 twelve Kalotes in my census planted citrus trees. This was still the period of tentative experiment, and most people who planted before 1954 were full-time farmers, with land and water enough to support experiment. Between 1954 and 1960 another fifty-four Kalotes planted citrus; that is, some 45 per cent of the men I sampled had gone into citrus to some extent (see Table 7). During the 1960s it simply became obligatory for any young man, whether farmer or not, who had a piece of land to plant citrus trees on it. A man who failed to do this was regarded as a fool. One hundred or two hundred trees is considered a small number. Four hundred or five hundred is beginning to be a useful number and one thousand trees or more takes one into the village elite.

Since citrus cultivation assumes such importance in the village, it is useful to outline what is involved. A *donum* of land is usually planted with fifty saplings, of a wild strain. After some eighteen months, these wild saplings receive cultivated grafts, obtained either from mature trees in the village, or in the case of certain new strains, from commercial growers of young trees or from government farms.

Saplings need irrigation during the normally rainless months of May to October. Roughly every twenty days, either the trees

TABLE 7

Second Wave (1955–60) Citrus Growers,
by land at marriage

DONUMS	GROWERS		NON-GROWERS	
	NO.	%	NO.	%
Under 10	9	16·6	28	34·5
11–15	9	16·6	24	29·6
16–25	21	38·8	15	18·6
26–50	13	24·0	11	13·2
50+	2	3·7	3	3·7
	54	99·7	81	99·6

themselves must be sprinkled with water, or, more commonly the whole field will be flooded for a short period. The water used is always from underground, pumped to the surface by diesel engines and conducted through concrete or earthen channels (*avláchia*) to particular fields.

Trees also need cultivation by tractor, both to keep down weeds which would otherwise compete with them for nourishment, and which inevitably grow rapidly in the irrigated, fertilized soil; the breaking of the soil by tractor ploughing also serves to conserve water, since it fills in the cracks and fissures in the soil through which in summer the irrigation water would otherwise rapidly run off. The newly ploughed earth keeps water near the surface of the soil for a longer period, and thus enables the tree roots to use it. Ideally, tractor ploughing would benefit the trees before each watering, but for reasons of economy, and because they fear to damage the tree roots by excessive ploughing, most farmers only have their fields ploughed every six weeks or two months.

In addition to ploughing by tractor and irrigation, trees need fertilizers, regular pruning, spraying with various pesticides, and if the trees are not protected at the edges of the fields, some form of wind break, which is often of light cane, planted in strips. Heavy winds, or hailstorms can cause serious damage to crops, either at the flowering stage or when the flowers have dropped and the first tiny fruit have formed. At the time of my fieldwork no one in Kalo had yet taken out any form of insurance against such natural hazards.

About the fourth year after planting, trees bear from about a dozen to fifty or sixty fruit. These fruit are fully mature and good to eat. From the fourth year to the tenth or twelfth, depending on type of tree and other conditions, the number of fruit produced increases. A Valencia strain (the commonest tree in the area) will when ten or twelve years old produce an average of five hundred fruit. Exceptionally high-yielding trees can produce over one thousand fruit. Even though a Jaffa orange commands a higher price, Valencia trees are more profitable because they produce many more fruit.

In 1968–9 the cost of cultivation was usually estimated in the village at 10/- per tree per year, after three years of age, and slightly more before then. But by late 1969 some farmers had recalculated the costs and were working on a figure of 12/- a tree. These calculations were made by men who needed to know precise figures, or men who either because they were white-collar workers, or because they lacked water, a tractor or some other essential, needed to work out how much money they would need to have for raising their trees. Many men, and in particular the full-time farmers, do not need to calculate in this way, since they have all the things they need for cultivation. These men think much more in terms of *ad hoc* expenses, such as a bill of £40 for repair of a tractor, or of lump sum debts, that they owe a total to all sources, of—say—£1,500.

Different people will have to pay in cash different amounts towards the care of trees. A white-collar worker who is unwilling to do even the lightest manual work to his trees must pay labourers and specialists for all stages of cultivation. A full-time farmer will do as much as he can himself, and only employ some-one else for some highly specialized job, such as the one-off task of grafting cultivated strains onto wild stocks. Between these extremes are a range of possibilities. Men who do not own tractors must pay men who do, to plough their orchards. Men with tractors but no water of their own must buy the water. Salaried men who do not mind spreading fertilizer, or driving a relative's tractor may avoid cash payment for these services. The hardest job, and that which educated men are least willing to do, is irrigation, for this involves hours working up to the knees in water channels, handling a heavy, long-handled shovel (dialect, *pthkíari*) to open and close the small mud dams. But even in this attitudes change and individuals differ: at the time of my field-work, a young man returned with a degree in Mathematics from Athens, positively delighted in irrigating his own fields. This was partly because he liked doing it and partly because his self-consciously progressive views suggested to him that it was a job worth doing.

The less a man does for himself in caring for his trees the less profitable to him they will be. But in spite of this, trees have still been attractive enough for a number of town-dwellers to go into citrus cultivation, including some high government officials, as well as sons of the village who have inherited land there. This economic interest in land within the confines of the village is one factor which adds to the sum of transactions between village and town, and which maintains in an active state ties between kins-men otherwise separated by distance.

The services just described can all be had on credit, although everyone in the village wants cash payment. But since many men are seeking to increase their holdings, and since the whole village is possessed to some extent with a 'boom' mentality, many services are supplied for credit, and a man may go several years without paying for water he has used, for tractor ploughing or for fertilizer from the Credit Co-operative. Villagers who supplement their income through providing citrus-related ser-vices must therefore take a great interest in the credit-worthiness of their co-villagers. The passionate interest in the small-change of daily life, gossip about tiny details of personal be-haviour is not gratuitous, but meets certain needs in the village as a whole.

The widespread use of credit does not suggest that credit may readily be had by all, and the issue of granting, withholding or terminating credit is a lively source of disputes. In this as in many other things, the poorer men are at a big disadvantage. A man with land, and growing trees, can be seen to have a possible future source of repayment. A man without these things has only his labour to offer. The chief factor which stops poorer men from getting in on the citrus boom is the problem of credit, or capital formation. For since trees do not begin to cover their cumulative costs until they are six or seven years old, the poorer man has greater difficulty in carrying his debts over this period of time than has the man for whom citrus is only a profitable sideline, and not the main source of income.[4]

When villagers talk about growing trees they say, 'After six years you just start getting your expenses back.' They do not mean getting back the full investment up to that point; they mean getting back those years' overheads. In any case, their statements usually take it for granted that a man has paid nothing to acquire his land.

CONCLUSION

The main concern in this chapter has been to describe the primary constraints on villagers which land ownership and work provide, and to suggest how four main categories of villagers enjoy different political roles as a complex result of their economic situations. Educated men tend to enjoy economic security and political power both in external village affairs, and within the village. Full-time farmers are economically secure, but are hampered in external affairs by their lack of education; within village administration and political leadership they are dominant over the remaining two categories. Skilled men have less economic independence than the full-time farmers, for they need customers, and wages to supplement inadequate land holdings. They are by no means barred from political activism and leadership, but are less likely to be pre-eminent. Unskilled men are the poorest and most insecure category, and the least politically active. They are never leaders, and always clients both inside and outside the village.

The secondary concern has been to give a brief picture of economic life in the village, and the system of social evaluation with which it is involved. In doing this, the analysis of politics in the village has been obliquely advanced, for what has been discussed will later be shown to be the central prizes for which village families are competing. Villagers are still in the main more concerned with the good opinion of their co-villagers, than they are with that of the world outside; this is not to say that the village is in any economic or political sense self-sufficient, for demonstrably it is not. It is to stress the village as a moral community, that is, a community where everyone shares some common notions of what social prizes are worth competing for. They do not in any sense share judgements about who deserves such prizes, still less who has won them. The outcomes of status contests are not the object of village-wide consensus. The consensus is confined to the fact that there is such a system, and that it has certain broad differentials. Such shared assumptions (like all social rules) leave room for endless disagreement over particular applications, but to understand this, the reader must be briefly introduced to the organization of kinship and marriage in Kalo.

NOTES

1. See Appendix 3 for certain aspects of changes in land tenure in Kalo.
2. Throughout, *donum* refers to government *donums*, which are roughly one-third of an acre. 'Village *donums*' were roughly twice the size of this, and were based on the amount of land a man with two oxen could be reckoned to plough in a reasonable working day. It was inevitably a rough measure.
3. Campbell (1964) has shown how the sex-linked constituents of honour (*timé*) contribute to a family's prestige in the eyes of other families. Wealth, strength, skills and other factors also contribute to prestige, but do not have the same dominant position in Greek values as *timé*. That is, the actors themselves are more concerned with *timé* than with other factors, appeal to it and justify their actions in terms of it. The fact that I devote so little space to the notion of honour is precisely because it has been so well analysed by others, most notably by Campbell (1964), Pitt-Rivers (1954), Lison-Tolosana (1966), and Davis (1969). See also (ed.) Peristiany (1965) for a number of papers on the subject.
4. A man would have to carry expenses of roughly £25 a year per *donum* (50 trees) for tractor ploughing, water and fertilizer. After seven years, this sum would be close to the cash value of the land itself (£350 in 1969). Poor men find the capital cost of the land a major obstacle to getting richer. It is clearly a much bigger problem than the running costs of citrus trees. A very rough reckoning of income from oranges is this: if a ten-year-old tree produces 400–500 fruit, and prices average £4 per 1000 fruit, then one *donum* might gross £75 to £100 a year.

4

Family

For the purposes of politics there are no individual actors in Kalo; there are only members of families, so for several reasons kinship and affinity must be discussed before we consider political processes. First, through these institutions individuals acquire their key statuses in the village, and the most compelling rights and duties which affect their relations. Secondly, nearly all actions are conceived of and justified in terms of furthering the interest of a man's dependants. Thirdly, the political culture of Kalo—and in fact of Cyprus and Greece generally—cannot be understood without an analysis of how far and in what contexts individuals regard themselves as members of family units. For Kalotes, in so far as it is conceived of at all, citizenship is mediated by kinship.

Certain formal aspects of kinship organization in Kalo are very similar to those described in Campbell's classic analysis of mountain shepherds in Epirus (Campbell 1964): the bilateral kinship system does not produce descent groups, the largest corporate unit being a three-generation family; a person's relations with mother's kin and father's kin are fully symmetrical in all respects; the kindred is not in any sense a corporate group but a category of consanguineal relations; it is precisely defined and within it a person may not marry.

But in other ways, kinship organization in Kalo differs from Campbell's material. There is normally no co-operating group of married siblings in the village economy. Kin and affines are not dispersed, but concentrated within the village, so they are less a scarce resource to be cherished, than a fact of life, to be judged on merits and usefulness. The relations a man makes with his wife's nuclear family are more relaxed, affectionate and co-operative than reported for the Sarakatsani; and finally, there is no binding obligation on members of one elementary family to present a united front in their political alignments; married men are also free to pursue their own alliances, and if these differ from those of their fathers, brothers or affines, this is not thought remarkable. These differences in no way alter the value of Campbell's analysis, for they do not affect the basic structural principles he isolated. However, they do suggest that Epirot pastoralists need not be regarded as in any sense an ordinary or standard adaptation of the principles, but due to the harshness of their situation an extreme case. Campbell's analysis of kinship and affinity nevertheless remains the best general guide to these institutions in Kalo, and it is only the fact that I can refer the readers to his work that allows me to treat these topics in a cursory fashion here, in order to advance more quickly to the analysis of politics in the village.

BASIC VALUES

In traditional times, when mixed farming dominated the village economy, the domestic group lived in a large courtyard (*avli*) in which there were several dwelling units and out-houses made of mudbricks, the whole being enclosed by a high wall which kept livestock in, and curiosity out. More recently as building land has become expensive, most Kalo families have stopped keeping oxen, sheep or donkeys; however, what has not changed is the cultural preference for a nuclear family to have a separate dwelling unit, and domestic economy of its own, from the first day of marriage if possible.

The phrase 'dwelling unit' is used advisedly, precisely because under traditional conditions of large courtyards, a family could, if short of building land, divide the courtyard into two, thus allowing a marrying child a yard and dwelling unit of its own. Similarly, if a number of children had been married off, and were living at some distance from their natal courtyard, the last child to marry often took over the parental dwellings, and the big yard, while the old people retired to a corner of the courtyard, in a small purpose-built separate mudbrick unit. This meant that they were still within call of a child, in case of difficulties, but could also lead an independent life. In the days of mudbrick building, old parents could easily move after a few years from the courtyard of one child to that of another, thus sharing the duty of their provision equally among their children.

In Kalo today, the majority of households contain a man, a woman and their unmarried children; a minority of households comprise a married couple, their unmarried children, and one or both elderly parents of either the man or the woman. To say this is to ignore the difficulty already suggested—those households which contain elderly parents are not in one sense households since the old people might, if cooking for themselves and living off their own savings or work, be counted as a separate household.

The villagers' wish that a married couple start life in a separate household is linked to three other features. One feature is the freedom a married couple have to make their own decisions; another, which underwrites this freedom, is the fact that the couple receive most of the property they will ever get from their respective parents at marriage. Thirdly, and obviously related to the first two points, parents gain or lose social prestige by the provision they make for their children's marriages. Taken together these features produce a complex process in which married adults work throughout their lives to gain their position in the prestige system of the village, which is only finally decided when the marriages of all their children can be evaluated by their fellow-villagers (Campbell, 1964: 146). People in Kalo are competing in two areas: first, they compete for resources (land, wealth, jobs, cash, influence) which they see as being in short supply; they also compete to obtain the best marriage partners for their own children. Both types of resource are in the control of their fellows, and success in the material sphere is usually followed by success in the critical prestige test—the acceptability of an individual and by implication his family, in marriage. The competition is particularly fierce since the final judgement is made by a person's rivals.

To the burden of provision for children, and the fierceness of competition with one's co-villagers, must be added the fact that rights to physical resources (land, houses) are derived from kinship status. In the most obvious way, a man depends on his parents and other kin for the advantages or lack of them with which he starts life, and on the relatives of his wife for any additional material or moral support he achieves in later life. Everyone who is not a consanguine or affine is, to some extent, a hostile competitor. In the next chapter the minimal rights and duties between unrelated co-villagers will be analysed; here it is enough to say that all critical resources and support depend on a person's kin and affines; they command his only categorical loyalties; in them are his strongest rights, to them his strongest duties.

In such situations, people invoke the notion of *synféron*, 'self-interest' or 'advantage' as the final logical and ethically compelling justification for what they have done or must do. This, it must be stressed, is not acceptable in the meaning of *individual* self-interest, but only when meaning the self-interest of a person with dependants. In the rhetorical give-and-take of self-justification, it sometimes appears that any kind of behaviour at the expense of another is morally justified if it can be held to advance or protect the well-being of one's dependants. This being the case, it is not surprising that people appear extremely mistrustful of others in most situations, and that such trust as is extended to others is normally greater between related than unrelated persons.[1]

SOME ASPECTS OF KINSHIP RIGHTS AND DUTIES

Census and genealogical materials showed that roughly four out of every five marriages in Kalo were between two persons born there.[2] It is a village where most people seem to have married within village boundaries fairly consistently for at least ninety years. This has naturally led to a situation where many villagers are highly interrelated. Only 44 per cent of 191 marriages in my census were between men who could trace no permitted consanguineal or affinal link to their wives. Of the rest, 33 per cent could trace a distant consanguineal link to their wives, for example, being third cousins collaterally, or even one link closer. Another 23 per cent could trace an affinal link, that is one of their consanguines was known to be married to a consanguine of their wife's.

This is to some extent brought out by the data in Table 8 which show that among selected informants the average number of first cousins resident in the village was twenty-three, while people with large kindreds have over forty first cousins in Kalo. This being so, it is likely that (allowing on average four second cousins for each first cousin) many villagers have from eighty to one hundred and sixty second cousins within the village. It is not surprising, then, that kin are not perceived as scarce, and that although people speak as if the fact of being related modifies social behaviour, in practice the right and duties between different categories of kin weaken roughly as the numbers in each category increase. I do not propose to treat kin categories either systematically or exhaustively here, but shall briefly note differences in rights and duties between three kinds of collateral kin—siblings, first cousins, and second cousins.

TABLE 8
The First Cousins of 24 Selected Informants

INFORMANT	TOTAL COUSINS	TOTAL IN VILLAGE	TOTAL OUTSIDE
1	40	35	5
2	59	Informant married into Kalo	
3	7	Informant married into Kalo	
4	25	16	9
5	30	20	10
6	34	27	7
7	46	43	3
8	55	25	30
9	26	17	9
10	16	12	4
11	30	22	8
12	11	10	1
13	27	21	6
14	19	14	5
15	21	16	5
16	35	30	5
17	26	23	3
18	35	23	12
19	57	41	16
20	36	19	17
21	36	31	5
22	11	5	6
23	43	38	5
24	50	20	30
	775	508	201

Average per informant: 32·4
Average in village: 23·09

Relations between unmarried siblings are strongly solidary with particular duties to economic support in domestic life, and to physical support in quarrels. A brother should defend the social reputation and physical person of his sister, to the point of death. A brother should avenge the killing of his brother. Siblings are expected to make sacrifices to help with the education or marriage of their siblings, particularly brothers for their sisters. However, after marriage, siblings have a new set of loyalties to their dependants, which conflict with their previous loyalties to their brothers and sisters. These conflicts become prominent late in a man's life, when he may dispute with his married siblings over residual portions of parental property. As many observers have pointed out, the cycle of relations between siblings in Greek culture is one of declining solidarity, with marriage as the turning point.

Between first cousins relations should be warm, and solidary, 'like siblings'. However, in terms of support and co-operation it is not possible to be on the same terms with twenty first cousins as with a handful of siblings, although in any case realistically no one expects this to occur. First cousins are not expected to support each other to the point of death, although if present during a quarrel they should support their kinsmen; likewise they should be alert to gossip about the reputation of their kinswomen. There is no expectation of economic support between first cousins, but nor is there a cycle of declining solidarity, for first cousins do not usually have common interests in property. The relationship has neither the costs nor the benefits of that between siblings. However, it does provide a basis for solidary relationships, should individuals desire them, and it is common for a man to have several first cousins among his closest friends. Normally first cousins are invited to all major life-crisis ceremonies.

Second cousins are formally members of a person's kindred, both in the eyes of the Church, and in village custom.[3] They are the most distant relatives who may not marry (a man may marry the child of a second cousin) and in this sense, in a village in which people compete for village-born marriage partners, they are something of a liability. For a man with many female second cousins can be heard to complain 'I could hardly find anyone to marry here, for they were all relatives . . .' There seem to be few benefits from second cousinship, except the vague notion that a person should show some small preference or greater trust in his dealings with a second cousin than he would with a completely unrelated person. There is no expectation that a man must invite all his second cousins to a baptism or engagement party and in these matters they are more like unrelated persons, than they are to first cousins.[4]

The following example illustrates forms of support between

siblings, and between first cousins. I know of no comparable examples of such support between persons whose main relationship was that of second cousins.

In 1968 Kounnis was charged by the police following a complaint by a woman neighbour that he had tried to assault her. The woman's reputation had been damaged, and in the scuffle Kounnis had slightly injured a young kinsman of hers with a knife.

Kounnis's wife was sister to Sklyros, one of the leftist leaders in the village. He was very angry with Kounnis, but at the same time his sister's well-being was at stake, and if Kounnis went to prison, as seemed likely, she and her children would be in difficulties.

Sklyros and his half-brothers went to a nearby village, and talked to a man who was their first cousin, and through his EOKA activities, was locally influential. He agreed to help, and visited a friend of his, a senior policeman in Market Town, where the case was due to be heard.

On the day of the hearing he appeared in the courtroom, in his best clothes, although he would not normally have had cause to be there. During the hearing the police decided to alter the charge from one of indecent assault, to attempted indecent assault. This charge does not technically exist in Cyprus law but the judge made no comment. Kounnis, after some uncertainty, pleaded guilty and was fined £40. He was thought to have got off very lightly.

This was considered by those concerned to have been a fairly strong demonstration of kin solidarity. The woman whom Kounnis had been charged with assaulting had a doubtful reputation in the village, and came from a small weak family. Kounnis, on the other hand, though a man of no account himself, was related by marriage to influential men, who were ready to help, less for his sake than for their sister's. The half-brothers of Sklyros had long-standing EOKA connections with their first cousin, and with him politically were clients of the same important urban politician. Their staunch support for this politicians' party in the 1970 Legislative Assembly elections was one way of repaying the favour which was thought to have occurred over the police charge.

PROPERTY TRANSFER AT MARRIAGE

In the village all children of both sexes, if not seriously deformed or handicapped, must marry, and do marry. It is also considered proper to marry them off as young as legally possible, and to have no unmarried daughter over twenty-five or unmarried sons over thirty. Children should also receive a share of their natal family property at marriage which is ideally an 'equal share' with the one their siblings will get or have got. Obviously, if there were no rule about order of marriage, such structural principles could easily result in a number of siblings all wishing to marry at the same time, and competing for the same scarce resources. In fact things are handled somewhat differently.

First, marriages are arranged: the decision that a person will marry is a collective family decision, not that of the young person alone. Traditionally, parents arranged marriages over the heads of their children, who were not granted even a power of veto over marriage partners. More recently, children (especially boys) and particularly those in more prosperous households, have the right to refuse to marry someone they do not want. However, marriages are still arranged by collective family action, and tentative approaches to other families are normally made through trusted third parties.

Not only are marriages arranged by collective decisions, but there is also an accepted set of rules about order of marriage which can be reduced to the idea that children marry in order of seniority, but that normally a girl should have an unmarried brother to protect her honour and help with her dowry. That is, a younger girl will marry before her older brother if there is no mature younger brother to protect her interests. The idea that there are such rules does much to limit short-term conflict between unmarried children.

It also helps create a situation in which younger unmarried children have a vested interest in helping economically to get their older siblings married off quickly, for that is the only way the younger ones can expect to marry. In effect, since siblings are typically separated by about three years, a domestic group is able economically to focus its resources on each marrying child in turn. Labour, surplus cash, and personal networks can all be mobilized in concentrated efforts to get a child successfully married off. A young brother may borrow cash from an employer to help finish the dowry house of his older sister, even though he knows it may take him five years to clear the debt, and start to save for his own marriage.

If a married sibling wishes to help one who is marrying, he must take care that this help is given discreetly, lest his own affines complain that he is diverting resources which should go to the children of the marriage. But if he can convincingly argue that by helping his younger siblings he is not alienating material resources from his own children, and at the same time building future support for those children in the shape of powerful or high-status uncles and aunts, then allowances will be made by the affines. In the case which follows a number of the themes of this chapter are illustrated: the rules of marriage order among brothers and sisters, the focusing of family resources on different individuals in turn and the sorts of calculations which a family must make in provision for members. The case is not typical, for the Fanos family have succeeded from a very weak economic base in advancing the fortunes of its members far more successfully than have most other village families: the family can be seen to have moved from the bottom to the top of the village prestige scale in a single generation; it is the process, not the particular statuses achieved which is characteristic.

Fanos and his wife had almost no land and their income was £20 a month from his salary as secretary to the village cooperative credit society. They had six children—three sons followed by two daughters, and a fourth son. The first son finished Gymnasium and got a clerical job in the land registry office. He did not in fact help his parents very much over the education of the younger children, but at the very least his academic success and his good fortune in landing a reasonable job encouraged the old people. The second son then completed Gymnasium and also got a civil service job. He turned over most of his salary for the education of the younger children, for since there were now always three at Gymnasium the school bills came to about £60 a year. The third son went from Gymnasium to the Teachers' Training College and after two years there received his Diploma and started work as a primary school teacher. He too made over most of his salary towards the cost of educating the three younger children. About this time the oldest son got married. The family now had a clear strategy for the problem of the remaining children. The fourth child, a girl, was also sent to the Teachers' Training College, and when she graduated and started teaching there were several requests for her hand from men in the village. In spite of strong family pressure she vetoed several candidates; it was understood that in order to build a dowry house she would need to take a loan of £3,000 from the benevolent fund of the school teachers' trade union, and that any man marrying her would accept the necessity of her working for a number of years to pay off this sum. During this period the second son also got married, to a rather wealthy girl in the village. Like his older brother he was soon in debt in an effort to increase the citrus plantation his wife received from her parents at marriage.

The third brother had now also taken out a large loan of £1,000 from the teachers' benevolent fund, in order to keep pace with the mounting costs of the two younger children. For the fifth child, another girl, had been sent to university in Greece for a five-year course in Philology. This alone was costing more than £300 a year.

The girl teacher got engaged to a young clerical worker, and they started building the new house in the village. The girl was a little more prestige-conscious than she was wise, and the house cost £3,500. Her sister finally completed the university course, and with some difficulty, which included important help from the husband of a first cousin, found a teaching job. She got engaged soon afterwards to a fellow teacher. Her unmarried older brother at 28 was nearing the age when village opinion felt it was high time he married. He met a girl—again a teacher—from a distant village and they got engaged. Now only the youngest child remains and the family have persuaded him, after many councils, to study medicine in Greece. He will have his fees met if the worst comes to the worst by each of the married children contributing about £5 a month, even though all of them have substantial debts to pay either on their houses or their citrus trees.

In this account it is important to note that the younger children have tended to receive more education and so qualification for the higher status occupations. The difference in age between the oldest and youngest children of this set is at least fifteen years, and the chances are that the oldest brother will be preparing to marry off his first daughter about the same time as the young doctor is ready to marry; since in this case there is no property left it cannot be the cause of dispute. In any case the prestige

TABLE 9
The Careers of Fanos' Children

CHILD	AGE 1968	YEAR MARRIED	AGE MARRIED	EDUCATION	JOB	SALARY 1968	COMMENTS
Boy	35	1961	30	Finished secondary	Junior civil servant	£860 p.a. (after about 15 years service)	His education cost about £150. He didn't help his parents very much.
Boy	32	1963	29	Finished secondary	Middle level civil servant	£900 p.a. (after 10 years service)	Education cost £150, but he helped his parents with the younger children on and off for seven years, with cash.
Boy	28	1970	30	Secondary plus 2 yrs. Teachers' College	Primary school teacher	£600 p.a.	Took loan of £1,000 from Teachers Union Benevolent Fund to help costs of educating younger children, and to study by post for a degree. Education cost £150.
Girl	25	1969	26	Secondary plus 2 yrs. Teachers' College	Primary school teacher	£500 p.a.	From Teachers' Union Fund she has borrowed £3,000 to build her own dowry house. Education cost £150.
Girl	23	1970	25	Took degree Athens University	Secondary school teacher	£900 p.a. in first year.	Failed to get State teaching job, since no more jobs in her subject (Philology). Currently faces problem in finding money to build a house. Education cost about £2,000 in all.
Boy	18	Single	—	Started studying medicine in Athens	—	Nil	Education will cost not less than £3,000, from start of secondary school to medical qualification. Some of this will be met by his married siblings.

for the sibling set of having both a Gymnasium teacher and a doctor in the family will act as a powerful sanction in maintaining co-operation. It cannot be said that many other families in the village have succeeded in elevating so many children from such an inauspicious base; it is more common to find that several of the older children have taken up manual work of some kind; but the principal strategies are the same in such cases. The particular leverage the Fanos family obtained was in the ability of the children who took up teaching to obtain substantial loans through their trade union. In a later chapter this family is described facing a serious crisis when the father was in danger of losing his job, which event would have seriously disrupted the pattern described here.

CO-OPERATION BETWEEN AFFINES

Campbell (1964: 140) describing how close affinal relations among the Sarakatsani only gradually come to approach the relations of trust which characterise close consanguines, writes:

> Yet even after the passage of years, close affinal relatives of the same generation must behave in a dignified and restrained manner in each other's presence . . . Affines do not laugh and joke together.

But in the situation he describes affines may only meet once or twice a year, and opportunities for close and continual economic co-operation are few. In Kalo, where a man meets his affines daily in the coffee-shop, relations appear to be much more relaxed, and economic co-operation more frequent. Indeed my impression is that with a successful marriage a man may find in his wife's father and wife's brothers a quality of informality, and support pleasantly free from the authority and competition of his own natal family. In any event, there is no lack of economic co-operation between affines. Twenty-four informants interviewed in depth about sharecropping and other partnership arrangements yielded sixty-eight instances of serious economic co-operation. These include both situations where one partner put up land, labour, cash or seed, against a complementary contribution from the other, as well as cases where two men jointly owned and operated a truck or tractor. Cases where an unmarried boy worked for his father were excluded. The sixty-eight cases were distributed as follows:

23 cases were between affines (a man with his wife's siblings, his wife's father, or some other affine)

15 cases were between consanguines (a man with his parents, with his siblings, or with his cousins)

26 cases with unrelated persons

 4 cases with *koumpári* (wedding sponsors, or the god-parents of one's children)

——
68
——

Data from women's work groups suggested similar proportions. A survey of ten agricultural work groups called by individual women (February–March 1969) yielded eighty woman-woman relationships; of these twenty-three were between consanguines and twenty between close affines. There is thus no reason to regard co-operation between affines in Kalo as less likely than between consanguines.[5]

In addition to economic co-operation, affinal relations create new networks which individuals can use to align support in particular situations. Marriage provides a man with a set of new contacts, which supplement those of his natal family. Obviously, a man's relations with his wife's kin are much closer than those of his siblings with her kin, but the Kalo data differ from Campbell's material (1964: 140): effective co-operation through affinal links can be extended widely, and this is not unusual. For in the final analysis, by definition any help given to an affine is mediated by the helper's link to his own blood relative—in helping affines one is helping one's own kin. That is how people justify co-operation when they wish to co-operate. The following case illustrates such a situation:

Sklyros has been married to Ploutis's sister for twenty years, during which time Ploutis has become very wealthy. Sklyros uses his tractor to cultivate Ploutis's citrus groves and Ploutis is content with this arrangement for his trees get good attention while the money he pays is of direct benefit to his sister's family.

Sklyros has debts of several thousand pounds; in 1969 he was thinking of starting a pig farm and went to a Market Town Bank for a loan. The manager would not normally have been willing to consider this, because Sklyros has mortgaged all available land, and is financially over-extended. But since Ploutis had agreed to guarantee the loan, the manager was ready to make it. If Sklyros fails to repay it, Ploutis will be liable.

This case then shows the ambiguity at the heart of much affinal co-operation by helping a brother-in-law a man is also helping his sister. However, in some cases it is possible to find help being given for more general notions of solidarity rather than simply 'to help the sister':

> Andreas had a younger brother, Yiannis. Yiannis's friend was involved in a serious court case, and to help him out, Yiannis gave false evidence. This was discovered by the prosecution, who decided to proceed against Yiannis. This would have cost him his white-collar job and a gaol sentence.
>
> Andreas heard of his brother's difficulties, and went to his wife's brother, Petros, a professional man in a town. Petros is married to the daughter of a wealthy merchant, who regularly goes drinking with a high government official. This man was persuaded to use his influence to get the case dropped.
>
> The links involved were friend/friend; brother/brother; brother/wife's brother; son-in-law/father-in-law; father-in-law/friend; friend/friend; and a final unknown link.

KINSHIP TIES AND POLITICAL ALIGNMENT

In the first chapter I mentioned the way in which national party politics and issues have penetrated the world of the village; it is now proper to pose the question of how far such new opportunities for alignment with forces outside the village have affected the traditional loyalties between kin and affines? In one sense the question is premature, since the actual benefits of political alignment, and the different types of individual response to national politics, have yet to be analysed. For the moment it must be enough to say that there are significant material benefits to be had from political alignment, although they are scarce and their supply is somewhat unpredictable.

The most straightforward answer is that villagers constantly speak as if it is unthinkable for related men to quarrel over politics. Anthropologists are well aware that what people say is 'unthinkable', often in fact happens, and that to say something is unthinkable is probably a device to stop it happening too often. However, in this case, the labelling of such quarrels as unthinkable seems successful as a form of social control at the very least. I collected detailed dispute data from twenty-four selected informants which yielded 120 disputes. Classified by cause, there were only five about politics, and of the five only two were between kin or affines.

This appeal to numbers is misleading by itself. What villagers mean by 'unthinkable' is that a man must be very foolish or short-sighted to jeopardise the long-term resources of kinship loyalty, for the short-term and more uncertain resources of political align-ment. Of course, in a few situations, there can be direct conflict of interest between a man's kinship or affinal relationships, and some benefit offered by his political alignment, and later in this book there will be examples of such conflicts, and the way villagers handle them. At this point in the book the interim answer to the question of how villagers handle politics must remain on the level of abstract rules and a few instances.

A married man is considered free to pursue any alliances that will benefit his dependants. There is no requirement that he will align himself with the same patrons or political allies as his father, his wife's father, his siblings or his wife's siblings. In for-mal terms, then, the autonomy of a household head is complete.

The limit on that freedom has already been hinted at: a man should not allow such political alignments to interfere with, dis-rupt or take precedence over the categorical loyalties of kinship, or the contractual loyalties of affinity. To do so would be to allow the smaller to dominate the larger interest. The following case is an illustration of adherence to this principle:

In 1963 Vakis, a leftist, was a committee member for the village Co-operative store. The village militia, dominated by rightists, was collecting money to buy guns. Vakis gave them £20 as did his older brother Anemos. But the collectors also took from the Co-operative store a box of shotgun cartridges, without asking. This annoyed Vakis, who told a friend of his, a civil servant, about it, and later some official inquiries were made.

The village militia leader was Moustachas. He and Anemos are *síghambri*, men married to sisters, but their good relations had deteriorated because of an unsuccessful co-ownership of a tractor. However both men were clients of right-wing urban politicians.

When Moustachas heard that Vakis had complained about the cartridges he told Anemos, 'Your brother needs shooting for doing a thing like that,' by which he meant bringing the village militia into disrepute with powerful outsiders, and his anger was double because Vakis was a leftist.

Anemos shouted back at him, 'You better not lay a finger on my brother,' and for four years after that the two men were cold towards each other. In public they concealed their coldness, and Anemos continued to behave normally to his wife's sister and the children. Anemos's readiness to oppose Moustachas is the more impressive because the militia leader is considered a dangerous man to offend.

Such an example of blood being thicker than political alignment is how villagers would like things always to be. I have already given in an earlier chapter an instance of how a right-wing nationalist father found himself in political opposition to his communist son (page 38). Recollections of this event had probably mellowed with time, and it is not possible to say much more about it than that it happened. But during 1968 there was a chance to see what happened when a young man (who was the client of Moustachas) was suspected by some of his first cousins of carrying tales about their political activities, to his dangerous patron. There was considerable anger expressed, and the cousins continually warned each other not to talk about politics in front of this young man. Whenever he turned up in the houses of relatives there was the suspicion that he was 'spying' and one family which contained several leftish brothers believed that he was reporting back to Moustachas which papers they read. These events were probably the legacy of earlier political cleavage in Kalo (see ch. 7, The case of the Lyssarides Group). What struck me when observing the reactions of the people involved was the bitterness over the fact that a close kinsman could do such things. Even if the men were wrong about the extent of their cousin's activities, the strength of their feelings clearly expressed the ground rules of kinship loyalty.

The issue can perhaps be made clearer by Figure 1. The senior generation, aged fifty to seventy, show a range of political ties. Most are simply 'nationalists' and not differentiated into left, centre or right-wing nationalists, since these distinctions have only become meaningful and clear in the last ten or fifteen years and the older people's 'nationalism' predates the distinctions. However, one woman from the group of siblings married a man who was already a communist in 1940. She in 1968 described herself as left, and had voted left in the past. One of her brothers had called himself a communist between 1945 and 1950, but later had switched alignment, probably under the influence of his wealthy

FIGURE 1

Political alignment in two generations

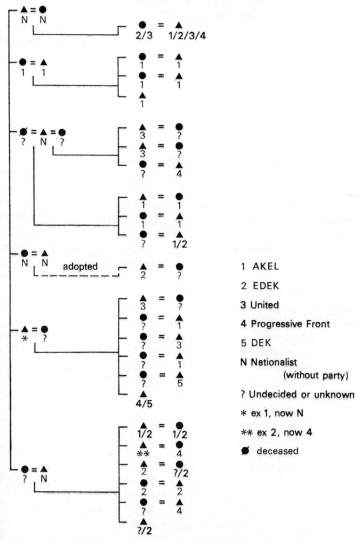

1 AKEL

2 EDEK

3 United

4 Progressive Front

5 DEK

N Nationalist
(without party)

? Undecided or unknown

* ex 1, now N

** ex 2, now 4

⚫ deceased

Since most parties emerged only in 1969, many longstanding Nationalists had no particular party affiliation. For a guide to parties see Table 14, p. 239.

D

elder brother, a staunch right-nationalist. One left-wing brother, not shown on the diagram, emigrated from Cyprus in 1930.

The second generation includes two sets of siblings who share the same political alignments, and two which have diverse alignments. There are 23 first cousins and their 20 spouses. Between them, they cover the five main political parties which contested the 1970 elections for the House of Representatives. In the instance just described the young man thought to have been 'spying' was the unmarried man whose alignments are shown as both 4 and 5.

The situation represented in the diagram does something to suggest the complexity of the alignments which may exist in one small section of a kindred.[6] In 1969 I examined the range of alignment among different sets of married brothers in Kalo. Nine sets of brothers had roughly the same alignments in national party politics; another four sets of brothers had alignments which were too ambiguous to be classified; and some ten sets of brothers had alignments which were quite clearly diverse. Here alignment covers situations where villagers were the clients of national political leaders. It does not mean paid-up membership in a party, but rather known and public support for a party or its leader. This shows that no simple rule of solidarity in political alignment operates between married brothers.

Even if such a rule *did* operate, the system of kinship and affinity is such that it would lead to conflicts of loyalties very quickly. If all brothers in a set aligned in the same way, what would happen to their affinal relations? How would they behave to the brothers and fathers of their wives? If a rule requiring men to marry into families which shared their alignments were to hold good over time, the village would end up as two in-marrying blocs (assuming two major parties, left and right). This might be a practical possibility if Greek Cypriots had kinship rules which permitted some form of marriage *within* the kindred. As it is, the rules force marriage with persons more distant than second cousins. The logic of such a system is such that it could only keep two unrelated blocs going; it cannot produce them from a village where people are already highly related. Kalotes were closely related before the distinctions of national politics entered their lives, and it is unlikely that they will invent rules to make life harder for themselves in this particular way. Besides, they have invented a rule which has already been discussed—a man would have to be stupid to quarrel with relations over politics.

However, the arrangement of marriage presents certain opportunities for political alignment to be taken into account. Some families are clearly more concerned than others that their daughter should not marry a man of the left, or of the right. Many villagers said that they would ignore political alignment when considering marriage partners for their daughters, and that only 'fanatics' would be so concerned. This does not provide proof that this is how they really behave. The fragments of evidence obtained suggest that alignment is taken into account in the same way that other factors are—age, wealth, education, job, family reputation and personal qualities such as strength, looks, willingness to work and so forth. There were certainly a number of striking cases of marriage across political alignments. During fieldwork a marriage was arranged between the daughter of old Tsingounis, a man who was a leading right-wing nationalist, and the son of a man who was one of the more mature and dedicated communists. The rightist was on several important committees, and part of a nationalist faction based on several linked nuclear families. The leftist was one of the largest landowners in the village. The two senior men were close neighbours in the village. No one seemed to think the match was in any way remarkable.

Another similar example involved Borris, a leftist on several important committees. In 1969 he was on the committee of the Credit Society, and left leaders regarded him as reliable. However, Borris allowed his daughter, the second of seven children, to get engaged to a young man of strong nationalist views, who is the client and supporter of a political leader known for his anticommunist views.

A final example: one of the left leaders, Tangos is married to another daughter of Old Tsingounis, just mentioned. He remembered that during his engagement he had argued with his father-in-law about politics. But he added that other old men in the village didn't really understand modern politics, 'If you ask a lot of them if it's true that the son of Old Tangos is a communist, they'll say it isn't possible . . .' He meant that given his father's relative wealth, and traditional nationalist views, old men would have found it quite implausible that his son could become leftist.

CONCLUSION

In social life and more narrowly in political life, the inhabitants of Kalo village must be understood as members of families, rather than as isolated individuals. The notion of *synféron*, self-interest, is normally interpreted to imply the interest of a man's dependants. Through kinship and marriage a man obtains his most important rights (to property or support) and acknowledges his most pressing duties, the adequate provision for his dependants. Each married man is economically and jurally independent, and the nuclear family usually lives in a separate house.

The villagers are highly intermarried and a man may have large numbers of his kin and affines present in the village. He cannot maintain equally close co-operative relations with all his kin. Before marriage relations between siblings are normally solidary, with strong co-operation, but as each person marries his loyalties to his wife and children compete with and inevitably weaken his loyalties to his siblings. Late in life, married siblings may come into conflict over residual family property, particularly since they will now have children of marriageable age who need provision. The decline in sibling solidarity over time makes the relation one with initially high benefits, but later with equally high costs.

First cousins rarely have a common interest in corporate property, nor do they experience early co-operation within the domestic group. The relation provides a sound base for enduring friendship and co-operation, with no inbuilt structural tension. It is a low cost relationship, with potentially high benefits. In contrast, second cousins within the village are so numerous that they are little regarded. The relationship carries few structural benefits, and can be costly in so far as men seeking marriage partners are barred from choosing among their often numerous second cousins.

The arrangement of marriage provides an arena for the competition for social prestige which so deeply concerns villagers. A family is judged by the acceptability of its children as marriage partners, and it is at marriage that most children receive their major share of family resources. A great deal of a married man's energies and calculations are involved with the best possible provision and marriage of his children; no man regards himself as free to undertake commitments which might jeopardise the well-being of his dependants.[7]

Marriage adds to a man's stock of allies; co-operation between a man and his wife's close kin is normal and expected.

Kinship and marriage as institutions are expressive of a man's long-term and categorical loyalties. Yet his autonomy as a household head leaves him free to seek any alliances which he perceives as likely to benefit his dependants. In political matters, men are not expected to align themselves with the same persons or parties as their parents, brothers, or affines. In fact, it is common to find men closely related to have different or opposed political alignments, and it is argued that the rule of exogamy and the high degree of interrelatedness of villagers, taken with the bilateral organization of kinship, make diverse ties inevitable. The likelihood that political interests between closely related men might bring them into conflict is reduced by a strongly held value which requires the long-term interests of kinship and marriage to dominate the short-term interests of political alignment. For closely related persons to fall out over 'politics' is said to be the height of foolishness. But as we shall see later, such definitions—items of social control—are sometimes strained by circumstances. Norms are easier said than 'done'.

NOTES

1. The reader will note the resemblance to Banfield's (1958) description of 'amoral familism'. This concept has been widely discussed and criticized. Here it is enough to say that throughout this book there are examples of villagers with a very similar set of core values, managing to cooperate, organize, and participate in formal organizations in a number of ways. This suggests, in view of the recent prosperity of the village, that these values (far from explaining 'backwardness') are more properly explained by it. When the Kalotes become more sure of their prosperity, they will behave less and less like 'amoral familists'. Indeed the younger people in the village—who have only known full employment and full bellies—criticize the suspicious watchfulness of their elders.
2. It is of course possible that the collection of genealogies distorts the situation, for elderly informants would be likely to forget those of their parents' (or grandparents') siblings who had married out of the village, if this resulted in breaking off contact. Also, some small kin groups which have left the village may be completely forgotten. There is also reason to think that before 1930 (an approximate point of cut-off) the rate of marriage within the village was lower.
3. A man may not marry any woman to whom he is related within five links of consanguinity, counting the relationship between siblings as one link. He may not marry a second cousin, for example a mother's father's sister's daughter's daughter or a father's father's brother's son's daughter, or any similarly related relative. Nor may he marry the child of a first cousin, for example, a father's brother's daughter's daughter, or even a father's brother's daughter's daughter's daughter. Nor could he marry such unlikely persons as his father's mother's sister's daughter's daughter. I heard of one case where second cousins married (after obtaining a

dispensation from a 'stranger' priest who may or may not have known the facts) and this was regarded locally as scandalous.

4. As one might expect when second cousins meet in town, or abroad (Athens, London) there is a tendency for the relationship to be given more value.

5. There are obvious difficulties inherent in such an analysis. For example, co-operation between unmarried siblings is inevitable in an agricultural household, but this is masked by the fact that resources are corporate and not individually owned. I am concerned only with situations where individually owned resources are being staked.

6. The situation would become much *more* complex if the various affinal connections of the 23 first cousins are included. As has been frequently noted, such exercises have no logical boundary, and this is why it is preferable to discuss actual transactions. But the formal description of alignments for a small number of persons is useful in itself.

7. In Cyprus during the last forty years it has become customary for daughters to need a well-appointed dowry house at marriage. This is a crushing burden on poor families with many girls, and has profound consequences for the village and national economy. These and other aspects of marriage and property transfer are discussed in Loizos (forthcoming).

5

Contracts

Economic constraints and family obligations account for a good deal of a man's behaviour, but by no means all. Certain kinds of social relations are achieved—*koumpariá*, and friendship; others result from membership in common categories—as with neighbours, men of the same age, or who do the same job; yet others derive from the simple fact of membership in the village. All these types of social relationship need to be analysed before any description of politics in the village can make sense, particularly since it will be a main theme of later chapters that there is a degree of tension between villagers' collective interests in preserving the peace of the village, and their individual interests in seeking new benefits which reach them when they align themselves with certain external agencies or leaders. The hottest debates of politics in the village are concerned with claims to specify how binding and extensive relations of incorporation are to be (Barth 1966: 4) and at what point they stop, and transactional relations begin. To this extent I think politics in Kalo can be fruitfully analysed with ideas derived from more complex and large scale units, and seen as debates and compromises about the proper way in which a defined social unit is given social order.

The most direct way to understand the essential content of social relations involving villagers is to grasp that all relations are thought of either as between equals in power or status, or as between unequals. Naturally, villagers do not always agree about the quality of relations which exist or ought to exist between two persons, and this follows both from the competitive nature of the status system, and the belief that most things worth having are in short supply. One thing that can be denied to someone else is equality, for by the denial the speaker raises himself (in his own eyes if in no one else's). Villagers are not 'competing to remain equal' so much as competing *to become as unequal as possible.*

Some writers on Mediterranean villages, impressed by the
values of honour and shame which are widespread, have tended
to stress notions of equality-in-honour.[1] That is, men are born
with equal quantities of honour which cannot be increased, but
can only be blemished or lost. This is generally true of Kalo. But
if such an approach suggests that villagers see each other as
basically the same, or that they wish all to remain at the same
status level, then it is very misleading. Kalotes are not levellers:
they do not want other people in the village to be 'the same'
in power or status as they themselves. But they are opposed to the
pre-eminence of other villagers being asserted, and they try their
hardest to pull anyone down if he can be pulled down. Each man
is perfectly happy to stand head and shoulders above his fellows
if he can, so 'egalitarian' would not be helpful here. Nor would it
be helpful to describe as any kind of democratic tendency the
fact that men who regard each other as equals in status are prone
to shout each other down with great vigour in coffee-shop debate.

It is easy to see contradictions and paradoxes in the way villagers behave, and the difference between this and what they say
they do. For example, a poor man when asked about his political
alignments may reply, *íme anexártitos; dhen anígho kanenoú*—I
am independent; I don't belong with anyone. Yet he knows that
the listener knows this 'independence' is sharply limited by
poverty. 'Fierce pride'? Or a sensible refusal to discuss something
as dangerous as politics with an inquisitive anthropologist? Or a
fantasy? Or a way of saying simply, that all options are being
kept open, against the hour of need?

Village social relations can be understood in terms of perceived
power. Villagers fear and defer to those markedly more powerful
than themselves; they treat those they see as equals with an
aggressive equality; and from those who are obviously much
weaker they expect some deference. To this must be added that
in a public, face-to-face situation men act with caution, and they
are often unwilling to say what they really think about powerful
persons or dangerous issues, if there is any chance that a hostile
remark will rebound. This regard for power relations is made
clear in many small ways; for example the use of pronoun and
verb forms which convey either distance and respect, or the
intimacy of equals (Brown and Gilman, 1960); another way is in
the giving of commands and the response to them; and a third is
in the way a man does or does not speak out on sensitive topics
in the arena of the coffee-shop.

It is often remarked that although it is humiliating to have to show deference to someone of roughly equal power, when the gap between two persons is greater, a weaker person can show deference without loss of face. If a relationship between persons of unequal power becomes institutionalized, by a continual exchange of goods and services between them, then the concept of patron-client relations becomes appropriate. In what follows I shall mostly be concerned with relations between equals, for the analysis of leadership, power, the benefits of political alignment, and the things exchanged between patrons and clients are left for the next chapter. Here they will only be discussed where essential to preserve some order in my argument.

KOUMPARIÁ

Marriage and baptism in the Orthodox Church of Cyprus create *koumpariá*, two core relationships expressed by a single word, wedding sponsorship and baptismal sponsorship. Traditionally a groom invited a male friend to sponsor him at his wedding, and the two men from then on used the reciprocal term *koumpáros* (plural, *koumpári*) to each other; the bride invited a female friend to do the same, and these women in Cypriot dialect called each other *kouméra* (plural, *kouméres*). Normally, the *koumpáros* and *kouméra* took it in turns to baptize all the children of the marriage to whom they became godparents.[2]

Since about 1930 in the Kalo region the numbers of wedding sponsors have increased apparently without any impetus from the Church. At first couples invited two sponsors of each sex, then three, four, and five, until in 1969 most couples had fifteen or twenty, and some boasted a hundred. This inflation of sponsors has led in the village to an informal ranking order, in which the first ranks highest, and *koumpári* after the fourth or fifth are thought of as little more than *koumpári* in name—the important rights and duties do not affect them once the wedding is over. The first four or five *koumpári* will baptize the children of the marriage, in turn, although the strict rank order is sometimes broken, and it is possible to invite a person who was not in fact a wedding sponsor to baptize a child.

Every adult wishes to baptize a child, and nearly all succeed. To be asked to baptize is an honour; to ask parents to be allowed to baptize their child is to make them an overture of friendship which they will consider carefully, and will normally only decline through a face-saving excuse, such as saying that the child has already been promised to someone with a closer claim.

Baptism creates two different kinds of new roles—those between the adults involved, and those between godparent and the godchild. In both situations the sponsor undertakes duties of support and protection. To the child the sponsor must be spiritual mentor in the Orthodox faith; to the parent, the sponsor must be especially ready to grant help, favours or support of any kind. The parents must reciprocate with similar readiness to help, and with additional respect and deference. Traditionally, a man seated in a coffee-shop would rise when a person who had baptized his child approached. This respect is due for both spiritual and material reasons because the sponsor meets the costs of the sacrament and the festivities which follow it, which nowadays in a modest ceremony include meat and alcohol for some twenty people. A person should have at least £20 available before agreeing to baptize a child; a man in 1969 earned £1.10.0 by a day's unskilled labour, and a woman earned 15/-, so this was no small outlay.

Koumpári should help each other, and they should carefully avoid quarrelling; there is reason to think that the religious and customary sanctions against dispute between *koumpári* actually work, for out of 111 disputes I collected, only four were between men who admitted to being *koumpári*, a proportion markedly lower than between consanguines, affines, or ordinary friends.

In Kalo over half the cases of baptism recorded involved invitations to persons who were kin or affines with one of the parents. Of the rest, most were still co-villagers. Less than 5 per cent of the godparents were not resident in the village, and less than 10 per cent of them were of obviously different status from the parents. This contrasts with Campbell's data from the Sarakatsani, well over half of whom were outside the shepherd's community and of higher status. Why should the same institution be put to such apparently different uses?

There are a number of reasons. Kalo is not isolated, but a short journey to the capital, and villagers have kin contacts there; the village is relatively prosperous, and the government's agencies relatively efficient and accessible. Younger villagers are nearly all literate. These reasons add up to a lack of pressing need to use *koumpariá* relation for external and asymmetrical purposes. I suggest that the preference for sponsors who are co-villagers and equal in status is also an index of the extent to which villagers look to each other both for economic exchange and the granting of social rank, i.e., status. Those who use *koumpariá* to create relations with powerful outsiders are often aspiring to village leadership, or with aims outside the village arena.

There is another kind of reason however, and that is made clear by the remarks of an informant with seven children. Six of them had godparents in the village, of the same status as their father. But the seventh had a Nicosia physician as godfather. My informant commented, 'He never comes to see the child. Once he sent him a piece of clothing, but nothing since. My kid says "Who is my godfather?" It would have been better to have a villager baptize him, and then the kid would have got to know him, and if he got a bob or two out of it from time to time, it would have been fine. The godfather should be a second father to the child . . .' The complaint here was about a complete lack of content in the relationship. The same man pointed out that a highly placed *koumpáros* could (and normally would) show preference to his godchild, and help him in different ways.

This shows the problem and danger for a villager of gambling on a relationship with a powerful person; it can be a complete waste of what should be a valuable relationship. The problem is one of prediction. The further away people are from the world of the village, the harder it is for a villager to say how they will behave. To have an indifferent *koumpáros* is to be mocked for having had pretensions. Most Kalo villagers seem to work on the principle that a bird in the hand is best.

PHILÍA[3]

Philía means friendship, by which villagers understand a relationship of mutual liking between people of the same sex, entered into of their own free will, and without intention of personal gain; it does not mean to them a relationship conceptually contrasted with kinship, and close friends are often close kin as well, but they are kin first and friends second. The idiom of friendship is frequently that of kinship: 'I love him as I love my brother', where what is implied is *aghápi*, non-sexual love. Esteem, *ektímisis* and respect, *sevasmós* are also appropriate sentiments towards friends. The final constituent definitions of friendship in Kalo are that friends help one another and that true friends, *gnísii phíli*, or friends of the heart, *kardiakí phíli*, must be distinguished from the varieties of false friends, those who are friends in pursuit of advantage.

Friends who are not kin must be on their guard against jealousy of the relationship from close kin who may claim priority in rights over resources. Secretiveness is one such mode of caution. Men freely admitted to owing sums of money as large as £5,000 (indeed they took pride in their debts); but they were very unwilling to tell me the names of people to whom they had loaned even £20. 'My relatives might be jealous and angry if they find out I lent him money' they explained. People often warn their kin against trusting non-kin, saying that people posing as friends may cheat or exploit them.

Friends have several areas where they can help each other: economically in cash loans; exchange of work; being each other's customers; socially; by support in quarrels; by advice; and by the use of network links, that is by putting information and contacts with people at each other's disposal. These need little comment, except to point out that in a community where people are quick to mock at innovation or eccentricity, advice from a friend may be greatly valued, since it allows a man to test response to an idea without risking public ridicule.

It is a commonplace that friendship is both expressed and reinforced by exchanges such as those just mentioned. Such transactions can be reinforced by eating and drinking together, whether at home, or in public. The honour-and-shame complex of values is so strong in Cyprus that to invite an unrelated man to the home, where he will meet one's womenfolk, is an act of real trust. On the other hand, to offer a man a meal in the coffee-shops has the advantage of a public gesture of friendship. Eating between unrelated persons is highly ceremonial, in that it is not hurried, and is accompanied by a number of formal phrases exchanged between host and guest. But more than this, there is the expectation that the very act of eating and drinking together creates an element of friendship where previously no relation existed. Men describing the emergence of a friendship often say *epínamen tch' 'etró'amen mazí, tch' ephilépsamen*, 'We were eating and drinking together and we became friends.' The suggestion is of a finite act, an event which in a small space of time altered the nature of a relationship. The implied gradualism of north European friendship is absent.

Friendships are also maintained through drinking groups. These tend to be fluid in composition, in a way which makes precisely balanced exchanges unlikely. A man invites another to drink with him. They are joined by several men, and the first man, or less commonly the first two men, pay for the whole evening. This sets up the general expectation of being similarly invited by each of the other men at some future time. The man who pays gains prestige, and men who avoid paying are themselves avoided. The more prominent political leaders in the village tended to be frequent participants in drinking groups. Such participation usually goes with a measure of economic success, but the educated men tend to feel that public drinking in coffee-shops is beneath their dignity.

True friends are usually equals in power and status, men who feel *sympáthia*, liking, for each other; the things they do for each other spring from this liking, and not vice versa. That is the way the villagers see it. They tend to describe a friendship between those not equal as *pseftikí philía*, false friendship, and this is their way of describing what to an anthropologist are patron-client ties. Both villagers and anthropologists are describing a situation in which what is exchanged is different both in quantity and quality. Two friends use intimate singular forms of address; a client uses polite plural forms to his patron, who does not seek his client's company for pleasure, but only when he or the client want something. A client usually takes some small gift when he goes to see his patron—fruit, potatoes, a chicken; patrons do not give such things to their clients. Instead they do them favours on request, favours which the clients could not conceivably do for their patrons, favours which depend on wealth, power, or personal contacts.

A client may try to insist that his relationship with his patron is 'true friendship'. A Kalotis called Yiannos during the EOKA period met a man who later became a minister in the government. This man then bought some land in Kalo, and paid Yiannos to look after it for him. Yiannos refers to the minister as his friend, and has taken a number of villagers to meet him when they needed small favours done. But other villagers sneer at Yiannos' claim, and say: 'What does the minister want with a man like Yiannos? Yiannos is his employee—nothing more.' Yiannos is widely believed to carry tales to the minister about people in the village who like or dislike him, who support or oppose his polical party. It is also believed that Yiannos could use his relationship with the minister to exclude certain personal enemies in the village from social security benefits. Yiannos is also believed to have told the minister the names of certain villagers after the minister's property had been damaged. Depending on the speaker's relations with Yiannos, the relationship is described either as genuine friendship or false, self-interested friendship.

OTHER BASES FOR ASSOCIATION

Koumpariá and true friendship are institutionalized relations, in different degrees. There are other bases for association which must be sociologically distinguished.

A man's social life is largely public, conducted in the several coffee-shops at the centre of the village. There were never less than four centrally located during my fieldwork, and sometimes, depending on the whims of certain individuals, five or six. Men commonly visit a coffee-shop at least once a day, and for most men, when not eating, sleeping, or in the fields, the coffee-shop is the natural and proper place to be. This is so much a part of the proper male role that a man who doesn't put in enough time in this public world is likely to have said behind his back: 'What sort of man is he? He prefers hanging about the house with the women!'

From 5 a.m. till about 8 a.m. and again in the evening from 5 p.m. to 8 p.m., the coffee-shops are an important clearing house for information and men deliberately go there to seek it, to find work or workers, to get a lift to Market Town or to the capital, to do any one of a number of things which involve other people. Unless he lives close to his house, a man will look for another in the coffee-shop, as visits to houses might give occasion for gossip.

Men come into the coffee-shop area where others are sitting at ease, and ask: 'Have you seen X?' 'He hasn't come yet.' 'He's over there at Y's place.' 'He's already left for Nicosia.' 'He's watering that big field of his down by the river.' 'He's sick at home.' Any man will answer who knows; and the question is often asked generally of all who are seated, since the speaker is less interested in who answers than in getting a useful answer. This need which each man has for a degree of civility and information from others is complemented both by the public character of the coffee-shops—they are open to all—and by a particular custom of hospitality associated with them: put in its baldest terms if a man B arrives and sits down near another man A, then A will normally order and pay for a coffee for the newcomer, *without there being an especially close relationship between them.* Major differences of age, wealth, or education may allow the second man B some scope for saying, 'It isn't done ...' but as a general rule common civility between co-villagers requires A at least to try to treat B to refreshment and B can only properly refuse it by stressing a social difference between himself and A, since the grounds for the gesture is that both men are co-villagers.[4] Although in this way the coffee-shop supports a minimal co-operation between co-villagers, this does not of course create universal harmony: there is no lack of dispute, tension, conflict or competition between villagers, nor in any sense are adult men 'randomly' engaging in social relations. Men on bad terms simply avoid sitting near each other, or indeed avoid going to the same coffee-shop.

Another basis for association in the village is through neighbour-hood, both in the sense of those whose houses, and those whose fields, are close. '*Mián pórta*', 'One door', is the way men describe having adjacent houses, and when they do so they rub the outside edges of their two index fingers along each other, in the same gesture they use to describe the relation between siblings. Since a man has his fields scattered in many places around the village, the idea of neighbourhood through adjoining fields is more diffuse, but suggests, as with the house situation, relations in which casual contact, borrowing and lending of implements, helping to raise a heavy load, and the exchange of gossip or agricultural information, may all take place. Women make even more use of house-neighbourhood than men. Men typically work alone most of the time. They also have access to coffee-shops, where they are free to select people to talk to. Women are gener-ally working in the house area both for reasons of domestic duties, and the honour-and-shame values already discussed.

Common occupation is yet another basis for association, and is particularly important among the teachers. Men with common activities and common skills have certain obvious reasons to seek each other out, for the exchange of relevant information. For example farmers ask other farmers about problems of cultivation; they would not normally ask policemen or white-collar workers. Farmers are also likely to meet around the village at odd times of the day, when other men may be working away from the vil-lage. But the teachers are the only category in the village who show signs of developing a distinctive life-style. They make less use of the coffee-shops than other villagers, and tend to hold them-selves back from what they see as the rougher side of coffee-shop life—drinking, spitting, swearing and gambling. These they complain of, and lament the 'dirtiness' of the coffee-shops, and the crudeness of village manners. Ordinary villagers point out behind the teachers' backs that they are paid well for doing little, give themselves airs, and are loth to put their education to the service of their villages. In a later chapter this latent cleavage is analysed, when an occasion arose for the possible institutionalization of these differences of association in a proposal by a teacher to found a club for those with secondary school education (see chapter 7).

MEMBERSHIP OF THE VILLAGE

The word *chorianós* means co-villager. It applies first to anyone born in the village; then to anyone who has married a co-villager and lives in the village. It can be extended out of politeness or for other reasons to anyone resident in the village or to anyone normally resident elsewhere who had a parent from the village.[5] In the jural sense, any person owning property in the village and paying tax on it becomes eligible to join the various village-based associations, to vote for their committees, or even to stand on them. In the final analysis, people are socially members of the village if villagers so behave towards them. On one occasion an important meeting took place (described in chapter 8). The man asked to chair it was resident in the capital, born in the next village, but married to a woman from Kalo, and through this a major holder of Kalo land; another man prominent in the meeting was born in the village, but had not been a village resident for a long time. But had any person with no recognized status been present at the meeting, his presence would have immediately been questioned.

To be a member of the village then entitles a person at very least to some degree of social recognition, and to the freedom to venture his opinion in open village meetings. It also provides another strong identity for individuals, weaker than that stemming from the family, but for most people far stronger than that of Greek nationality as such. In one sense this identity becomes most important when a man is away from his village, but even within Kalo there are continual references to what are thought of as the characteristics of Kalotes. They often contrast themselves with members of Kammari, a mile away. Kalotes, they say, love feasting, avoid strict accounting, help each other in a crisis, and are innocent of political fanaticism. A favourite hypothetical example involves an accident in which a Kalotis might need blood. 'Then you would see everyone here, related or not, friends or not, right-wing or left, pile into cars and drive off to the hospital to give blood. Now in Kammari they aren't like that. They only help those they have close relations with. . . .'

The Kammarites of course have another view of the matter. Kalotes' love of feasting and pleasure, becomes a proneness to drink too much, and quarrel, and go around bawling with one's shirt hanging out. Lack of strict accounting becomes a fiscal sloppiness which leads to accusations of cheating and so to quarrels. Kammarites point out that a number of Kalotes have been in prison for theft or violence. But the views of Kammari need not any longer detain us.

Loudon (1970: 301) has talked of small-scale communities having 'export-models' of their behaviour, and stresses the element of social control in such emphasis on local standards. One essential component of the Kalo export-model is that whatever else goes on in the village, this is a village where men do not interfere with each other's womenfolk. In fact there are instances of what amounts in the village to sexual misconduct but these are very rarely mentioned in public, and strenuously denied to outsiders. This is for two reasons. First, such issues can still cause trouble, and in general members of the village are for good reason concerned to dampen and control conflict. Secondly, villagers in the act of denying gossip to non-Kalotes, are defining the social boundaries of Kalo. Village gossip is the complement of the village status contest.[6]

If the village keeps its gossip to itself, this solidarity also implies the power of social control. One of the commonest reasons for not doing something is that if one does it 'they will laugh'. The word *gheló* means I laugh, or I cheat. The passive *ghelióumai* means, I am deceived/laughed at. Villagers are continually wary of doing things which because they are unorthodox might make people laugh at them. They avoid planting a new crop, wearing different clothes, going for a walk with one's fiancé, or going sea-bathing. It is the very unpredictability of public response which makes people cautious. Yet often the action which last year was the subject of mirth, this year (or next year) is the object of fashionable pursuit. Sexual transgressions are the area most likely to produce mockery; and one man told me that he had refused a large sum of money from a man he surprised with the wife of another, rather than forgo the pleasure of telling the story in the coffee-shops. But anything which causes another person to look a fool will be round the village in a few hours. The knowledge of 'how they will laugh' is one of the surest forms of control, but it also implies that the actor cares for the opinions of the community. When the matter is trivial, gossip is scarcely an aspect of social control, but when the matter is serious, gossip as a sanction must be considered as on the same scale as forms of physical violence, to which in fact it sometimes leads. Words, unlike other missiles, simply cannot be avoided, although their wounds can be suffered with dignity, and the pain they cause, denied.[7]

Nicknames are also expressive of village membership. One reason that they arise is undoubtedly because the simple patronymic system of naming used by the villagers gives rise to a situation in which many people have the same name. There are at least 30 men called Yiorgios, 21 called Charalambos, 18 called Yiannis, 14 called Christodoulos and 8 called Dimitris in Kalo. Some men (often first cousins) share the same first name, and the same second name. Nicknames then help differentiate villagers; and some of them are merely variant forms of the owner's first name. It is notable that men with very distinctive or rare first names didn't have a nickname. Nicknames only occasionally express moral evaluations and most of them are used to the owner's face, by those he regards as his equals. Among common nicknames used in Kalo in 1969 were: the Bat; the Cheese-eater; the Fat Man; the Russian; the Dark Man; Gandhi; the Deceased; Satan; the Needleman; the Cat; and the Old Man.

Nicknames are of course not generally known to outsiders. If the telephone rings, the nearest villager answers it and asks who is wanted. The operator probably replies 'Yiannis Mikail'. 'They want Yiannis Mikail—who's that?' 'You know, the Rat. The son of the Cheese-eater . . .' The fact is that many villagers simply do not know each other by their full legal names, but only as (nickname) the son of (nickname). As has been suggested by Pitt-Rivers (1954: 160–77) nicknames are an expression of local purposes, and local interests. Like access to gossip, they define members of the village against outsiders. One of the favourite 'export-model' stories the villagers tell involves attempts by British soldiers to catch the village EOKA leader. They had learned somehow that his nickname was Moustache, but this was all they knew. They rounded up everyone in the coffee-shops, put them against the walls, and asked them: 'Where is Moustache?' To which everyone replied: 'Which Moustache do you mean? Look, there's a man with a moustache, and there's another one. There are many of them . . .' And so, the story goes, the EOKA leader was not discovered even though he was sitting there all the time 'because there were no traitors in Kalo'.

If an outsider comes to the village and asks for someone by his nickname this suggests a degree of familiarity with that person which serves immediately to break the ice. Knowledge of the nickname acts as a visa, giving the user a qualified protected status for a short time, in addition to that which he must inevitably have on entering the village as a stranger; for the same word which is rendered *guest* in English is also used to render *stranger* —*xénos*.

There is a sense in which common membership of the village comes to mean more on occasions *outside* the village than inside, and this is complemented by aspects of kinship behaviour. The issue is the relative scarcity of resources. In the village, a man with married sisters who needed a meal would not feel free to eat in the house of a female first cousin. If he had no sisters, his aunts would be next in order of natural preference, and accepted rights and duties. In the unlikely event of his having no closer female relative he could eat in the house of a female second cousin, or female first cousin of his parents. However, away from the village close relatives may be scarce or distant. It therefore becomes reasonable to activate more distant relationships. In precisely the same way, if two persons from the same village come into contact away from the village their relationship takes on an additional moral quality, a limited obligation to mutual help in the face of whatever common problems a hostile or at best neutral environment provides. To put this in more concrete terms, all Kalotes know that in the town of Limassol, some two hours' drive from the village, there is a man born in the village who is a police sergeant. Anyone from the village who found himself in difficulties in Limassol would, if he had no closer contact who would be likely to help him with his problem, turn to the sergeant for help. This holds for each major town in Cyprus, for Athens and for Saloniki where there are students from the village studying; and for London and the U.K. in general. The existence of co-villagers does not *assure* help for any particular person at a particular time. But a request for help could not be totally ignored in good conscience, whereas the same request between the same persons in the village might be regarded as eccentric.

There is one further feature which attaches to membership of the village, but it is more elusive than the sharing of gossip or use of nicknames. This is the general value placed on limiting physical violence between co-villagers, and the commonly expressed notion that relations between co-villagers should be peaceful and controlled. This norm can be seen in action when fighting breaks out in a coffee-shop or at a wedding, for when this happens, the braver bystanders always attempt to separate the combatants *whether they are related to them or not*. There is no idea that they should be left to fight it out, and this is slightly surprising since in many ways villagers seem to take malicious pleasure in the misfortunes of others. Of course, sometimes violence is stopped precisely because third parties are closely related to the antagonists, but there is a belief among villagers that fighting—which can quickly lead to killing—should be prevented within the village no matter who is involved.

In spite of such a norm (or perhaps because of it) fighting occurs, but usually it gets stopped quickly. Earlier in this century fighting seems to have been more common than today; and this may be to do with the increased efficiency of communications and the police, as well as the wider availability of fire-arms in recent years. There is also the likelihood that fighting is common enough because men are fairly sure they will in fact be restrained by onlookers.

Fighting is the final sanction between people who find their views or interests in conflict, and anthropologists have described many societies where fighting between or even within small groups is commonplace, and not regarded as a deviation from the group norms. It is then by no means self-evident that a village will contain people who act as if personal or corporate disputes should be handled without violence. Kalo is not a community of perennially peaceful, co-operative, like-minded citizens. The violence of gossip, the readiness to attribute bad faith and deception to others show that *verbal* aggression is commonplace. Obviously for men about to fight, the risk of injury might act as a deterrent; but why should the bystanders feel the need to intervene? Much of the material in later pages will describe political competition and sometimes how the peace of the village is violently disturbed in the course of this competition. For the moment, it will be useful to see what common interests villagers have which might make them see the limiting of violence as desirable in itself.

THE BENEFITS OF VILLAGE SOLIDARITY

By 'village solidarity' two things are meant: first, the traditional sense of solidarity, that members of the village identify strongly with each other vis-à-vis outsiders and suspend internal antagonism to deal with external threats; secondly, that villagers attempt to limit violence, and the intensity of competition, by stressing controlling norms, and by active interventions and mediations in disputes. Obviously, then this is an abstract and relative notion, which applies in specific contexts, and not in others. Men do not go about their daily lives showing with every gesture that they value village solidarity; but in certain crisis situations the norm of village solidarity is publicly invoked. When villagers are attempting to persuade each other that it is better to compromise than to disrupt the peace of the village they are seeking to assert that relations of incorporation should prevail (Barth 1966: 4). That is, they are behaving as if they were members of a corporate unit in which for certain specific benefits all the members either prosper together or not at all. Most of the time (especially in day-to-day economic exchanges) villagers see their own relations as what Barth would term transactions: that is, as exchanges governed by the general idea of reciprocity, in which each party tries to make sure that he gets at least as much as he gives. The transactional side of Kalo social life is shown in the constant appeal to *synféron*, self-interest, which has already been discussed. On relations of incorporation Barth reminds us that 'there are limits in most cases to the losses, or inequalities of gains, which people are willing to bear through such incorporation', (1966: 4) and this raises the question of why the villagers should ever be prepared to give up self-interest for even a short time, to suspend the right to vengeance, self-justification and the redemption of honour?

The answer is that village solidarity is not a free-floating value, but firmly grounded in other values and relations. The villagers believe that land, cash, and children, should be kept inside the village, and they usually manage to so keep them. The way in which villagers depend on each other for confirmation of status has already been discussed, and this is the more important precisely because recent economic and political change have brought the village out of its more isolated traditional past into closer contact with external agencies of all kinds.

The extent to which villagers have managed to keep land

within the village is easily shown from figures. The 1969 tax list, for irrigated land, listed 4,529 *donums* (about 1,500 acres). Only 278 *donums,* or 6 per cent were owned by people who were neither village residents, nor children of the village. In 1968 I counted 66 persons not resident in the village who owned some land there; all but three of them lived in the surrounding villages, and often turned out to have close kinship links with Kalo. Villagers actually say that it is bad for the villagers to sell village land to outsiders, and when one Kalotis sold some land to a minister in the government, he was criticized for this in the coffee-shops.

Children receive land from their parents at marriage, so there is a close fit between children marrying within the village, and land rights remaining there. It is natural then, that youngsters (in the role of marriage partners) are spoken of by older people as a resource to be conserved within the village, as one following episode shows. A Kalo man with a rather attractive daughter received a number of offers for her hand from within the village, all of which were refused. Finally, a highly eligible young Kalotis, handsome and with a good white-collar job, approached the family, confident that he would succeed. He too was rejected, and immediately went off to get engaged in the next village, Kammari, which happened to be his mother's birthplace.

The reason that all the Kalo suitors had been rejected turned out to be that the girl's father had very large debts and was planning to marry his daughter off to a wealthy outsider, who didn't demand the customary dowry house from the girl's family. But this cut no ice with one villager, to whom I listened the day after the last rejected Kalo suitor had been engaged in Kammari. With many a curse he bemoaned the loss of such a fine young man to the village. 'And there's even a shortage of young men in our village. So now you know what will happen? A Kalo girl, who could have married that boy, will now have to take some penniless bloke from the mountains.' Sometimes when villagers discuss among themselves how things might turn out in the future, land and marriage are linked explicitly. 'Suppose I sell you a piece of land one day when I'm hard up. Then years later my son marries your daughter—we become affines. So one day that piece of land comes back to my child and grandchildren.' This would not happen if the land was sold to an outsider, and the fact that villagers use such an idiom to talk about projected co-operative relations suggests just how village-centred are their main interests, in both the more common senses of the word, 'interests'.

Children and land are not the only resources which should be kept in the village—labour and cash and the potential for profit should also be kept in the village as much as possible. So a man building a house finds it convenient to have another villager do some of the building work, and to use a third villager for trucking the materials. Obviously such relations can become subject to strain when one side feels it is being exploited, and in such situations people break off relations. However, there is a strong feeling that if a reliable village man is around and able to perform the service needed it is better to employ him than an outsider. Once again people use future marriage as a rationalization for this: 'Even if he gets rich, perhaps one day a child of mine will marry a child of his.' This statement was made when villagers were pressed by me to explain why in the context of their competitive individualism they choose to 'help' unrelated co-villagers. The other justification for the action is that greater trust exists and better chances of reciprocity between co-villagers than between strangers. Most villagers sell their oranges to one of the four Kalo middle-men although they could use middle-men in Market Town or from one of the other nearby villages. Often they are dissatisfied with the bargain they strike, and complain that all the middlemen are crooks. But they do not seek outsiders next year. If all middle-men are crooks, then outsiders are likely to be bigger crooks than those who have to go on living in the same village as the people they cheat. The coin that has solidarity on one face has social control upon the other.

The emphasis on keeping exchanges within the village can be seen in many situations to pay off handsomely. To take one example: during the carrot harvest Kalo imports poor women to work, who arrive from many miles away in buses. During this period Kalo women work, but there is no time of the year when Kalo women travel in buses to work in the villages of others. The furthest a few of them ever go is five miles away to the CITCOP Packing Plant or the nearby Box Factory. The poorer women of the village are able to work in or near their own village partially because of the prosperity of others in the village. The manager of the Box Factory was for a time a Kalo man and he was always careful to give as many of the available jobs to Kalo men and women as he could, even though the factory was sited in another village whose people complained about his favouritism. Another example: in poorer districts of Cyprus men and women who have no land or skill, work on the roads or other public works; this work is rough, poorly paid, and requires travel, as well as being under the supervision of a foreman. In Kalo few people undertake such work, because there is better paid, easier work available within the village, on the land of those white-collar villagers with citrus holdings.

Although the villagers do not think in terms of the cases just outlined, they are aware of their easier position in comparison with other villages. The poor do not enjoy being poor in Kalo but they see that in certain ways it is better to be poor in Kalo than in the mountains. To the observer it is clear that the village, while increasing in population, has also increased in organizational complexity, and the villagers now experience greater economic interdependence than in the period of traditional agriculture.[8] Although agricultural prosperity was produced by imported machines and products—tractors, cars, trucks, diesel pumps and fertilizers—for many other economic transactions the villagers still turn to each other. They buy meat from village butchers; have clothes made by village tailors; sell oranges to village middle-men; employ fellow villagers to work their land; buy and sell land among themselves, and finally expect to marry their children to those of their co-villagers. When competition looks like getting out of hand such common interests provide a strong basis for controlling norms which invoke a notion of village solidarity.[9]

NOTES

1. Pitt-Rivers (1954) and Peristiany (1965).
2. The use of *koumpariá* terms is in fact considerably more complicated. If a man A baptizes the child of another man B, then A's wife will also call B '*koumpáre*' and B's wife '*kouméra*'. The terms are sometimes extended to more distant kin, and are often used in situations where no institutional relationship exists at all, much as unrelated men in working-class London call each other 'mate'. As in Britain, such usage can express or mask hostility, as well as readiness to be intimate.
3. My debt to both Pitt-Rivers (1954) and Campbell (1964) is particularly great in this chapter. More recently Paine (1969) has reviewed some of the peculiar difficulties involved in analysing friendship.
4. As with many other items of village behaviour, the meaning of offering light refreshment changes in terms of the structural relations between the actors, and these themselves can change in different contexts.
5. The word *chorianós* was used of me in this way, since I was temporarily resident, and my father had been born in the village. However, I have no doubt that had my behaviour greatly offended village opinion, people would have stressed the *contingent* nature of my claim to membership.

They would have said, 'His father left the village 35 years ago. His mother wasn't Greek. He's really more of an Englishman ... etc.' See Appendix I.

6. Frankenberg (1957) has described particularly vividly how Welsh villagers deny gossip to those they wish to define as 'outsiders'.

7. I am grateful to Antony Forge for suggesting that gossip and physical violence can be usefully thought of together.

8. I cannot therefore accept as necessarily general the point made by Bailey (1971: 298) where he suggests that there is a higher degree of interdependence in communities where people all make their living in the same way, than in those more occupationally diverse. He continues 'The diversification of ways of making a living which comes about through incorporation into a larger economy, automatically cuts down the frequency of exchanges, restricts the flow of information. ...' My own material seems to me to suggest the *opposite* effects of diversity, nor am I alone in this, for Cohen (1965: 57–9) reports an essentially similar situation. Diversification changes the form and content of co-operation, but it need not cut down the frequency of exchanges. Anthropologists are usually *guessing* at such frequencies when they write about the past, whatever yardstick they use. But I agree that villagers do not co-operate 'with the object of modernizing their own communities'—unless of course they can benefit as individuals in the process.

9. There are three other sorts of occasions when villagers act in a way which underlines the importance of common membership in the village. First, when a funeral procession passes through the village everyone rises and unrelated men often help carry the coffin to the graveyard, one taking over from another every so often, since the coffin is heavy and men tire quickly. Secondly, when someone is to leave the village for a long period or returns after a long absence, he goes around the coffee-shops shaking hands with everyone he meets and exchanging ceremonious phrases. Thirdly, in the last twenty or so years it has become the custom for all families to go to the marriage celebrations of all other families (unless serious hostilities exist); previously these festivities were attended only by close friends and kin. How far these practices are maintained between the Greeks and Turks I am not sure, but the one Turkish wedding I saw in the village was well-attended by the Kalo Greeks, and Turks returning to the village were warmly greeted by many Greeks.

6

Politics

INTRODUCTION

Up till now the main concern has been to analyse organization, structure and values of Kalo village essential to an understanding of villagers' political behaviour. From now on the emphasis will be on things more obviously political in the traditional sense— office, leadership, the factors which give men political power, the organizational and ideological differences which distinguish different political groups, particularly the left and right wings, and the ways in which these groups reach accommodation with each other. At the same time, the costs and benefits of political alignment will be made clear, as well as some of the rather specialized forms of political behaviour, such as the formation of clandestine support groups of national leaders, and their effects on village life.

The material in this chapter suggests certain modifications to Bailey's distinction between local and national political structures.[1] For Kalo village shows numbers of people operating essentially mixed strategies in politics, with a double, or two-tiered set of values. Like the inhabitants of Pisticci in South Italy[2] the Kalotes sometimes behave like people in small-scale pre-literate isolated communities, and sometimes behave like citizens of a modern industrial state. The intermediate nature of Kalo political structure and political culture is shown in the extent to which left and right ideologies have a hold on some villagers, who nevertheless may employ certain traditional tactics to seek many of their goals.

FORMAL OFFICES

A number of administrative offices exist for the conduct of village affairs; their powers and duties are formally defined by a body of laws, and are thus part of the governmental framework. Some of the officers are elected, others appointed. There are a small number of paid posts, which are attractive for this reason, but rather more posts are unpaid, although travel expenses may in certain cases be recovered. The power, in the sense of the ability to secure performance of one's wishes resulting from the authority of office, is in most cases highly specific, and limited. Village office gives little opportunity in Kalo for direct personal advantage; in a community where gossip and criticism of third parties is always lively, there were few occasions where office holders were accused of furthering their own material ends. Later in this chapter, when the social characteristics of committeemen are discussed, I shall explain that the main reason why men take office is because it confers prestige, through the notion of giving service to the village.

The *múktar* is appointed by the Ministry of the Interior; he is a junior government officer, present in the village, and always a village resident. His main duties are the registration of births and deaths, and the collection, with the help of the paid rural constable, of a number of taxes—land tax, irrigation tax, slaughter-house tax, and school tax. He should also report any illegal acts to the police and call on them when needed to maintain law and order in the village. His signature is needed on a number of documents required by villagers to certify that they are of a certain age, residential status, wealth category, that they have a certain number of dependants, and that they follow certain occupations. The *múktar* is sought out by visiting officials and dignitaries, and should normally be present if any matter of communal interest is to be discussed. He is paid by a fixed percentage on the volume of cash he collects through legal taxes. It is clear that in a society where literacy and knowledge of civil rights are only now becoming widespread, some *múktars* are able to use their powers in an arbitrary manner. This certainly occurs in many villages. The *múktar* of Kalo had held the post since 1958, having been assistant to the previous *múktar*. He is widely regarded as honest in his conduct of affairs. But even were he not so, the presence of large numbers of villagers with secondary education would seriously limit his ability to abuse his office.

The *múktar* is assisted by a *dímarchos* (village functionary), a paid post with specific duties regarding the cleaning of the village streets, the maintenance of lighting, and the supervision of the slaughter-house, used by the village butchers. The *dímarchos* is like the *múktar* an executive post. The *múktar* is also assisted by four *azádes* (singular, *azás*) and together *múktar* and *azádes* are

formally known as the *horikéh archéh*, the village authorities.
The *múktar* has the right to choose his *azádes*, but the government has the right to refuse a man so selected, though it rarely
does so. The *azádes* are merely consultative—they have a general
duty to consult with and advise the *múktar* on matters of communal interest, and he may call them when he wishes. In Kalo
this proved to be not more frequently than twice a year. The
commonest reason for calling on the *azádes* is the occasion
when the *múktar* must revise tax lists. Certain taxes, particularly
the school tax, are assessed *kata dynámin*, according to a man's
economic position. To reach their assessment, the village authorities take into account land owned, other sources of income, number and age of dependants, and may take into account exceptional
circumstances such as the costs of marrying a daughter or educating a child. The range of school tax payments was from 10/-
to £8, most household heads being assessed at about £3, and
certain destitute old people being excused. It is obviously an
advantage for the *múktar* not to make these decisions alone, since
there are always some complaints and requests for reassessment.

The office of *múktar* in most other villages I visited seemed to
be held by the wealthier and more articulate villagers, and often
they are shown a considerable degree of formal respect by other
villagers. In Kalo, most villagers were polite to the *múktar*, and
went so far as to address him as 'Mr. President' but he was not
looked on as a powerful man or a particularly dynamic one
(except by some of the poorest villagers to whom the smallest
administrative act appears a major undertaking). He came from
a poor family, and had never himself amassed money or land. His
predecessor had been wealthy, articulate, and widely known outside the village, and was held responsible for having brought certain benefits to the village and to have helped a number of
villagers get government posts. This suggests that the qualities
of the incumbent are at least as important as the rights and duties
of the office.

The Church Committee consisted of five men, elected at three-
yearly intervals, who had charge of the small sums of money
raised by the church through the sale of wax tapers during services, and the sums payable to the priest for officiating at services.
It was not the subject of any discernible interest among the villagers, and one man had been re-elected without interruption for
forty years. There seems to have been no competition for office
on this committee at the most recent elections, which took place

after I left the village, but complaints reached me from committee members that only a handful of villagers had attended the elections. It would seem, particularly from the conflict over the voting rights of communists discussed in the opening chapter, that at earlier periods the church committee had attracted more interest.

The Co-operative Store Committee runs the affairs of the store, which was set up in 1954. Householders became members, paying 10/- per share; at that time there were 223 shareholders, who held 679 shares between them. This share capital formed the basis for the store, and the only other resource available to it is credit from merchants. In 1969 the store employed three full-time sales staff, and a full-time Secretary, responsible to the committee for the overall management of the store. It owned one large modern building, rented another space, and was handling a turnover of some £50,000 a year. Shareholders receive fluctuating dividends of between 2 per cent and 2½ per cent on their annual purchases, and elect the committee members every three years.

The store is then, by village standards, a major enterprise, and all but a handful of household heads are shareholders. Its activities are controlled by a special body of Co-operative Laws, and there are regular audits carried out by employees of the Co-operative Commissioner's office. The Secretary travels twice a week to Nicosia in the store's pick-up van to purchase stock, and the store keeps gas stoves, refrigerators, diesel fuel, as well as all kinds of clothes and foodstuffs. The main activities of the committee in their weekly meetings, are to carry villagers' comments on stocks and prices to the Secretary, to oversee the general management, and to discuss and decide on new appointments, as well as the salaries of existing employees. The committee acting on information supplied by the Secretary, also agrees on the annual dividend and new investment.

The Credit Co-operative has a paid secretary, and a four man management committee. Its main functions are to act as a low-interest source of short-term loans for agricultural activities, and it also supplies bulk fertilizer to villagers, at prices competitive with those of private merchants. Its third activity is to act as a local savings bank for villagers with spare cash, and village girls who take paid work, saving for their dowries, have started to use it for this purpose. They now receive 6 per cent on deposits, although five years ago it was only 4 per cent.

The main work of the committee is to meet, normally every week, to decide on applications for new loans, and to check on outstanding loans to see that they are being paid off in time. The limits on unsecured loans are set by the Co-operative Credit Bank, which is the higher administrative unit for the village branches. The bank decides on a limit by estimating the return on agricultural production in a particular village. In 1968 in some poor villages the limit was £150, but at this time in Kalo it was £500, which in 1970 rose to £750, which gives an idea of the relative economic standing of the village. The rate of interest on unsecured loans in 1968 was 7 per cent. In 1970 there were 465 members; the reason that there were half again as many members as household heads is that married women (who usually own land) may join individually, thus increasing the borrowing power of their households.

In making its decisions the committee tries to foresee the difficulties a man might have in repaying a loan. The rationale given by members for their activities is that they must protect individuals from themselves, and the organization from exploitation. Since, they argue, in the village everyone knows a good deal about everyone else's business, they are in a good position to know what debts a man should and should not be able to take on. They argue that the problems faced by the head of a household are fairly similar, and that they all have experience of meeting them. Everyone is aware that occasionally a man seeks a loan ostensibly for agricultural purposes, which he intends to use for building a dowry house for his daughter. I saw such cases come up in meetings. The decision tended to go on whether the man would be able to keep out of financial difficulties. No one on the committee was bothered by the building of a dowry house, since it was a problem they could all imagine facing. In their work the committee are in fact continually making assessments of their co-villagers, and this assessment differs from that made by the *horikéh archéh* about tax ratings, for it involves some measure of prediction, whereas the tax rating is current or retrospective.

The Carrot and Potato Association was set up in 1960 as a producers' co-operative which organizes the local washing, packing and through its national administrative unit the marketing of member's produce. It is village-based and in 1964 the villagers built—at a cost of £3000—a packing house. The association has two committees of villagers, who are elected by members; one committee is the executive, and the other a supervisory committee which meets less frequently. The task of the executive is to manage the packing house, which includes the fixing of hourly wage rates for those women who work there during the short but hectic period when carrots and potatoes are harvested (April–June), and the drawing up of schedules to determine the order in which member's produce can be handled. This last item is the occasional cause of friction since members are extremely anxious about the speed with which carrots can deteriorate in the fields, and there is great pressure to get produce washed, packed and trucked to the port as quickly as possible. In such an atmosphere, charges of favouritism or minor injustice are sometimes made, and here the committee need a good deal of tact and authority to deal with such crises. As with the other committees mentioned, while the actual work calls for responsibility in decisions over one's fellow villagers' affairs, there seems relatively little scope for personal gain, and there were very few adverse comments made about the way committee members handled their duties which survived the day of the particular occurrence. In chapter seven I deal at length with events accompanying election to the committees of the association, but here it is enough to note that the elections were contested on party political grounds, rather than on previous performance in office or personal conduct.

The Irrigation Committee has been in existence since before 1930 and its main duty is the use of the tax money paid by the villagers at the rate in 1968 of 10/- per *donum* on the 4,529 *donums* of irrigated land within the village area. This yields an annual budget of around £2,500, which is currently spent in two ways: existing irrigation channels must be cleaned out twice a year and this is done by paid labour from among the poorer or older men in the village. Secondly, under a system of matching grants from the government, new irrigation channels of concrete are being built. Concrete channels save water loss by seepage and by evaporation, both serious problems with the slower earth channels. But the concrete channels are expensive and there is a large area of village land still without them. The committee also has the duty of representing the village's interest in any dispute over water use or rights with other villages, towns or the government. During my fieldwork the committee and those of several neighbouring villages became involved in some special activities regarding the representation of village interests to the central government, and these are the object of extended analysis in chapter eight.

This description of formal office in the village raises the question of why men seek office at all. They stand to gain little or nothing financially; the authority of office is limited, and does not ramify outwards into other affairs, except in the case of the few men who hold several offices, who are thought to be good people

TABLE 10
Overlapping leadership

SKLYROS
(i) Carrot Association Committee
(ii) Secretary, Co-op Store
(iii) Irrigation Committee (resigned 1968)
(iv) Co-ordinating Committee
(v) Village representative on 1964 School Committee, Market Town
(vi) AKEL Village Committee
(vii) Credit Co-op Committee

PATRIS
(i) *Azas* (appointed)
(ii) Co-op Store Committee
(iii) Carrot Association Committee
(iv) Irrigation Committee
(v) PEK Village Representative
(vi) Credit Co-op Committee

VOURROS
(i) Attempted to organize Graduates' Club, 1962
(ii) Co-ordinating Committee (1964)
(iii) Co-op Store Committee (1969)
(iv) CITCOP Committee (1969)
(v) Advisory Committee (1969)

IOANNIS
(i) Church Committee
(ii) Co-op Store Committee
(iii) Credit Co-op Committee

GIORGIOS
(i) Church Committee
(ii) Irrigation Committee

ANDREAS
(i) *Azas* (appointed)
(ii) Co-op Store Committee

DIMITRIS
(i) *Azas* (appointed)
(ii) Irrigation Committee

PETROS
(i) Irrigation Committee
(ii) Carrot Association Committee

MICHAILIS
(i) Irrigation Committee
(ii) Credit Co-op Committee

to consult on a range of subjects. One reason why men accept office—few show active signs of seeking it—is that it is a mark of general village approval. In a competitive, individualistic community, where it is standard practice to cast doubt on the motives of others, election to village office shows a qualified trust. I do not wish to make too much of this, because the low turn-out at the elections observed weakens such an interpretation: it could equally well be argued that men are elected through the apathy of the village at large, and the sycophancy of particular cronies. This explanation is rejected on the simple grounds that it goes against what was observed. Some prestige can be had by holding office; that it can also be lost serves to dignify the holders who succeed.

However, as Table 10 makes clear, there is another crucial reason for analysing village committee recruitment: men prominent on the administrative committees are also in general men prominent in other leadership situations, and particularly as village representatives of national political groupings. That is not to say that committeemen are the *only* political leaders in the village. But several of them appear in a number of different situations. Later in this chapter it will become clear that the administrative committees are not in any simple sense free of national politics. They can be cockpits or arenas for alignments which are derived from the nation, and not from problems of village irrigation, or agricultural credit. Also, a recurrent theme of village politics is the attempt to keep the administrative committees 'out of politics', or in the idiom of the villagers, to prevent politics from 'colouring' the committees.

THE CHARACTERISTICS OF OFFICE-HOLDERS

In this section I shall consider in more detail the social characteristics of the persons who hold office in village economic organizations. The simplest facts about them are that they do not include women, unmarried men, or illiterates. Furthermore, Table 11 suggests that men whose main occupation is farming dominate the committees and these have already been shown to be men with substantial land holdings. Since, among married household heads alone, there are over 300 men who could stand for office in most cases, the reasons why a few full-time farmers dominate the committees must be examined.

The landless men and those with little land do not obtain

E

TABLE 11
Kalo Committee, 1968–9

1. IRRIGATION COMMITTEE 1967/68

   Old Sklyros—farmer
   Sklyros   —farmer
   Y. Tangos —farmer
   Kirkos   —farmer
   Kanellos   —farmer

   IRRIGATION COMMITTEE 1968/69

   Patris   —farmer
   Glykis   —farmer
   Yorgios   —farmer
   Kirkos   —farmer
   M. Tangos—farmer

2. CO-OPERATIVE RETAIL SHOP 1968

   Secretary: Sklyros   —farmer (paid)
             Tsingounis—farmer
             Patris   —farmer
             Ktistis   —farmer
             Akis   —bulldozer driver (owns land)

3. CO-OPERATIVE CREDIT SOCIETY 1968

   Secretary: G. Fanos   —ex-shoemaker (paid)
             Patris   —farmer
             Sklyros   —farmer
             Borris   —farmer
             Kirnos   —farmer
             Akis   —bulldozer driver (owns land)

4. HÓRIKEH ARCHÉH (VILLAGE LEADERSHIP) 1968

   azas: Glykis   —farmer
   azas: Patris   —farmer
   azas: Akros   —farmer
   azas: Tsingounis—farmer

5. CARROT AND POTATO UNION EXECUTIVE COMMITTEE   (re-elected uncontested for 3rd time, 1969)

             Patris   —farmer
             Tsingounis—farmer
             Kanellos   —farmer
             Tangos   —farmer
             Sklyros   —farmer

office for a number of reasons. They need all their time and energy to support their families. But almost as important, they are inhibited by their own low view of their status, from seeking office, which they rightly suspect will be denied them. For in the values of the village, administrative competence begins at home, with the management of the affairs of the domestic group. If a man has not succeeded in securing his families' positions through the acquisition of land, or a well-paid job, then he is unlikely to be much use in the handling of village affairs.

Government teachers and civil servants might be expected to take office, but they usually do not. First, laws exist which while meant to apply to party politics are widely interpreted to apply to village administrations as well, which appear to prohibit both these categories of peoples from serving. Secondly, work on these committees requires close contact and co-operation with farmers, which to some extent cuts across the notions of superior status which men with secondary education hold. Thirdly, there is the possibility that farmers themselves will be unwilling to trust management of those committees chiefly concerned with farming, to non-farmers. In later chapters I discuss a number of situations in which the relation of a person's education to his qualifications for office became lively issues. Here I wish to do no more than stress the ambiguous social position of educated men in village affairs—they hold values which distance them from farmers, they often comment on the 'backwardness' of villagers, but do not participate in the main in village administration.

A third possible category of persons who might seek office are merchants and middle-men, of whom there are five normally resident in the village. Not one had served in recent years on village committees; they rarely attended elections, nor were they proposed for office. The only occasion on which a merchant was entrusted with village business—the purchase of arms for a village militia—it turned out badly. (pp. 144–5) To some extent the explanation for their not holding office must lie in the notion villagers have that all merchants are *kléphtes*, 'crooks' (literally thieves). But another reason, which applies to the merchants, the white-collar workers, and landless men and craftsmen, is that all these categories tend to spend much of the day away from the village, whereas the full-time farmers, while often out in the fields, are available, and come in sometimes for meals. This is only a partial explanation since committee meetings take place often on Sunday mornings; but the activities of members are not confined to such meetings. The general availability of committee men to hear complaints, or merely to keep an eye on things, means that the full-time farmers are from this point of view most suitable.

There is no suggestion that the full-time farmers are a con-sciously organized group who run village affairs to suit them-

selves. I rather argue that in the traditional village land ownership was the chief concern of the village and that status within
the village still continues to go with those activities which are
directly related to the central activity of agriculture. The farmers
continue to see such offices as the appropriate forum for achieving
status. That the teachers and white-collar workers remain for
a number of reasons aloof from these committees, only serves
to emphasize the extent to which they face two ways—they are
more involved in a system of evaluation which has its roots in
the larger society. But as will be clear in later chapters, the values
implicit in the attitudes of teachers to village administration were
undergoing some change.

There are other characteristics normally possessed by most
committeemen. These include the ability to speak well in public
and a reputation for honesty or responsibility. Since these qualities are also those normally associated with powerful or important
men in general, and with political party leaders in the village in
general, I shall consider them in a little more detail.

Speaking well has several aspects. One is speaking forcefully
and persuasively. The villagers use the Demotic Greek word
syzitó which means 'I discuss' in a way which means 'I have an
argument with'; they use the abstract noun *syzítisis* to mean
argument verging on serious disagreement. The ethos of debate
in the village is well expressed in this assimilation of the moderate
meaning to the more harsh one. Committeemen need to be able
to argue forcefully in the free-for-all exchanges of coffee-shop
debate, to put across their point of view, and to silence others by
persuasion or sheer energy.

However, another aspect of speaking well involves mastery
of Demotic Greek, *Demotikí*,[3] a more educated form of Greek
than village dialect (*horiádika*), for this is considered appropriate
when dealing with officials, even though the officials themselves
know how to use village dialect. On this point it must be stressed
that not all the words now needed to conduct village business
exist in dialect, but this is not the whole problem—it is not simply
a matter of knowing *Demotikí* words, but a whole speaking style
which is at issue. In addition, the ability to speak and understand
Demotikí must be matched by some ability to read it, and to
handle official documents.

Another aspect of speaking well involves the restraint appropriate to behaviour in committee. Here, or with officials, the bold,
declamatory and aggressive way of coffee-shop debate is not

appropriate. A fellow committeeman should not be interrupted or shouted down, but allowed to have his say. His points should then be taken up politely and discussed. It is not appropriate to use nicknames in committee, or to swear. One does not even say *ma, íse pellós?* 'are you mad?' to express disagreement.

A reputation for honesty is hard to maintain. I mentioned in the last chapter that the village word for 'to cheat' is synonymous with the word to laugh at, *ghfeló*. In the main, villagers seem to admire cunning, and sharp practice, at a distance. Yet, as has been observed elsewhere (Davis: 1969) accompanying suspicion and admiration for the man without scruples, is a readiness to make verbal agreements with reliable men to which substantial resources are committed. Within the village each adult has what is in effect a credit rating for reliability (although of course villagers may not always agree about the ratings of a given person). Men who *are* reliable in this respect are known as *tímios*, in the sense of honest, *sovarós*, serious, or *varetós*, weighty (as opposed to lightweight). No man is expected to be reliable to the point of being *palavós*, gullible, for there are circumstances in which any honest man may break his word. I shall try to give the measure of this problem with a single example: the Secretary of the Co-op Store found at the end of the year that he was entitled to the highest dividend, since he had bought more at the store than anyone else; this was not surprising since, as founder of the store and a man ideologically committed to the co-operative movement, he does all his buying there whenever possible. However, he explained to me that he would reduce the amount of dividend due to him 'Because some people in the village are bound to say, without a doubt the Secretary must be stealing from the till, or else how could he obtain such a high dividend?' In order to preserve his reputation for honesty, he was claiming less than his due, to give no grounds for gossip. In the face of the suspicion accompanying all acts in the public domain, and the opportunistic gossip of enemies, a man with an eye to his good name must keep his wits about him.

OTHER BASES OF POWER

Formal office provides leadership roles, but such offices do not by any means exhaust the possibilities for exercise of power, and specifically political power, by villagers. By power I mean two things, which are closely related: a man's ability to control the actions of others, and his own relative independence from such control. As it happens, these two senses of the English word 'power' correspond closely to what villagers mean by the Greek word, *dýnamis*. They frequently say of a person *éschi tín dýnamin* . . . 'he has the power . . .' but they as commonly say '*oti théli, kámni* . . .' 'he does what he likes'. In the following pages I shall discuss the various factors which give a man power. Any single one may give him a measure of power, but if he can combine several together, his power will be the greater. Education, wealth, personal contacts with powerful people, and the use of force are the key factors.

Education was discussed earlier (pp. 52–4, 93–4); its importance for the analysis of power lies in the fact that villagers grant high status to the highly educated. Doctors, lawyers and senior civil servants enjoy the most prestige, and villages assume them to be rich unless proved not to be. Such professional men have power because of their status, but also because of contacts they made at earlier stages of their education and careers. These contacts with other high status and powerful persons in the capital, as well as the command of bureaucratic skills which their advanced education gives, are important in dealing with the urban elite on an equal footing, and for securing all kinds of favours through personal intervention in decision-making. A doctor, for example, need show deference to very few people in Cyprus, and most people defer to him. Because of this he can get many things done, and this means that villagers are prepared to become his clients or dependants. A doctor or a lawyer can waive his fees as a favour; a civil servant can waive 'red tape', or normal regulations.

Wealth also creates power: Rich men can acquire friends and dependants in many ways: by gifts, personal loans, the guarantee of a bank loan, or ostentatious use of their wealth in entertainment. In the village a common idiom used to describe how a man influences others is to say *taḯzi tous* 'he is feeding them', which means, he is bribing them. An old man described to me how he thought the murderers of his brother had managed to escape punishment in the 1920s. 'They fed the policemen, who destroyed the evidence and covered up for them . . .' In traditional Cypriot peasant society the notion of feeding someone expressed the creation of dependence, and scarcity of food gave force to the image. Today most men are not hungry yet the word still has this force for what is now at stake is not bare nourishment but luxury. Rich men today do not merely feed people, they *feast*

them. During my fieldwork the *múktar* of a neighbouring village
invited a powerful minister to baptize his grandson. He gave a
feast for over a hundred people at which his clients roasted the
meat and served the food and drink, which included whisky.
This feast cost several hundred pounds, but the *múktar* is rich.
He and the minister belong to the same political party, and the
múktar's office depends on the will of the minister, who could not
have helped noticing the numbers of people at the feast capable
of voting. It is not that a meal buys a vote (votes where bought
would probably cost a good deal more than a meal) but rather
that large feasts create for those who give them an atmosphere
of power, generosity and the ability to patronize.

Rich men occasionally regale close friends by making the
companionship of women available to them. Some wealthy men
are known to have 'closed the cabaret' for the benefit of their
friends. A cabaret in Cyprus is a kind of night-club where among
other things there are costly prostitutes for the pleasure of customers. The rich man pays the manager a lump sum (several
hundred pounds) to keep out the general public, and make the
club's women available to a select party of the rich man's friends.
This is regarded by some villagers (but not all) as one of the
more luxurious expressions of wealth and power.

The rich are powerful for other reasons; economic independence is the goal of all household heads, and is firmly supported
by the strong awareness of the difference between being one's
own man, and being dependent on another. But wealth carries
other overtones: the rich can behave unpredictably, in a dangerous sense. For a man's death can be bought, by paying £300
or £500 to someone ready to kill him. In one case which came to
my attention from another village, a man's daughter was seduced
and led into prostitution. The man wished to be revenged on her
seducer and paid money to someone from Kalo who shot him.
In general villagers are very careful not to make enemies of the
rich. For example, the richest man in Kalo made his money
through selling vehicles. His father was a shepherd, and he himself
when young had a flock. He has had little education, no refine-
ment, and swears heavily in normal conversation. He brings his
little son to the coffee-shop, and the son calls adult men *póushtis*
(passive homosexual), conduct which would get any other village
child at least a boxed ear. But this child is tolerated, and his
father is often called *kýrie* (a title not usually accorded to men
unless they have finished Gymnasium). Behind his back, he is

called less pleasant things, but few people are willing openly to antagonize him.

Readiness to use force makes for power, not only in the case of office-holders—who in a broad sense might be thought of as acting legitimately—but in the case of any individual who chooses to do so and take the consequences. The example of the man who avenged his daughter is extreme, but it is such rare and drastic events which are the keystone of the honour-and-shame values concerning female chastity. Men known as ready to use force—fists, chairs, knives or guns—when opposed or insulted, are treated with considerable caution and it is enough for a man to have violent friends to win him some measure of deference from his fellows.

Not only is force a factor which floats fairly free from normal structural constraints, but in one sense it is a factor which arises from traditional village norms and actions. The resort to force was—in more lawless days—the decisive factor which guaranteed a man some security of life for himself and his dependants. The authority of the state, which seeks to monopolize the use of force, is an intrusive factor which has become more prominent in recent times, and is directly related to modern, efficient government. Yet as with other aspects of central government, villagers do not regard either state intervention or the process of law as certain. Thus, readiness to use force can usefully be seen as a village-based value partly opposed to the values of the larger society.

Some committee men have been known to employ force effectively and this undoubtedly enhances their authority in office, and makes them more easily able to get things done. Patris, the most prominent right-nationalist leader in the village has on three occasions in the last twenty-five years beaten up men for assumed insults to his wife and daughters. Sklyros, the prominent left leader, has had one similar episode, as well as several fights with men over other matters. There is some reason to think that the prominence of both men is reinforced by their readiness to fight, and fight well.

The last factor which creates power is one that is clearly a synthesis of other factors, that is relations with powerful people, especially those outside the village. Up till now most of the emphasis has been on the village, and the internal relations of villagers, although continual mention has been made of the increasing dependence on the wider society which is central to my argument. But in case the reader should have received an im-

TABLE 12
Villagers' links with highly-placed persons, 1968–9

PERSON/OFFICE	MAIN LINK TO VILLAGERS
Minister of Interior (1960–68)	patron/client ties, from EOKA relationships.
Minister of Labour	mainly patron/client ties based on land owned by minister in the village, which his client cares for.
Minister of Justice	'friendship' based on fact that a young villager works in a government legal office.
Public Prosecutor	*koumpariá* (baptismal).
Minister of Agriculture	mixed ties: Minister from near-by Market Town, and organized the district militia in 1963/4, thus coming into contact with village militia.
Army Commander	mixed, but basically patron/client ties based on fact that one young villager is an Army Officer.
District Commissioner	the previous *múktar* knew the commissioner well when he was a junior civil servant.
Ministry of Education	kinship: one villager has a high post in the Ministry.
Forestry Department	as above.
Commissioner of Co-operatives	one villager works for the Commissioner's office, and is essentially his client.
2 doctors, 1 dentist, 1 lawyer	kinship; all born in village.
Political Party Leader A	*koumpariá*, 'friendship' and clientage.
Political Party Leader B	the same.
AKEL (Communist Party)	formal membership by a few villagers over at least 20 years.

pression of an isolated, self-sufficient village, the next few pages will sketch-in aspects of the relations between villagers and the wider society, to suggest how certain villagers enjoy particular power from their ability to mediate such relations.

To start with an economic example: until the middle of the 1940s, oxen were used for ploughing, but they came gradually to be replaced by tractors. Tractors are sold and serviced in

Market Town; and most buyers of tractors need some contact with a bank in order to secure terms of purchase. Thus the change to tractors inevitably involved some villagers in new and wider contacts. The use of buses, cars, and trucks complements and parallels the use of tractors in terms of consequences for the villagers; increases in access to secondary education also take villagers outside the village, for the nearest secondary schools are in Market Town, and some of the better ones are in the capital. Good medical care, like education, is not to be had in the village (except in the marginal case of visiting doctors or the government-licensed midwife); the villagers use Market Town for emergency medical care or trivial problems, since there are several undistinguished physicians and a cheap government clinic there. But for anything in the least serious, for pre-natal care, specialists, and operations, they go to the capital.

Links with the outside are also apparent from the occupational histories of village heads. An analysis of the first one hundred informants in my census shows that 72 per cent had some history of prolonged work outside the village. Some 28 per cent had always worked only within the village. Of those who had worked outside at some time, over half were working regularly outside the village, or had done so until they stopped work altogether— 39 per cent of the whole sample.

There are also links through specific relationships to people in positions of power (see Table 12). In 1968 there were close relations between particular villagers to the Minister of the Interior, the Minister of Labour, the Minister of Agriculture, the Minister of Justice, the Commissioner of Co-operatives, the Cyprus Army Commander, and the senior civil servants for Nicosia district. There were also links with well placed civil servants in the Land Registry Office, the Forestry Service, and the Ministry of Education. The village boasted of having produced two doctors and a dentist, all Nicosia residents, and a newly qualified young lawyer, who was to set up practice and live in Market Town. There were known to me ten primary school teachers and seven secondary school teachers who were usually village residents. A son of the village also held posts in the Co-operative Bank. This list is not exhaustive.

There can be little doubt that this formidable array of links to highly placed persons comes partly from the small scale of the island, partly from the nearness of the capital, and partly because Kalo, a wealthy village in a wealthy region, has sent some of its children into the urban elite. The Minister of the Interior had baptized several village children; the Minister of Labour had land near the village; the Minister of Agriculture was a local man from Market Town. The links to the Land Registry, Forestry and Agriculture were all Kalo or Kammari villagers who had achieved important jobs. The Co-operative Department has several major enterprises near the village, and employs one Kalotis and so forth.

The Cypriot civil service is often very efficient, and cases of cash bribery for minor transactions are to my knowledge rare. Nevertheless, in spite of this, villagers (and townsmen) seek access to civil servants and powerful people to get certain decisions made to their satisfaction, so neither the presence of major inefficiency nor flagrant corruption in any way explain how villagers relate to these government agencies.

One reason for seeking alliance with civil servants is that the older villagers in particular often do not know what their legal rights are, and even if they do know, do not expect to get them if the decision rests in the hands of an unrelated, unknown person. That is, the impersonality of civil service norms strikes many villagers as a cause not for security but for anxiety. A man is more likely to look favourably on a request (whatever its legal status) if he is in some sense, one's friend.[4]

Another reason for seeking such alliances lies in the hope that where the law is apparently against a villager, a sympathetic civil servant can find a loophole, or bend the law slightly. Undoubtedly villagers are encouraged in these attitudes by their own perceptions of Cypriot political culture. They see the society in terms of alliances, and competing power groups; they see no reason to think that a civil service post precludes a man carrying over his politics into his daily work; thus it is sometimes worthwhile to suggest that one already supports the same cause, or is ready to support the same cause, as a partisan civil servant.

Certain links with powerful people were created in other ways which spring out of the historical legacy of colonial rule. During the 1955–9 Emergency, people active in EOKA were inevitably involved in relations which ranged beyond the village, and the dangerous clandestine and ideological nature of the EOKA struggle perhaps helped some of these relations to endure. When Independence came in 1960 EOKA members were able to meet freely and here the small scale of the island, the modern roads, available motor transport, widespread telephones and the

magnetic appeal of the major towns, all made such meetings both
easy and attractive. Young militants from Kalo travelled around
the island meeting old comrades-in-arms, and some of them became frequent companions of ex-EOKA leaders in Nicosia, at
night-clubs, offices, and elsewhere.

Contacts with powerful people, like the use of force, are in
some ways free-floating, and can be captured by individuals who
are not necessarily privileged in structural terms. However, a
man with such a contact does not squander it, or make it freely
available to the village at large, for to do this would soon weaken
a strong link. Such contacts may be put to use for particular
relatives, friends, or for men who share political views. In the
struggle for advantage villagers compete fiercely to monopolise
and conserve any special resources they have.

LEFT AND RIGHT

Numbers of villagers answer the question 'where do you stand in
politics?' with answers which use the Greek words for left
(*aristerós*) or right (*dhexiós*). They may use other words:
'nationalist' tends to be a synonym for right-wing, and 'progressive' for left-wing. The use of the words suggests several
difficult problems—what do the labels mean to the villagers, how
do they relate to the apparently similar words used by national
leaders in Cyprus and in other societies, and how far do they
explain how villagers behave? The first of these problems will be
approached in the following pages; the second is left virtually
untouched, and the third will be indirectly dealt with in later
chapters.

It is difficult—if not impossible—to make systematic remarks
about how far people believe things they say, how far they understand the implications of what they say, and so forth.[5] Village
leaders and activists use refractions of left- and right-wing
ideologies to attack each other in debates, and they organize
and vote under these labels in national politics. There is no reason
to think they use the labels cynically to wheedle benefits from
national leaders (although a few opportunists certainly do this).
Nor does the fact that some villagers obviously receive all kinds
of benefits from supporting one side or the other mean that their
support is different from that of electors in western industrial
countries. Some Kalotes are political altruists (or in their own
words, ideologically stable) in that they stick to their parties

through thick and thin. Others are more concerned with supporting a party which represents their interests, as they see them, at the moment.

Since the leftists have a longer history of stable organization, and since in my view it has for many years been more dangerous to be a leftist in Cyprus than a moderate nationalist, I attacked the problem of structural bases for political alignment in the following way: From my census it was possible to check declared leftists against non-leftists (who inevitably include the politically unaligned). Of the leftists, some 68 per cent had started marriage with less than 16 *donums* of land (5 acres); of the non-leftists some 46 per cent had started marriage in this situation. Only 26 per cent of the leftists were full-time farmers, against 38 per cent of the non-leftists. Of the leftists 22 per cent were labourers, whereas only 12 per cent of the non-leftists were in this category. Finally only 2 per cent of the leftists were civil servants, such as policemen, firemen, clerks, etc., whereas 12 per cent of the non-leftists fell into this group.

The suggestion is clearly that men who started marriage with little land, who were labourers or manual workers, were *more likely* to support the left; that correspondingly civil servants and full-time farmers were less likely to be leftists. Such conclusions are hardly surprising, but even so, need the following qualifications: The civil servants, for example, may simply be afraid openly to support the left because they believe it will block promotion in their jobs. Some of the labourers may simply stay with the left because they joined its trade unions before right-wing unions got going. Finally, some men have deserted the left since 1945 and while this may be because their economic situation changed, it is equally likely that they did so because they simply doubted the power of the left to give them what they wanted—protection and security in an uncertain world.

Certain wealthy farmers, who have been wealthy since childhood, are staunch leftists; certain very poor men, labourers with little or no land, insist they are anti-communist, and 'with' the right. These exceptions are already dormant in the figures just given. There are two obvious explanations, which do not exclude each other, for these 'exceptional' cases. One is that a man may be sincerely attracted by the ideology he supports; the other is that a man may have little or no political philosophy of his own, and may simply (as client of a more powerful man) be parroting his patron's views.

Earlier I distinguished four different political roles (pp. 44–7). The link between that economic analysis and the present discussion of leftist and rightist may now be made clear: relative occupational position is a partial predictor of a man's political alignment in terms of left and right. It is a somewhat more sure predictor of his being a leader, patron, or a client within the village, a village representative in external relations, and so forth. Leadership, and independence cut across the left/right cleavage. In village terms, a leftist *leader* may get a grudging respect from the right because he is a leader (though not because he is a leftist). A poor man who is a client of a right-wing leader will be dismissed by the thoughtful leftist with these words: 'His poverty has turned his mind: he is blind to his real interests.' There is a constant attempt by villagers of all kinds to reduce the left/right distinction to a poor/rich distinction, yet this is belied by the facts, as they well know. In terms of the wider society, all are 'mere villagers'; and the ideologies of the wider society are partly confounded by the fact that the village leftist leaders are men of substance and good sense.

In one very obvious way right and left need each other, define each other, and cannot exist without each other. Much that goes to make up the political position of either is produced by conscious opposition to the assumed position of the other side. I shall now examine the formal positions which each side takes up.

Men who describe themselves as nationalists, or as rightists, stress that they are practising Christians, loyal to Greece and ready to die for her, who wish passionately for the Union of Cyprus with Greece (*Enosis*), who are strongly anti-communist, and often strongly anti-Turkish. Some rightists also strongly support private property, and private enterprise. The strongest claim of nationalists is that they speak for and support the largest and most important unit a Greek can belong to, over and above his family—his Nation (*to Ethnos*). This Nation is defined in terms of adherence to Greek Orthodoxy, the Greek language, and a body of Greek culture and custom.

In stressing their distance from the left, whom they fairly indiscriminately dub 'communists', the right charge leftists with being atheists, with only pretending to believe in God, and with dislike for and rejection of things Greek. They further charge communists with a secret or open loyalty to the U.S.S.R. and a readiness to put that power's interests before those of Greece or Cyprus. Rightists insist that leftists either held back from or betrayed EOKA's struggle against the British. No leftist, they insist, can be a true nationalist, but are more commonly traitors to the nation. Rightists, for obvious reasons, delight in taunting leftists with anything to the discredit of the U.S.S.R., or communist parties anywhere in the world.

In certain ways the position of the left complements that of the right. Where the rightists seek to monopolise the Nation, the left claims to speak for and support the Masses (*o laós*), or 'the ordinary people' or 'working people'. In this they are at a slight disadvantage, for whereas The Nation is by definition inclusive of everyone, The Masses includes only a section of The Nation. Leftists insist however that the right have no monopoly of patriotism, and that a leftist can love his country and his nation just as well as can a rightist, or even better. Leftist claim to be democratic and progressive, as opposed to the undemocratic and reactionary nature they attribute to the right. Democratic is taken to mean having a preference for consulting people in general over decisions, as opposed to accepting leadership from the wealthy or powerful: however, educated men still receive considerable deference from leftists if they are not violently anti-left. By progressive is meant open to new ideas in agriculture, technology and education, but also it is simply a general term implying that one has leftish, modernizing ideas.

Leftists rarely choose to discuss Christianity, except to make criticisms of the wealth and influence of the Church. They insist that one can criticize the Church without being against religion. Only a staunch village leftist will deny that he believes in God, and very few leftists in Kalo fail to attend church for baptism, marriage or funerary ceremonies, when their families or friends are affected by them.

Leftists are usually strong supporters of the U.S.S.R., and strong critics of the U.S.A. They support the co-operative movement in its various manifestations, and a few speak wistfully of the need for agricultural collectives, but there have in fact been very few attempts co-operatively to exploit land in the island.

These values are expressed in coffee-shop debates, and reinforced by newspapers. Leaders and active supporters usually subscribe to a newspaper, which they sometimes take home for the benefit of their families. It is the expression of the appropriate set of values which defines a man in the village as leftist or rightist, rather than his formal membership in a party or other grouping. Village leaders know who is and who is not a member of their party, but that is by no means the end of their interest. The position a man takes in argument, and how ready he is to make his views known in support of his side, are in the daily life of the village just as important as formal membership. From this point of view leftists and rightists are given these identities from the behaviourist judgements of other villagers. They are attributes of people, in their social placement within the village. In the same way, those who are 'indifferent' to politics, or are thought to be insincere in what they say, are defined by other people's observations. These differ from person to person. Some people assured me that a man who said he was left, was 'really' right, and vice versa; or that a man who appeared in public as 'indifferent' was in fact a secret supporter of one side.

For those who are open supporters of the national groupings there are a number of ways of demonstrating support, some major, and some almost—to the foreign eye—trivial. Trade union membership is an obvious measure of support, and although the left have the lion's share of members (about two-thirds) the parallel right-wing unions have the remainder. Some of the island's soccer teams also have political identities; at one time one such team being almost exclusively manned by policemen thought to have been appointed by the then Minister of the Interior, Yorgadjis. Certain villages (though not Kalo) have two soccer teams, one right and one left; some villages have coffee-shops which are party-political, their walls festooned with party symbols (red for the left, blue for the right) where it is said only those of the correct views are made welcome. Even preference in consumption may be political. Some makes of brandy are produced by a left-wing co-operative, LOEL, and leftists pretend to prefer this for drinking groups. If some rightists are also joining the groups, there may be some playful bargaining over whether 'capitalist' or a 'socialist' brandy is to be consumed. The Co-operative Shop stocks various things from socialist countries and on one occasion a leftist leader said to his son: 'Go to the Co-op and get a tin of pork-meat. You know, the Chinese one.' The same man told me that the Russian *Lyto* condensed milk had more sugar, fat, and vitamins, according to its label, than the 'Cypriot' *Gala Vlachas*. (It is in fact made by a Swiss firm.) He had at least taken the trouble to compare the fine print. However, his wife, like many village women, reserved the right to give *Gala Vlachas* to young babies, since as the oldest brand it enjoys a reputation among village mothers as being 'better for babies'. Such preferences are not entirely serious, but then, they are not entirely frivolous either. Political support in Cyprus can take many forms, and it is natural to villagers, who are often competing for very small advantages, that support in any economic activity can be witheld from 'enemies' and granted to 'friends'.

Perennially, soccer teams and youth clubs spring up and die down in villages. Just how far these are politically exclusive depends on the local situation. Kalo had a soccer team in the 1920s which was not political, as now remembered. It lapsed after a few years. In the late 1940s, during the high-tide of left influence in the village, there was another soccer team which was recalled as 'leftist' in the sense that most of the players were left supporters. The nationalists tried to form a rival team but found that not enough good players remained, and dropped the idea. The left team lapsed, probably soon after the EOKA campaign began. In 1968 there was a soccer team in Kalo, but this seemed to have no political overtones, in that young men of both sides played in it together. There was also a branch of THOI, a church-supported youth club; on one occasion I saw a strongly right-wing schoolmaster who was on its committee rebuke a young man for smoking in the club, by saying: 'If your father wasn't a communist you wouldn't behave so badly.' This teacher was laughed at behind his back by the youths, for his 'fanaticism', and there was no move to restrict attendance at the club's recreation room to the right.

Data from other studies[6] make it clear that when there is a high degree of political polarization in a village, all sorts of other activities get politicized, and in certain ways the village draws apart into two exclusive and hostile camps. This does not seem to have been the case in Kalo for many years, but this description should make it clear that the potential for such cleavage is present in the institutional behaviour of the villagers. The organizational bases for full cleavage are present and ever ready.

THE COSTS AND BENEFITS OF ALIGNMENT

There are a number of tangible advantages and disadvantages to being an open supporter of the left or the nationalist right; to discuss them is not to suggest that ideology plays little part in village politics: a personal commitment to a position does not exclude receiving benefits from it. It is also worth stressing that tangible benefits are in short supply, usually available only to those who have held leadership positions or have shown firm support for a long period; but the risks of open support are more evenly spread.

The possible benefits for leftists include scholarships for their children to study in Eastern European countries. One young man from the village went to study in Czechoslovakia in 1969, and several other children of prominent leftists hope for similar scholarships.[7] Occasionally, these countries also offer free or subsidized medical treatment for difficult cases which cannot be accommodated in Cyprus. Several Kalo leftists have been on visits to socialist countries in Eastern Europe with most of their expenses paid as delegates of the agricultural organization of the left, EKA.[8] EKA also organizes cheap air charter flights to Britain at Christmas and Easter, through which students in the U.K. can visit their families, or relatives visit emigrants living in the U.K. There are also the normal benefits of trade union membership for those villagers enrolled in PEO, the leftist federation of unions, which include the fruits of collective bargaining, subsidized medical attention, and pension schemes. Finally, since the left organizations have a number of paid administrative posts, there is the possibility of steady employment for a few individuals, although during my fieldwork no one from Kalo held such a post.

There are serious disadvantages to being a known leftist, which include difficulty in getting certain highly desired jobs: leftists are unwelcome in the teaching profession and the police; government departments are reputed to deny promotion to such leftists as slip through the net and get employed. The sons of known leftists are often said to get posted relatively far from home during their military service, and to get more than their fair share of fatigues, punishments and hardships. There are even said to be special army camps to which the leftist's sons are sent, the better to keep watch on them. To complete the list of drawbacks, there have been sporadically since 1954 a number of acts of violence against leftists, including beatings, occasional killings, and bombing of buildings belonging to left organizations. Known Cypriot communists find they are unwelcome in Greece, where the communist defeat in the Civil War was followed by a succession of right-wing governments.

The following example makes clear how careful villagers feel they need to be: in 1968 a group of young men returned to Kalo from Athens where they had been studying. At a wedding they expressed strong support for the military dictatorship in Greece. Later several men told me that one of them had previously been a strong leftist. A prominent leftist told me that the boy had wanted a scholarship to an Eastern bloc socialist country but had failed to get it, and out of pique had turned to a right-nationalist politician, who had perhaps helped him to get a scholarship to Greece. I told this man that I'd heard the boy was still a leftist at heart but was hiding his views because of the danger from the Greek government that he would at very least be stopped from studying in Athens. 'No. A leftist is a leftist, and never hides it.' I said this was a little hard, given the obvious difficulties for leftists in Greece. He agreed but added that the boy had not been 'ideologically committed'.

Later the boy himself gave the following account: He had once been a 'fanatic leftist'. In Greece, before the military coup, he had seen the extent of political conflict, and the extent of political surveillance and favouritism, even by the Papandreou government. He was sure the Papandreou authorities had opened a file on him. Once the Junta came to power, he certainly wasn't going to stick his neck out after all his family's sacrifices. 'Did you hear any boy from the village speak against the Junta? You do realize there are spies in the village?' He described his own position as centre-left. He denied having a scholarship, but said he knew of a boy from the village who had got a scholarship through the support of a nationalist politician.

To be a strong nationalist has certain advantages, some of which complement those of the left. The right-wing trade and farmers' unions, though much smaller, exercise similar functions to those of the left. They also organize visits to foreign countries, and charter flights to the U.K. Since their organizations tend to be more weakly institutionalized, there are fewer jobs available in this area, but this is more than matched by the much better prospects a moderate nationalist enjoys when seeking jobs in the police, teaching, or any branch of the civil service.[9] There are scholarships for study in Greece made available through nationalist channels, and for the few opportunities to study in the U.S.A. nationalists stand a much greater chance than leftists.

Perhaps the greatest single benefit to being a nationalist is the least tangible. It can be summed up by saying that the nationalist under normal circumstances appears in a completely legitimate light, as the upholder of Greek cultural values, which are strongly bound up with the profession of the Orthodox faith. In a society where traditionally under Turkish rule the Church was the political representative of the Greek people, and where an archbishop is the popularly elected head of state, the nationalist usually can place himself, in argument at least, in the mainstream of the society's values. The leftist is permanently upstaged, both by the ambiguity of his position over religious belief, and the problem of the relationship between the communist party and the U.S.S.R. The exclusion of the left from EOKA both symptomized this political weakness, and further contributed to it.

For leaders and activists of both left and right wings, there are certain other benefits, which are harder to describe. The nuclear family, with the key moral appeal to the idea of *synféron*, self-interest, is the basic structural unit of village society. Unrelated men meet in a climate of fiercely competitive individualism. It seems reasonable to see such competition as psychologically exhausting, and the relative isolation of the individual as threatening, and stressful. In such a climate, an alliance with a larger and more powerful unit than the nuclear family may provide certain types of satisfaction, which could be thought of as an additional supportive social identity.

In a period of rapid social change, the left offer the individual both a strong organizational vehicle to which he might attach himself, and a secular philosophy which expects, indeed predicts, change. This philosophy also explains certain unpleasant features of the social world, such as the unequal distribution of advantage, and suggests certain remedies for them. The most serious difficulty for a Greek about identifying himself with the left focuses on the problem of religion: can a man be both a good leftist and a good Christian?

The right has always been organizationally weaker than the left, and its theory of change, is a fundamentalist assertion of the overwhelming importance of Family, Christianity and Hellenism. If the right loses something through its less flexible and less coherent set of answers to the problem of change, it gains much from being more directly and unambiguously the inheritor of traditionalist Greek culture.

THE CONTAINMENT OF RIGHT/LEFT ANTAGONISM

What weight should be given to the identifications, left and right, in the village? The terms are in daily use when villagers refer to each other, and also as terms of address. At the same time the apparent violence of tone in newspaper editorials (particularly those of the extreme right) makes it at first sight hard to see how the use of the terms in the village does not lead to more frequent open conflict, if only between the leaders and activists. Even granting that there may be a cultural factor which allows villagers to discount heavily the rhetoric of the daily papers, there still seems to be a gap of some size between what the papers say and what the villagers do. I shall now briefly discuss factors which contain left/right antagonism; further material will appear in later chapters.

Since 1955 the island's Greek leaders have been preoccupied first with the British rulers, then with the Turkish minority. The response of the left has been in the main to give firm support to Makarios, to call for unity of all Greek political groups, and generally to appear as a party of order. Since Makarios is generally popular, and since the left has much to lose from any taint of illegality, this tactic has served to protect it from harassment from extreme anti-communists. The right also supports the call for unity, while still keeping up a hostile tone towards the left. This, then, is the framework of Greek communal unity which surrounds any particular event.

In the village this general situation has been reproduced by the avoidance of hard contests between the two main groups. The administrative committee elections, which take place every three years, have not been matters which mobilized all possible support in the village. A turn-out at these elections of between thirty and fifty people was typical in the elections I attended, and this seems to have been normal, from informant's comments. The possible number of voters varied from 300 or more for the Co-op Store Committee, to 450 for the Credit Co-op. In fact, throughout the 1960s there has been a long-standing *implicit* agreement among village leaders not fully to contest these committees, but to have agreement of rough parity between right and left representatives. This still leaves some scope for manoeuvre, as I shall describe in the next chapter; but such tacit procedures have the result that most villagers—who are in any case more or less indifferent to these elections so long as their affairs are handled both reasonably fairly and efficiently—are not involved in them. A full-scale contest would mean that both sides would attempt to use all kinship, friendship, ideological and other ties to line up their supporters, and the cross-cutting ties which involve most leaders, and indeed most villagers, (p. 282) would be strained and tested.

The fact that hard contest was avoided, does not mean that right and left as political categories were irrelevant to, or not invoked in these situations. It means instead that explicit recognition was given to their importance by agreeing parity of representation. There is something called 'the left' which must be given two positions on any committee; it cannot be ignored. There is no need to give up two seats to something which doesn't exist, or is irrelevant in village life.

However, this control of contest is made by another conscious activity of village leaders: they define these committees as 'not political' in their purposes, but solely concerned with 'village business'. 'We don't want to allow party politics to get mixed up in village business' was a statement made on many occasions, and specifically made to prevent political contest. The easiest way of doing this, since neither group of leaders will stand by and let the others dominate anything in the village, is to agree tacitly or openly on a division of committee jobs in advance.

If political identities of the left/right order were of less importance in village affairs, one would surely expect individuals regarded in other contexts as spokesmen for these positions, to be able to stand as 'independents' on village committees, or to be able to show their ability to segregate their loyalties to an institution outside the village, from their conduct of village affairs, by reciting some suitable formula. As it is, the efforts to control the extent of political contest suggests that no simpler means is available; and even the device of defining areas of activity as out of the scope of politics showed signs of a breakdown on a number of occasions. These incidents will be made the subject of extended discussion later.

A further factor which has limited the conflict between left and right is again related to the national system. In short, for the period 1960–70 the developing lines of most intense political cleavage in Cypriot society have been between two groupings in the right-wing nationalist camp, which in 1969 became openly institutionalized when political parties were formed. In their inception these events are related to a struggle between certain national leaders. One result in Kalo was that the intensity of conflict between the leaders of left and right was modified, since the right were often too busy with their internal differences, and the left were careful not to unite them by obvious provocation.

This was a village level counterpart of the AKEL national leadership's policy since 1960. I shall have more to say about this in the next chapter.

OMÁDHES: THE DISRUPTIVE POTENTIAL OF POWER FORMATIONS

Omádha (plural, *omádhes*) means a group or, in a military context, a unit. *Omádhes* were often spoken of by villagers, and their presence (real or imagined) had clearly played an important part in village political life. *Omádhes* suggest power formations in their simplest, purest form—numbers of devoted supporters who will, at a leader's bidding, become an action group.

Sociologically, an *omádha* is an ego-centred category of recruitment, which might (Mayer, 1966) be called an action-set; they are the supporters of a particular leader, having a minimum of coherent organization, and who may or may not all know each other. In a single village it is highly likely that they *will* all know each other, but what makes them both interesting and divisive in village political life is that other villagers may not necessarily know who they are. *Omádhes* are often clandestine, and have some historical roots in Cypriot culture. Reports of early elections suggest that politicians were often accompanied by groups of coercive supporters. More recently, the 1955–9 EOKA insurrection relied on island-wide loosely organized teams of secret guerrillas. Later, in 1963–4 villages, including Kalo, formed militia units to fight against the Turks. The Kalo unit came under the authority of the district commander, based in Market Town.

However, after 1964 various *omádhes* which had originally been formed by various Greek leaders to fight the Turks, became the subjects of factional disputes at the national level. In the press and in debates in the Legislative Assembly, there were endless references to 'private armies' and these were continually linked to the then Interior Minister, Yorgadjis, to the left-nationalist physician Lyssarides, and the right-nationalist newspaper editor and former EOKA militant, Sampson. *Omádhes* loyal to General Grivas were also thought to exist. Arguments about the relative legitimacy of these different 'private armies' were endless. It was widely believed that President Makarios authorized the formation of these units by Sampson and Lyssarides because he feared the growing power of Yorgadjis, and of Grivas.

Such issues can hardly be dealt with authoritatively here, for *omádhes* whether in town or village are by their nature usually invisible and uncountable. Sometimes they are more talked about than real. It is certain, however, that there were new *omádhes* in 1969–70, one of which, the *Éthnikon Metópon*, (National Front) was responsible for a number of raids against government buildings and officials but ended with the arrest of seventy men, and the trial of some twenty of these. The Greek Army was also suggested as the source of yet other groups, and this was explicitly linked to the *Éthnikon Metópon*, when the Greek Army officer General Yerakinis was sent back to Greece at the request of the Makarios Government. However, it is impossible to know for sure what was the relationship between the General and the *Éthnikon Metópon*.

Omádhes threaten village solidarity because they represent an extreme form of commitment to individuals, or institutions outside the village, they also suggest a capacity for action considerably more powerful than that arising from ordinary ties between individual clients and their patrons. A basic distinction in Cyprus is between *dhikós mas*, our man, and *xénos*, the stranger, or unrelated man. In the context of *omádhes*, the phrase *ánthropos tou Yorgádji*, Yorgadjis's man, implies a man who will do Yorgadjis's bidding even against a neighbour in his own village. Just what that bidding is depends on the leader's whims and the national situation; it is not derived from village goals. EOKA units went on missions against the British, and suspected traitors. The village militia of 1963–4 trained in the Pendedactylos Mountains, and fought against Turkish units near Kokkina as well as taking part in an assault on a Turkish village ten miles from Kalo. These are known activities of a concrete nature. But groups which have existed at other times have been involved perhaps merely in the notion of group membership carried about in members' heads, plus a certain amount of surveillance, alertness and general intelligence work.

National leaders, whether public politicians or more or less covert figures in army, civil service or private life, wish to be kept informed about the movements of and support for their opponents. Village activists, linked to such leaders, wish to show their loyalty and vigilance. Thus there appears to be a continual flow of traffic in information between villages and urban leaders. Sometimes when the information is of low grade this has curious results. A young school-teacher of cautious disposition and no known political position was surprised to find himself transferred to a distant village in a poor region; since he had done nothing that he knew of to displease his superiors, he asked a close kinsman with good government connections to find out why. His kinsman went to a trusted government official high up in the security services. This man told him that his kinsman the teacher was a member of an illegal political group. The evidence was that he had been seen one night at a petrol station with a police uniform in his car. When challenged with this 'evidence' the young man admitted to having had the uniform, not to impersonate a policeman but because he was taking part in a school play!

Another example from the EOKA period: the teacher Vourros was told by a close kinsman that he was suspected of having contact with the British security forces, and thus being a traitor. He was badly frightened, and asked his kinsman to find out what the evidence was against him. The answer came back that he had been seen going into a British Army building in Nicosia. The army building was in fact the Ministry of Education, which had British soldiers stationed outside it, as did all government offices during the Emergency. But the villager who had reported Vourros' activities did not know or understand this.

An example of a more serious nature will show how villagers are inevitably unsure of the purpose and direction of some groups: Dhaskalos had been active in a village EOKA shotgun group, but had had some personal differences with its leader. Later, in 1964 he was working as a teacher in a village fifty miles from Kalo when one night he heard in the dark the voice of a Greek mainlander giving weapons instruction. Next time he went to Kalo he made inquiries, and learned that a village *omádha* of about thirty-five men had been formed and was drilling. He was angry because he had not, in spite of his EOKA experience, been called on to join this group. He went to see a powerful EOKA leader in a nearby village,[10] and asked what was going on. This man was hesitant, and said nothing. 'Don't take me for a fool', said Dhaskalos. He was then told that official but secret groups for defence against the Turks were being organized through the Nicosia M.P. Koshis, a close friend of the Minister of the Interior, Yorgadjis. Dhaskalos then went to Nikos Sampson, who was by this time a political critic of Yorgadjis, and asked him if he knew about these activities. Sampson said that he did but had authorization from the President to form official groups of his own, and that if Dhaskalos wanted guns for such a group he could have them.

In the village, the existence of an *omádha* is seen as a centre of power, and whatever its ostensible purpose, it is potentially threatening to rival political supporters. In the next chapter I shall discuss the consequences of one such *omádha* being formed in the village. Here it is enough to say that the existence, real or imagined, of such groups seems to have produced a further degree of tension and sometimes sharpened cleavage in village relationships; and that whatever the combination of tangible benefits, personal loyalties or values induces villagers to join groups, the origin of the groups lies in political competition in the national arena. Groups are the stuff that coups are made of; some of the events in recent Cypriot politics involving assassination attempts, and rumours of planned coups, sent reactions through the villages, where segments of supporters existed who saw themselves as directly affected. When for example, during my fieldwork, a senior police official was shot a few miles from the village, a number of villagers were arrested because it was thought they belonged to a group hostile to the Minister of the Interior. Later, when the *Éthnikon Metópon* was launched, the village was thought by some to be a hotbed of supporters for this illegal underground organization, and was again the scene of arrests, and full-scale house searches. Extra-parliamentary political activity plagues both the national and village arenas in modern Cyprus, but it is probably more immediately disruptive of social relations in the smaller arena, the village.

CONCLUSION

The administration of village affairs, which takes place within a formal governmental framework defined by the state, provides a number of posts open for competition to villagers. In fact only a limited category of those eligible actually fill these posts, the full-time farmers. These men are always in the village, are economically sufficiently secure to undertake additional responsibilities, and by that very fact have, in the eyes of their fellow villagers, the essential managerial skills. In addition to being full-time farmers, the committee men are usually able to speak well, are generally thought to be honest, and may sometimes have shown that they can effectively use force.

However, power is not confined to the committee men (who in fact enjoy very limited power from office itself). In addition to being a good speaker, a man may have power through education, through wealth, through contacts with powerful people, particularly in the capital, or through his known readiness to employ force. Each of these bases for power can be achieved; they are not the monopoly of a hereditary power elite in the village.

Many villagers (but not all) describe themselves as right- or left-wing, identifications which have their origin in recent political developments of Cyprus, and international society. These distinctions are related to but not fully explained by differences of wealth and occupation. The ideology of the rightists involves emphasis on Greek nationalism, adherence to Orthodox Christianity, the family, private property. That of the left stresses different priorities—the claims of the working masses, the idea of progress (particularly in science and technology) and the notion of democracy by which is meant consultation of the masses. The ideology of each side is partly determined by defining its positive characteristics as the opposite of its opponents' negative characteristics. In this sense, each group invents the other, and depends on the other for the clarity of its identity.

Alignment with left or right may offer the chance of a leadership role, but also more material benefits which may further the interests of a man and his dependants. Access to certain jobs, scholarships, trade union benefits, cheap travel, cheap medical care may be available through national organizations; conversely, a man may be excluded from certain benefits precisely because he is a known supporter of a political party. In Cyprus both leftists, and extreme rightists of an anti-government persuasion, tend to be disadvantaged in seeking civil service jobs, and even if they succeed, their promotion prospects may suffer. Thus the alignments of national (and international) politics represent a high-risk commitment, which also holds out the tantalizing prospect of high profit. The very uncertainty of such political benefits will partly explain why villagers seek to control the scope of political conflict in the village. The peace of the village offers more certain benefits than the elusive prizes of political alignment.

It follows from this that the formation of *omádhes*, clandestine teams of active supporters for national leaders, is one of the more threatening events which can occur in the village. *Omádhes* are potential action groups which promise to break the bounds of village solidarity. In the wider society they represent the danger of extra-parliamentary political force, acting outside the state's monopoly of force. In the village, where the resort to force has been the traditional defence of the family unit, they represent crystallized power, but power which is not created for traditional reasons of family defence, but for reasons of identification with outside and so uncontrollable principles, forces or leaders. To most villagers the formation of *omádhes* is viewed as a dangerous breach of traditional control rules.

NOTES

1. Bailey (1969: 144–85).
2. Davis (1969), (1973), and Forge, A. (personal communications).
3. For a useful discussion of the development of and distinctions in Modern Greek, see Browning (1969). Villagers in Cyprus speak a distinct dialect. In school they learn a spoken language, *Demotikí*, and a written language, *Katharévousa*, which is used in most official documents, and formal speeches.

   Although some words are common to all three levels, there are also many important differences, and villagers do not usually feel able to cope with *Katharévousa*. Younger villagers, with secondary school education are at ease in *Demotikí*.
4. Campbell (1964: 213–62) has described in striking terms the relations between Sarakatsani, and government officials; Cypriot civil servants also try to enhance their status by treating uneducated villagers in a high-handed manner. But there is no doubt in my mind that in efficiency, and in the implementing of basic legal rights of citizens, the Cypriot civil service is well ahead of that in Greece. Younger men laugh at their elders for being in awe of minor officials and for not knowing their rights, saying they are 'ignorant and old fashioned'. The word *dhikáioma* 'rights' is often heard in the village.
5. For example, see Needham (1972); by writing of 'alignment' rather than belief, commitment, conviction etc., I have made the problem of what people believe seem to disappear, but obviously the disappearance is more apparent than real. On the basis of many discussions, I *infer* that some villagers (usually leaders and activists) take their political beliefs very seriously. I do not know how to show this or measure it.
6. See Boissevain (1965) Kenna (1971) Morin (1970) Tarrow (1967). (1967).
7. In 1972, Sklyros's oldest daughter received a full scholarship to study in the U.S.S.R., which she accepted.
8. Travel abroad is highly prestigious at all levels of Cypriot society. On one trip to the Soviet Union, Sklyros was accompanied by his rightist opponent Patris; afterwards Patris made certain criticisms in the coffee-shops of the things he had seen, and Sklyros was highly annoyed, saying he had picked on trivia.
9. Not only leftists suffer forms of discrimination in the civil service, Extreme rightists of a pro-Grivas persuasion tend to experience difficulties, if their accounts are to be believed.
10. This man is also mentioned on page 69 and page 266.

7
Troubles

INTRODUCTION

To this point my main concern has been to give the reader a
historical perspective and structural analysis of facts essential to
an understanding of politics in the village. This chapter marks a
turning point for from here on the concern with structure gives
way to concern with process, and in place of more or less isolated
events, we shall now follow in detail developing situations. There
is no way to analyse political processes without first describing
them, and this will take the form of extended case histories. It
should not be thought that these are in any rigorous sense a
sample of politics in the village; they are in fact trouble cases,
salient issues, events remembered by the villagers or events
which struck me, the observer, as vital to the interests of the village; and because men's daily lives are taken up with work,
family and relaxation, the reader must bear in mind that most of
the villagers most of the time are not greatly involved in the sort
of events which make up the rest of this book, which is concerned
with village political activists at their most active.

The six cases in this chapter[1] are concerned with the competition for political power between the villagers, and although
outside resources are often employed the main arena remains
the village and the main protagonists, the villagers. In chapter
eight the focus will shift to relations between villagers and the
larger society and the main theme will be the antagonism between
Kalo with several allied villages, and Market Town over the
proposed construction of a dam. Chapter nine shows the cleavage between Market Town and its satellite villages to be
operating at the same time as the dam issue, but over another
issue, the management of a major citrus sales co-operative, in
which many villagers and Market Townsmen are shareholders.
Chapter ten discusses the consequences for Kalo of the two main
right-wing party electoral campaigns in 1970, and how this
campaign tested the solidarity of leading Kalotes. Thus, each

chapter focuses on a different organizational level of Kalo politics. In real life several series of events were going on at the same time with the same personnel but for analytic clarity I have treated them separately since this better shows the relation of the various political fields.

THE CASE OF THE GRADUATES' CLUB

In which Vourros, a wealthy educated urban resident attempts to improve Kalo by introducing a social club for educated men only to find himself thwarted by the opposition of a poorer and less educated man, Moustachas who has authority in the village because he was a leading EOKA militant.

Vourros was born in the neighbouring village of Kammari, married the daughter of a former Kalo *múktar* and together they live in a big house in the capital. They have very large land holdings in the village, and a second house to which they often come. Vourros has a British university degree and teaches in a private school. His views on village life stress the need for thrift, hard work, strict accounting; he deplores the drinking, swearing, and spitting of the coffee-shops and the respect for physical toughness. He has fairly strong views on the need to 'develop' the village.

In 1962 he proposed to several other educated men in the village that they do what his own and several other villages had done—start a club for Gymnasium graduates, a *sýllogos apophytón*, in which villagers with secondary education could come together to chat, read newspapers, play chess, drink coffee, and perhaps occasionally discuss problems of the village. They might even invite outside speakers to address them. The club would, he hastened to add, be non-political.

He found those with whom he discussed the idea quite enthusiastic. He continued with the idea until he had sounded out most of the eligible men in the village. They got as far as agreeing a date for meeting to discuss a constitution.

In the event, nothing happened. Several people who had previously expressed enthusiasm approached Vourros and said on thinking it over they had decided that really the village was all right as it was, and they did not really need a club for those with secondary education. At first Vourros was puzzled, and when he pressed people, they became uncomfortable. Finally it came out that Moustachas, the leader of the village EOKA group in the 1950s, a right-wing farmer with substantial land and a small supplementary government job, had heard about the scheme, and said in his view it would be a bad thing for the village, because it would undoubtedly become political in tone. Having expressed himself strongly against it, and suggested to other people that they should see it his way, the previous support for the scheme simply evaporated. Vourros tried a direct discussion with Moustachas on the subject, assuring him of the club's political innocence, but Moustachas, who had not enjoyed secondary education, did not change his view. Privately he pointed out to others that several people interested in the club were leftists or left sympathizers, and he was sure they would try to take it over.

At this point Vourros might still have succeeded, because there was one man in the village who could have talked Moustachas round, or at least, acted as a counter-weight. This was the teacher Dhaskalos who was both a known right-wing nationalist, with a record of EOKA service in the village as well as being an educated man. Dhaskalos insists that Vourros, believing him to be hostile to the notion anyway, failed to approach him at the right time. Thus Dhaskalos simply stood back and watched. He believed a club would be good for the village; he thought Moustachas's view was wrong (he had in any case some personal differences with him which dated from the period of EOKA leadership) but he was not prepared to support Vourros. He took the simple step of not turning up to the initial meeting that Vourros had tried to organize. He did nothing so direct as to tell him either that he would not come, or why he would not come. Indeed he had told Vourros that he would come. That was the end of the Graduates' Club, but Vourros continued to think about it, and built up a picture of the village as a place where education was rejected, and only the ability to use guns carried any weight.

Why should the proposed formation of the Graduates' Club have produced Moustachas's determined opposition, and why should the event be regarded as in any way memorable by those involved? There are a number of reasons. First, Moustachas was undoubtedly sincere in his belief that the leftists might dominate such a club. For one thing it is part of the right's picture of the left that it is constantly engaged in a secret move to increase its power, secondly the right sees the left as working through literacy, book-learning. Sklyros, for example, is known to do a lot of reading in his spare time, and so did the village's first two communists. 'They read a lot, those cuckolds' was a remark I heard on many occasions. So to Moustachas the idea of a leftist take-over of the Graduates' Club was plausible.

He also had something to gain by his action. To have taken action which could be reported as vigilance in urban anti-communist circles was useful.[2] At the same time, to have demonstrated his power in the village was part of a self-fulfilling prophecy. Since the days of the EOKA struggle there do not seem to have been many opportunities for Moustachas to have laid down the law in the village. Here was a chance and he took it.

The reasons given so far are to do with Moustachas's personal power and position, and make him sound extremely calculating. This by itself would be misleading. There are other aspects which must be considered which may have influenced him but of which he need not have been consciously aware. At this period in Kalo there were no strongly institutionalized arrangements for social distinctions between members of the village. Although Vourros could not see it this way, his proposal to introduce a Graduates' Club was a proposal to introduce emphatic and institutionalized inequality into the village. It is clear in the discussion of land, occupation, status, life styles and the arrangement of marriage that the villagers are well aware of social differences, but this does not mean that they are keen to have such differences institutionalized. Since the actual decision to oppose the Club came from a single man, who was quite widely feared in the village, it would be incorrect to take his views as simply representing those of the village at large. Also, in other villages, such clubs have been accepted for many years. Some are political, others are not. It is important to note however, that whether or not the club would have become political in the way Moustachas said it would, it would have unambiguously symbolized a most important social difference between villagers.

It was argued in chapter one that during the early years of independence, there was a structural conflict in Cypriot society, expressed by individuals' statements that others were not entitled to benefits—jobs, scholarships etc. The individuals in question were members of certain categories, in broadest terms an uneducated rural mass with aroused expectations, and an educated urban elite.[3]

The episode in the village over the formation of a club for

Graduates has, as one of its several causes, shown the way in which Vourros and Moustachas represent the opposed values and characteristics of these categories. In this sense the dispute was a miniature version of a pervasive, general conflict within the larger society, which will become more sharply defined by the next case.

Before passing to it however, it is worth relating an interesting sequel to the event of 1963. In January 1970, a man in his middle twenties freshly returned from a university degree from Greece, and like Vourros a secondary school teacher from a wealthy farming family, tried to set up a Graduates' Club in the village. In a few words, his experiences turned out very much the same as Vourros'. Initially there was a lot of verbal support which however soon faded. He discovered that certain people were blocking the club, in the main the supporters of a right-wing nationalist party. He himself was an open supporter of a left-wing nationalist party. The men who opposed him were mostly uneducated farmers with solid land holdings; but they were supported by a few young men with secondary education, who now faced the difficulties of finding appropriate jobs in a shrinking market.

In 1971 a right-wing nationalist club was formed in the village, which no one had the temerity to oppose. But in these situations, nationalism is usually defined by nationalists as non-political and the club in theory is open to all.

The chief reason that Moustachas was able to get his way in the first place was because Vourros and the other educated men were afraid that he would use force if they persisted with their plans, and that his EOKA connections, and urban patrons among former EOKA fighters would support him in anything he chose to do. Vourros had already had a scare during the EOKA period (p. 135) and he was not prepared to take the matter further. It is very likely that Moustachas would not have resorted to force in this issue, the critical fact was that others thought he might. Later events will make clear why they thought so.

THE CASE OF THE CRETAN GUNS

In which the Kalo militia leaders raise money for guns but later find they have alienated village opinion; they call for an *ad hoc* committee to create an atmosphere of village unity, only to find that the committee is used to control them. Vourros again confronts Moustachas and his nephew, and

F

educated men are once again in dispute with less educated
farmers.

The fighting which broke out in December 1963 (pp. 18, 134) had
its repercussions in the village. One of these was that in the first
half of 1964 the Kalo EOKA group decided to form a volunteer
militia to protect the village in the event of a direct Turkish attack,
and also to take part in fighting generally in defence of the Greek
community in the island. It must be stressed that information on
such topics is hard to obtain, but the evidence suggests that the
volunteer militia groups were those already planned by Yorgadjis
and Koshis prior to the Turkish secession.[4] However, until the
return of General Grivas to Cyprus in June 1964, such militia
groups and 'private armies' acted with a high degree of local
autonomy. Several accounts agree that the Makarios government
had a serious problem in trying to control the behaviour of such
groups during the initial fighting.

Although Moustachas was the senior EOKA man in the village
involved with the volunteer militia he seems to have shared
the command of the militia unit with his wife's sister's son
Vasilakis, who partly due to his uncle's intervention had been
commissioned in the Cyprus Army. Several other prominent
EOKA people were also in command positions in the unit, and
some fifty or sixty village men volunteered as 'other ranks'. On
this occasion, unlike the 1955–9 EOKA struggle, known leftists
were admitted to the militia, the right-wing view being taken
that the national threat from the Turks was such that even leftists
could be relied on to fight wholeheartedly for their country.

The first job of the militia unit was to obtain guns. The government was very short of weapons at this period, so the Kalo unit
organized a house-to-house collection to raise money for the
guns. They used a system of assessment by the relative wealth
of each family, with a large landowner being assessed at about
£20 and a poor man at a pound or two. Even those who felt
that perhaps the purchase of arms at this point was ill-advised
and that such matters should be left to the central government,
were not inclined to resist the assessed contributions, since this
would have appeared unpatriotic, and most people were nervous
of arguing with the EOKA men in the village. In the end about
£1,000 was collected, and three men were sent to Crete via
Athens to buy guns. In due course they returned with some guns.
But some of the villagers felt that these guns were in poor con-

dition, were few in number, and that even when the essential expenses of the trip were taken into account, there was rather little to show for the money. They also heard from people in other villages who had sent similar missions that the guns were given away free by the Cretans. There was therefore some ill-feeling about the Cretan guns, and years later people were saying quite openly in the coffee-shops about the trip and the money *ephá'an ta* 'they ate it'.

Faced with a loss of support, albeit probably of a muted nature, the EOKA group running the militia revived a device which had existed in the 1955–9 period, the formation of a special committee, the Co-ordinating Committee (*Syntonistikí Epitropía*). It is possible that the initiative for the formation of this committee did not come directly from the leaders of the militia unit but from other members of the village. However, in any event the militia leaders accepted the idea and even agreed to the presence of several leftists on the committee. It is agreed by all parties in Kalo that the initiatives for the committee did not come from the central government or any other official body, even though in some other villages similar committees emerged during these months.

The minutes kept by the committee—which I examined—begin by specifying who are recognized as the leaders of the militia unit, and go on to specify the members of the committee. Of the ten men named[5] one is the *múktar*, two are the two most prominent leftists, Sklyros and Tangos, a brother of one of the three men to go on the Cretan trip. No one suggested to me that he would not be impartial. A fourth is Vourros. Patris and his brother were members and several other nationalists. The aims of the committee were listed as concerning (I quote):

(1) the agricultural and family problems of militia unit members

(2) political and economic problems, such as relations with the Kalo Turks

(3) general compensation to Kalo Turks for any economic losses suffered by them

(4) control of military activities, by liaison between the militia unit and the committee. The teacher Dhaskalos was selected as the militia leader responsible for liaison

(5) the committee to receive at least 48 hours notice from militia unit members of any agricultural work they needed[6]

(6) the committee to have the final say on the actual payments
   by unit members
(7) that good accounts are to be kept and audits allowed for all
   financial transactions
(8) the volunteer militia unit to give account for the outstanding previously collected money (the Athens–Crete trip)
(9) in the event of differences of opinion between the committee and the militia unit, the local district Legislative
   Assembly representative to be the arbitrator.[7]

Informants explained that one of the outstanding problems
of the volunteer militia was that during the absences of the men
for training or fighting (and it must be stressed that the Kalo unit
was involved in heavy fighting on several occasions) the agricultural work involved in their land holdings needed attention.
In the case of crops like potatoes and carrots, a day or two's delay
at critical harvesting times can lead to complete destruction of
the crop. For the village to handle such administrative problems
it was essential to obtain money to pay other people to do the
work, by taxing the village yet again. Clauses (6) and (7) are thus
to be seen as attempts to prevent the sort of dissatisfaction that
occurred over the Cretan guns. Clause (8) one informant insisted
was inserted through the efforts of Vourros. Vourros, and some
of the village leftists like Sklyros, also felt the issue of how the
Kalo Turks would be treated was in danger of being mishandled.
It seems that a few of the more excitable and extreme persons
connected with the militia were anxious that the Kalo Turks
possibly with the help of other Turks from outside, would try to
harm the Greek community. Since the Kalo Turks were outnumbered 30 to 1 and since Kalo is strategically rather far away
from a major Turkish concentration as well as being surrounded
by exclusively Greek villages, their fears may have been ground-
less, but in the atmosphere of alarm and vigilance of the period,
such views undoubtedly had some slender basis. At one point a
few persons were speaking of driving the Kalo Turks out of the
village, and Vourros spoke very hard and critically against such
views. Sklyros also used his baptismal *koumpáros* relationship[8]
with Moustachas to persuade him to go with him one evening
when the militia was preparing to go into action against a distant
Turkish village, and reassure the Kalo Turks, who were terrified,
that not only did the Kalo Greeks mean them no harm but that
in the event of outsiders coming to harm them, the Kalo Greeks

would defend them. These episodes cast light on clauses (2), (3) and (4). However, no one could remember if the concern and discussion about the Kalo Turks happened before the formation of the committee, and directly produced the relevant clauses, although the evidence suggests this.

Also at roughly this period there were undoubtedly certain personal animosities between Vourros and Vasilakis, the army officer. On one occasion Vasilakis said to Vourros, 'What you need is a bullet: not actually *in* your head, but just close enough to put some sense into it.' In terms of the way most village people speak to Vourros, this was at least highly disrespectful, and confirmed all the reservations Vourros had about the tendency of the villagers to turn to violence or threats of violence at the least excuse.

In this period of approximately six months, January–June 1964, Vourros had been engaged, using his professional skills in preparing hand-grenades for the use of the Greek militia in Nicosia. Vasilakis on several occasions asked him to bring some grenades for the use of the Kalo militia unit, but this he always refused to do on the grounds that he was acting under orders, and was accountable for all the grenades produced, and that these were under the direct control of the government.

It would be useful to place this series of events related to the Cretan guns trip and the formation of the Co-ordinating Committee in a precise time-sequence and to state the effect that each event had upon the others. This is not possible. To do so would be to transmute impressions—both mine and my informants—into the more weighty metal of certainty. In spite of this it is clear that during this period a number of incidents took place connected with the formation of the militia, involving some of the more influential people in the village, and that these incidents reflected real and divisive differences of opinion about how village affairs should be conducted.

The first recorded minute of the Co-ordinating Committee is entered by Vourros, and it thanks Vasilakis, as officer in charge of the militia for having co-operated in presenting the accounts of the Cretan trip, but asks if he could further provide the actual list of names of villagers and amounts collected because the amounts set down do not tally.

The committee decided to meet every Saturday evening regularly, and to have special meetings if needed. The next meeting noted that a list of tax-payers was being prepared, and that an

association of tractor owners had put the money owed to it at
the disposal of the committee. At the next meeting, among other
things decided, was that one member should take responsibility
for certain 'special losses' to the Turks of the village. These arose
when some shepherds had turned their flocks to graze in the
Turks' croplands, and later, when another villager Mangaras had
taken fifty lorry-loads of earth from a Turkish field without payment. Another item minuted was that the militia unit commander,
Vasilakis, was requested to attend regular committee meetings
as often as possible. The last item was a request that the accounts
for the Cretan arms trip be presented 'with the least delay possible, so that the unity of the village will not be broken'. At the
next meeting, neither Vasilakis nor his uncle Moustachas were
present. It was decided that the shepherds should pay the Turks
£5 for damage to their carrots, and the man who had taken fifty
lorry loads of earth to pay £5 for them, which was only slightly
under the market rate. This man was married to the half-sister
of Sklyros the leftist leader, who is also at this point writing up
the committee minutes.

At a later meeting, one committee man resigned in order to
allow his place to be taken by 'an educated man'. Four names
are put forward, in order of preference. All four are school-
teachers.

In the end, Vourros signed the accounts for the Cretan trip,
although he had great reservations about them. He saw himself
as having no practical alternative. At one point, when a villager
was refusing to co-operate with the committee, Vourros asked
some of the tougher members to deal with him, knowing that this
might involve force; another act of the committee was to resolve
to help the Turkish *múktar* of the village to find his wife, who
had gone off (in the last stages of pregnancy) with a Red Cross
medical team. At the last meeting minuted, it states that the
future of the committee was discussed, but no details are given.

The committee in fact lasted from March to November, 1964.
There are two quite different explanations given for why it
stopped. Some of the leftists claim that it became an efficient
instrument for conducting village affairs, and was about to start
looking into other matters of communal interest. They insist that
when the rightists realized this they decided to have nothing
more to do with it, and by continually staying away, effectively
brought it to an end. Sklyros is a proponent of this view, and is
particularly bitter about the issue, since he says that the right, by

which he means the militia leaders, Moustachas and Vasilakis needed the leftists on the committee after the Cretan guns fiasco, to give it new legitimacy in the village. His theory is that the leftists had a reputation for honesty, and that this was the only way the militia could retain the confidence of the villagers. However, since they as rightists hated to see the left succeed in anything, when the committee became effective, they undermined it.

Moustachas's account is different. He stated that once Grivas returned to Cyprus, in June 1964, and set about organizing through conscription a disciplined National Guard, the need diminished for a volunteer militia acting on its own. The committee folded up simply because its work came to an end.

There is no way of deciding between these two versions. There is no reason why both may not be substantially true, and complementary. The committee was an *ad hoc* measure, taken on local rather than governmental initiatives, and specifically designed to create a unified authority, representing all shades of political opinion among the Greeks of the village. The *múktar* and *azádes* could not do this because they were all non-leftists, and thought to be easily influenced by the more vocal nationalists. Once the national situation had become more normal, and a National Guard had been formed, the specific purpose of the committee would have come to an end. It would be galling for the right-wing leaders either to admit that they had depended on left support, or to go on co-operating with the left, so they effectively withdrew. If the right nationalists stayed away the remaining members could not act by themselves for the village, having neither any legal status, nor any legal authority to speak for the village.

The Cretan guns episode, the formation of the committee, the matters undertaken by the committee have a certain continuity with the issue of the Graduates' Club: Vourros is again involved. Moustachas is less prominent, but his nephew Vasilakis held very similar views politically. There are two sets of views and values, which can be inferred from these events.

Vourros represents the question, *quis custodiet ipsos custodes*— who will protect the rest of the village from the vagaries of its volunteer guardians? He represents a legalistic, bureaucratic position, like that of a conscientious ratepayer who wants to see public money properly spent. Through the minutes, and the committee decisions, some control is exerted over the use of money, damage to Turkish property, the convenience of the militia. The notion that the committee needed more educated people on it underlines these issues.

The militia views are not recorded in the minutes, but from the way the events were described to me, there was a good deal of resentment at the 'interference' of Vourros and other committee members, who were thought to be preoccupied with trifling details, hampering those who due to their military experience, courage and patriotism were engaged in the serious issues of village and national defence.

Before leaving this case, it is worth noting some of the other consequences. Future collections for weapons were on a more genuinely voluntary basis. Vourros had enough of village politics for some time, and withdrew from them. He did not really take much further part in things until 1969. In 1968 he was owed for two years' water by Moustachas and was not pressing for payment, although he would have liked the money. The reason was that he was still nervous of Moustachas. However, as I shall explain in the next chapter, in 1969 there was another opportunity for the village to throw up a special committee to meet a special crisis, and once again Vourros was prominent. Moustachas and Vasilakis however both stayed away from it.

THE CASE OF THE LYSSARIDES *omádha*⁹

In which the brothers Fanos form a support group (*omádha*) for Lyssarides, an urban politician, but find themselves threatened by supporters of an opposed leader. They employ an outside resource (access to a newspaper) which aggravates the dispute in the village, and Moustachas threatens them with violence. After much mediation and bargaining the issue is allowed to cool down but the support group started by the Fanos brothers virtually evaporates.

Before discussing certain events which occurred in Kalo during 1965, a few words are needed about Dr. Vassos Lyssarides. He is a medical doctor, trained in Athens, who for the last ten years at least has been Makarios's personal physician and close confidant. Lyssarides was in the 1940s a member of the communist party, AKEL but later withdrew. He seems to have had some connections with EOKA and certainly distinguished himself in the 1964 fighting by taking a group of men to storm a Turkish position on the Kyrenia range. He is a socialist, takes an anti-

NATO pro-third world stance, including strong support for the Arab countries. However, he also strives to include himself within what is called 'the nationalist camp' in Cyprus. Rightists who mistrust him for his leftism usually admit that by fighting he has proved himself an ardent nationalist. Lyssarides has also had two recurring themes in his political statements since 1964. One is that there are plots going on against Makarios, and the other is the theme of popular vigilance, suggesting that people's volunteer militias should be formed to protect the government and Makarios. In 1965 he was continually stressing both these themes and again in 1970. He implied that a coup was being planned by extreme right elements in the Cyprus Army, the police force, and among the Greek Army contingent.

During this period two young Kalo brothers, both gymnasium graduates, D. and L. Fanos (pp. 71–4) had come to know the doctor, and to be influenced by him. Since they worked in Nicosia they could easily visit him in his office where he always welcomed political supporters. They decided to form a small group in Kalo in support of him, and started to meet in various houses in the village. This sort of group was a variant of the *omádhes* described in the last chapter. Among others involved were Patris, the father-in-law of D. Fanos, and his brother, Oligos, both of whom had been EOKA activists in the village. There was also a school-teacher, who had been at gymnasium with Lyssarides and was his *koumpáros*. There were between fifteen and twenty people meeting regularly in this group, several of whom had been active in EOKA and the militia, and one of whom was a 'spy' in that he was not there in good faith, but for the purpose of reporting what was going on to the teacher Dhaskalos.

Dhaskalos's version of the situation is that Lyssarides at this period was suggesting that he alone was truly pro-Makarios, and that his supporters in the village believed this, and for this reason failed to invite either Dhaskalos himself, or the EOKA leader Moustachas to join the new group. They even suggested that Dhaskalos was not loyal to Makarios, which he regarded as a serious insult, and was angered. However, on his own admission, he—probably like many other ardent nationalists in the island—was in two minds over whom to support—Makarios or Grivas. When asked by a friend at this time what he thought, he replied 'We have to choose between a treasury and a pistol,' he meant that Makarios as controller of patronage was the treasurer, and Grivas the pistol. He was at the time attracted to the pistol, but claims he was acting independently of Moustachas and Vasilakis (p. 141).

There was another background issue which played a part, although a part difficult to judge precisely. A year or two previously, the Fanos family had been very friendly with Moustachas. He had often eaten and drunk in their house. They were undoubtedly hoping to obtain through him some form of scholarship for one of the younger children in the family, a girl, so that she could study at university in Greece more cheaply. Such scholarships were sometimes made available to the families of persons who had been closely involved in the EOKA struggle, and Moustachas's word as the senior EOKA man in the village might have carried a lot of weight. In the early years of the 1960s, Moustachas was consulted over the appointment of Kalo people to government jobs, especially on the all-important question of saying if they were communists or not. Eventually, however, it was his own daughter, a girl who, it was said, had done much less well at gymnasium than Old Fanos's girl, who received a scholarship to Greece. After this relations between the Fanos family and Moustachas were colder.

There was another personal matter. When D. Fanos became interested in supporting Lyssarides, he started arguing with various people in the village. Among these was Moustachas's nephew Vasilakis. They had a serious political argument some time before the events I am about to describe. My informant suggested that since D. Fanos was also in the militia and nominally under the command of Vasilakis as the officer, he may have felt the need for a more powerful ally in a quarrel with a military superior, and that this would have encouraged his stronger support for Lyssarides. The truth of such a view cannot be weighed but in itself accurately evokes the political culture of the village.

Information on the alignments of individuals at this time is less reliable than most of the data in this book, because since 1964 there have been major factional realignments both in the village and in the capital, which will be more fully discussed in chapter ten, and this caused my informants to try to put themselves in the best possible light. This must be born in mind in the next two paragraphs.

The militia group which was the subject of the last case was created by the Minister of the Interior, and the then pro-Makarios group of politicians. Since it was part of the Greek community security system it remained clandestine but 'official'. However, when Grivas returned in mid-1964 to Cyprus a dispute occurred between him and the Interior Minister, Yorgadjis, over control of the National Guard and the armed forces in general. There was growing hostility between Yorgadjis and another nationalist leader outside the government, Nikos Sampson. From the left, Yorgadjis was continually attacked politically by Lyssarides. Yorgadjis's power was feared, and he was believed to keep his rivals and their supporters under surveillance (pp. 18–20).

These rivalries and animosities among national leaders were probably reflected in village militias, and groups of supporting clients. However, in Kalo they were kept under control and kept quiet, partly because some village leaders were trying to keep all their options open, and avoided openly committing themselves to a single national leader. Moustachas for example had a government job, which Yorgadjis, as Minister of the Interior, could have taken away from him, but he was also *koumpáros* of Sampson, who was becoming increasingly outspoken in his criticisms of Yorgadjis. Moustachas was also linked, through his wife's sister's son Vasilakis, to pro-Grivas elements in the Cyprus National Guard; he was facing three ways. In what follows I assume that the village militia leaders were reporting to the Ministry of the Interior; but there may also have been an active connection with Grivas factions in the National Guard.

This, then, was the background: a number of members of the village militia were developing loyalties to different nationalist leaders and were watching each other, in an atmosphere of rumoured plots and planned coups in the capital.

One night the Lyssarides *omádha* called one of its secret meetings in the house of Patris. Members of the militia group claim that one of the subjects under discussion was of obtaining arms supplies, and that Patris's brother Oligos was appointed as the man in charge. However, the Lyssarides *omádha* probably had no weapons at this time. At some point during the meeting they heard a noise and on opening the door found several young men of the militia *omádha* outside, apparently listening to their meeting. Angry words were exchanged, and scuffles. One of the Lyssarides *omádha*, the young teacher, L. Fanos, tugged at the coat of one of the militia group and saw a sten gun was concealed under it. During the scuffle someone shouted out, 'This is the last night you meet here.'

The militia group's version states firmly that no weapons were carried, and that the meaning or intention of the phrase 'This is the last night . . .' merely referred to the intention of the militia group to allow no more meetings of a furtive political nature in Kalo by an 'unofficial' *omádha*. The phrase is not supposed to contain any threat of violence. The Lyssarides group version however is insistent that weapons were carried.

The cluster of angry people finally dispersed from the house, but all remained in a high state of tension. Among other things which had been said by the militia *omádha* was that the insults to Grivas must stop. This small detail perhaps explains some of what then occurred. The teacher L. Fanos went to Nicosia in the morning and reported the events of the previous night to Dr. Lyssarides, who was suitably angry at the way his supporters had been treated. Later L. Fanos wrote a small description of the event which with the help of another Lyssarides' supporter he managed to get printed on the front page in a newspaper owned by Nikos Sampson. It stated briefly that an attempt had been made to threaten a group of pro-Makarios people having a peaceful democratic discussion in the village of Kalo and gave the distinct impression that the militia *omádha* were *anti-*Makarios.

This move produced a very strong reaction from the militia group in the village. They were furious. First, they were being described as anti-Makarios. This was undesirable for several reasons: because Makarios has always held centre stage in recent Cypriot politics, and those who have strongly opposed him have been in weak positions: and because several of the militia group held jobs which were within the government—Moustachas, his nephew Vasilakis, who had actually sent the militia group members to watch the house, and Dhaskalos the teacher. The possible threat of loss of job, loss of promotion or transfer to far-off places always hung over their heads.

Another reason for anger on the part of the militia group was that they and the village in general were being brought into disrepute with the outside world for high-handed methods. 'An insult to the village' was a common line of their protest. In any event, night after night Moustachas sat drinking in the coffeeshops saying that when he found out who had written the piece he would shoot him. Dhaskalos went to see his friend Nikos Sampson and said, 'What the hell do you mean by printing a thing like that in your paper? We support your newspaper, and this is what you do. Is this what you mean by friendship?' He also asked Sampson to clarify the rumour which one of the leaders of the Lyssarides group was spreading—that Sampson was forming an *omádha* which would co-operate with Lyssarides's group. Sampson denied this categorically, and told Dhaskalos that if this had been the case, then as the chief Sampson supporter in the village he would have been the first to hear about it: and that he had not known about the newspaper story in advance, so was not directly to blame for it.

Because feeling was running so high in the village, various people made efforts to reconcile the two groups. Vourros was one of these. The District M.P. (who had been nominated as arbitrator in the relationship between the formal militia group and the Co-ordinating Committee) was approached. He was on good terms with leaders of both groups. There were a series of meetings involving different representatives of the two groups. One was in the house of the Kalo priest, at the suggestion of the M.P. At this meeting two documents were produced. One written by Dhaskalos, described the newspaper report and the whole event as a 'misunderstanding' *(parexígisis)* and asserted that no threat had taken place. The other document, prepared by L. Fanos stuck to the original story in its main outlines, that is, that a threat had taken place. Since no agreement could be reached, both versions were taken to the District M.P. to decide. Here once again accounts differ. The militia group claim that he decided in favour of their version, but that the Lyssarides group would not accept the verdict. They for their part claim he did not decide one way or the other. Debate dragged on in the coffee-shops for weeks and even months, about who was 'really' pro-Makarios and who was not, who had been in the right and who had been in the wrong, which *omádha* was 'official' and which was 'unofficial'. Some of those involved continued to be very angry and not speak to others for nearly a year.

Most of the versions of this episode also stress that at the several mediatory meetings Moustachas continued to complain that the people of the Lyssarides group had been going 'behind his back', and organizing political actions without consulting him. The essence of his complaint was that his authority, rooted in his EOKA and militia activities, was being eroded. In so far as he failed to get the newspaper item 'corrected' it could be said he failed to re-establish his position. Indeed the very fact that an issue which a few years before he might have settled with a few words in the right few ears, had now been referred *outside* the village in several different directions (to Lyssarides, to the M.P., possibly to Yorgadjis), was a clear indication that Moustachas no longer 'did what he liked' in the village. At the same time there is some slight evidence that the main decisions in the episode were not taken by Moustachas, but by the younger and politically more sophisticated man, the teacher Dhaskalos. There was also some tension between Dhaskalos and Moustachas from earlier differences. There is a further complication: one member of the militia unit who actually went to the house to spy on the meeting was the younger brother of Vasilakis, the Cyprus army officer. He argued that if he did not give his older brother full details of the meeting and the action taken, Vasilakis might get into trouble with his military superiors for failing to do his job properly, for failing to report on the formation of a left-wing *omádha*. Later, it was argued by some members of the militia group that the officer Vasilakis had tried to take all the credit for the episode as if it were all his idea. This point makes it clear that in some circles at least there was an idea that something had occurred *for which credit could be taken*, a thought that might not immediately strike an outside observer.

The Lyssarides group episode had several other consequences. First, the group as an active organization ceased to exist. One by one members dropped out. Only three or four of the original fifteen or more remained open supporters of the doctor. Among the most dramatic defectors was the leader, D. Fanos. His father-in-law Patris, and Patris's brother Oligos also dropped out, and are later in this book to be found as staunch supporters of other emergent and established political groupings of the nationalist right. This seems to have been the choice of most of the other members of the group. L. Fanos (the younger brother of D. Fanos), and a teacher who was Lyssarides's classmate and *koumpáros*) both remained quietly loyal to the doctor, hampered by their roles as teachers from more active support. It is probable that they were only emboldened to support the Lyssarides group openly at the time because the action could have been defended as related to national defence and support for the government and thus not crudely 'political'. This was certainly the rhetoric of Lyssarides's position.

The case then was a turning point in the career of Moustachas and in the life of the Lyssarides group in Kalo; both lost by it. For D. Fanos it was also a turning point but perhaps a more profitable one. He decided in effect to change patrons. Several

years later he was sent on a six months' trip for special training to
the U.S.A. by his civil service boss, who is also closely connected
with PEK, the nationalist farmer's party. It was for this party that
D. Fanos, his wife's father Patris, and Patris's brother, Óligos,
worked in the spring of 1970 (see chapter 10).

In a more general way the episode, apart from affecting the
positions of individuals and of factions, affected the whole village.
It was an object lesson both to the activists and to the village at
large of the dangers to village solidarity which arose from letting
commitments to political leaders and values outside the village
play too strong a part. Looking back on this period villagers said
to me, 'We were more fanatic then' (which is the same thing they
say about the late 1940s, when right and left had frequent confrontations both in the island and the village). The fact that
villagers remember the incident at all, and remember it as a kind
of failure, shows how a conscious interest in keeping the peace of
the village is a firm value.

Later in this account I shall describe how in June 1970 political
leaders in Kalo continually faced the possibility of new breaches
in village solidarity due to the intensity of political activity, and
by what methods they sought to restrain their followers. It may
well be that one of the factors which told most strongly against
Moustachas in the Lyssarides *omádha* affair was his open threat
to use force against the writer of the newspaper piece. This was
regarded in the village subsequently as having been a thoroughly
ill-considered action.

One important point which emerges from the episode is the
nature of the gap between events at the national and local levels.[10]
When Lyssarides was making calls for vigilance against a possible right-wing coup, he undoubtedly did not intend that one
direct result should be any loss of political support for himself.
Yet this was the result in Kalo, and there could possibly have
been results even more detrimental to Lyssarides's position such as
the killing of some of his supporters. This suggests that leaders
often have poor perceptions of the effects their actions will have
both on their followers and on those of their opponents. I shall
have more to say about this in other cases. Cypriot politicians
have been to some extent affected by British ideas of parliamentary democracy, and particularly enjoy the cut-and-thrust tradition of political debate. They also indulge in violent personal
attacks on each other, and a standard manoeuvre consists of
hinting at dark plots and evil designs by unnamed opponents. In

the capital, in newsprint or in the Legislative Chamber the immediate costs of such actions to the politicians themselves are low, and roughly speaking they understand the rules of this game. In the village, however, the same speeches and manoeuvres can have less predictable consequences. The costs of confrontation and encounter are potentially much higher and the rules of the game were designed to control indigenous home-made disputes, with home-made norms. They do not easily control norms and manoeuvres favoured by the elite, who in turn are looking abroad for their models, to Athens, London, Moscow and elsewhere. The fact that both groups in Kalo turned so quickly to mediation, and used the mediatory process as the means of seeking further advantage is in itself most important. But to what extent this was a purely village decision and to what extent outside leaders influenced it I unfortunately cannot say.

CARROT AND POTATO ASSOCIATION ELECTIONS

In which Sklyros, a leftist farmer and Patris a rightist farmer both seek to control an administrative committee without a costly contest. In the end Patris employs outside resources to gain the decision which is made on party political lines.

In 1963 Kalo formed its branch of the Carrot and Potato Association. The regulations for its administration, laid down by the Department of Co-operative Development, stipulated that there should be two committees, one for the actual administration, and one for general consultation. These committees were to have general responsibility for all matters arising out of the washing and packing of the carrots produced by village members. The duties and composition of these committees were discussed earlier (p. 108).

At the elections for these two committees the leaders of the right and left agreed to share the posts. It is worth noting that at the national level in this period, all nationalists were still loosely allied and apart from a few supporters of General Grivas, nationalists were united in support of the government. Leftists were also fully supporting the government. The major cleavage among Greeks was between left and right; but this was being kept to a minimum in the interests of 'national solidarity' in the early years of the Republic. Furthermore, the struggle between Greeks and Turks over the implementation of the constitution was in full swing.

The agreement to share the committee posts in the village was then a reflection to some extent of national policies. But when it came to the actual nominations, the two Kalo groups could not agree over procedure. The right leader Patris asked the leftist Sklyros as they sat in the village school preparing to vote, 'will you let *us* have the President of the Committee?', Sklyros said, 'We would like it'; Patris continued to ask for it, and finally, Sklyros decided to back down. At this point both groups thought that the President of the Committee, as opposed to the President of the *Council*, was the key post. Both units were composed of a president and four ordinary members. The committee, the actual workhorse, ended up with Patris as president, two other rightists and two leftists, one of whom was Sklyros. The President of the Council was a rich leftist farmer, two more leftists, and two rightists. Things were in complete balance, except for the slight primacy of the President of the Committee.

Having settled this quietly, they turned to the matter of the secretary of the Association. This post carried a small salary, and demanded a certain amount of general administrative and book-keeping experience. It was also a position of trust, but a non-voting position. Sklyros wanted it, partly for the salary and partly because he thought he would do it better than any rightist, and partly because ideologically he favoured any form of agricultural co-operative organization. However, it now turned out that the rightists and Patris in particular wanted to appoint Arklos, a first cousin of Patris. Arklos is one of the largest landowners in the village and is consequently usually very busy. So Sklyros commented 'Charon cannot find Arklos ...' that is, he is so busy that death (Charon) would not find him when his hour comes. The two sides were now in deadlock. Sklyros was not inclined to back down again. Patris would not change, so they both decided to stand, and put it to the vote. They each received five votes, and a new deadlock resulted. Finally they decided to toss a coin. Sklyros won, and they wrote to the Department of Co-operative Development describing the procedure and outcome. They received a letter back saying this was not the correct way to do things, and that they should try again.

To avoid further dispute Sklyros suggested as compromise that old Fanos be given the job. To Sklyros he is mother's sister's husband, and to Patris, daughter's husband's father, so the ties were close to both rivals. Old Fanos had many years practical experience as secretary of the Co-operative Credit Society in the village. Although thought of as a nationalist, he was regarded as politically inactive, and a man whose appointment could not really be construed as a victory for one side or the other. The only problem was that he was elderly and probably therefore a bit slow. When Sklyros suggested him, the right were pleased to accept. They again wrote to the Department of Co-operative Development and this time received a letter saying that old Fanos was not suitable for the job and that they should try again. Now they were again back in the deadlock position.

At this point versions of the case differ and details are confused. The rightists went off to see the Commissioner, since there seemed no way out of the deadlock. Sklyros looked up the rules of the Co-operative and discovered to his amazement that it was the village council, and not the village committee which had the casting vote in deadlock situations, and that therefore he could, if he wished, become secretary. Meanwhile, the Commissioner of Co-operatives had also come to this conclusion and told the rightists, 'The left have stolen a march on you . . .' The upshot of all this was that the department changed its mind about old Fanos and accepted him for the post but at a lower salary than previously suggested. Sklyros claims that instead of pressing his claim he now said nothing to 'avoid conflict'. Both sides remember the end of the affair as a small victory for the right, because a leftist had been kept out.

Right and left were actively opposed to the extent that they were contesting the positions on the committee; but they were co-operating in so far as they discussed in advance the allocation of positions between themselves. In this they were repeating, for example, the policy of the political leaders at the national level during the 1960 elections to the House of Representatives. Finally, they failed to agree over the precise working-out of the agreement and both sides tried to secure what they considered to be the critical posts for their own nominees. They referred the issue on several occasions outside the village, to the department of government responsible, and their own compromises were twice rejected by that department. Finally the right sought special access to the department and a decision resulted which favoured the right.

This last point needs explanation: Azinas, the Commissioner of Co-operatives, is a civil servant with very wide powers approaching those of a Minister; earlier in his life he had been the General Secretary of PEK, the nationalist-rightist farmer's union. PEK in

turn, had been closely implicated with the early phase of the
EOKA movement, and Azinas had been sent to Athens as political
liaison officer between Makarios and EOKA on one side, and
the Athens Government on the other. Azinas is known to be
strongly anti-communist—it is even said that a brother of his was
killed by the communists in the Greek Civil War. It is common
knowledge in Cyprus, though it never appears in print, that
Azinas is still the guiding hand behind PEK. As a civil servant
he may not openly take an interest in politics; he must have daily
dealings with left-wing committeemen on a number of co-operatives in the island, and in general is believed to conduct his purely
administrative work fairly, although he has been heard to
lament the dominance of the left in the co-operative movement.
Both rightists and leftists in Kalo believe that Azinas acted partially in the case just described. They see nothing odd about
this; rather it was a 'natural' event, and the right insist the left
would have done the same given half a chance and given a left-
wing Commissioner.

The remaining point to be made about this dispute is that
in a sense no valued resources were committed to or depended
on its outcome. I have never heard it said that there were any
significant spoils attached to control of the committee.[11] Why
then should the issue have been contested? There are several
reasons: one is that all such contests are a trial of strength. To
give the other side a walk-over looks as if one side is weak. A
political group remains organizationally alert by continued contest, no matter how quietist the policy on the national level.

Secondly, although nothing depends on the committee when it
is *shared,* if it were monopolized by one side, that side might
find opportunities to exploit the situation. For example, it would
be possible to make sure that rightists got their carrots washed
first; this would of course be a provocation, and after a period of
time (three years is the lifetime of the committee) there would
probably be an attempt by the disadvantaged side to rally support and change the entire committee. During times of co-operation, a mixed committee prevents such practices wordlessly. The
mere presence of the other side helps prevent anyone trying anything blatantly partisan. In addition the *atmosphere* of co-operation prevents people wanting to do so.

Thirdly, as has been shown here, the basic agreement to co-
operate over allocation of positions did not rule out a good deal
of manoeuvre. However, the intensity of the dispute was kept

within tolerable limits, and informants remembered it with a certain amount of humour. The incident did not seem to them to have involved a serious breach of any kind. It was merely the normal cut-and-thrust of everyday opposition.

IRRIGATION COMMITTEE ELECTIONS, 1968

In which the leftist leader Sklyros loses an election because he is in dispute with his sister's husband, a rightist called Mangaras Tangos. Beneath the surface of party politics are personal differences.

During the period of my fieldwork the national policy of the Greek Cypriot left was still full co-operation with the government, and a conciliatory posture towards the moderate nationalists. I do not have information about their instructions, if any, to village leaders on matters such as representation on irrigation committees. In the case to be described, my concern is more with the style of a village administrative election, and the undercurrents in it, than with trying to fill the gap in the information about the relation between national party policy, and local decisions.

The Irrigation Committee is re-elected every three years but several members had been in office for nearly ten years without change. One of them, Sklyros was on bad terms with his half-sister's husband, Mangaras Tangos, the man who (p. 148) had been made to compensate a Kalo Turk for taking earth from his field. Sklyros had been a member of the committee which ordered the compensation. Mangaras had been making allegations that Sklyros had been dishonest in administering the Co-operative Store, and Sklyros had replied with the charge that Mangaras had been involved in a series of robberies of Co-operatives in the area. On another occasion Mangaras had criticized the Irrigation Committee for not having done some of their work properly, and this view had found some support in the village. A normally staunch leftist friend of Sklyros had been heard to complain publicly on the same lines.

Sklyros in anger said to Mangaras Tangos in public, 'I fuck the whole thing: I fuck your family, and I fuck your Irrigation Committee.' In his own words, this was the same as resigning from the committee. There was another leftist leader on the committee. Y. Tangos, an older brother of Mangaras, but he had already announced his intention to resign, and was in the U.S.S.R. with a delegation of Cypriot farmers. He had served nine years on the committee. However, it was open to the left to replace these men with other leftists. The trouble was, their leaders were the men in difficulties, particularly Sklyros.

The first time the elections were due to take place, they had in fact to be postponed because of insufficient attendance. An official of the District Commissioner's office arrived on 1 July 1968 to supervise the second attempt. He called the roll; of some 400 persons eligible to vote since they owned irrigated land by legal title, and paid taxes on it, only 49 were present. The official called for nominations, and 13 people were proposed, and seconded. Two of these were leftists, the remainder either nationalists of various complexions or politically unaligned. The results are set out below:

elected:	Patris	46 votes
	Glykis	46 votes
	Yiorgios	49 votes
	Kirkos	43 votes
	Mangaras Tangos	44 votes
not elected:	Old Sklyros	37
	Kanellos	39
	(a)	36 (left)
	(b)	30
	(c)	36
	(d)	32 (left)
	(e)	34
	(f)	38

The voting system allowed people to vote for each and every candidate, and this they almost did, since 49 people cast a total of 510 votes. Each person seems to have voted for 10 people. This is characteristic of village public behaviour, in that a main aim is to avoid antagonizing people who expect one's vote for reasons of kinship, friendship and other ties.[12]

The re-election of Kirkos and the relatively high vote for Kanellos and Old Sklyros would suggest that there was no strong intention among those present to reject the previous committee as a whole. But it is possible that even in the event of strong hostility, the desire to avoid making enemies would have produced a similar result.

Perhaps more instructive than the voting itself were the comments made about the election by some of the interested parties. Sklyros believed that his half-sister's husband, Mangaras had deliberately organized people to come to the election 'and get out the leftists'. Jokes were certainly made to this effect in the coffee-shop. Sklyros was particularly bitter about this because his father Old Sklyros had not been re-elected. Now although Old Sklyros was an old man, and a strong rightist who had quarrelled with his son many times about politics, he was also an expert in irrigation matters, having for many years earned his living by digging underground chains of wells. Sklyros argued that Mangaras had nothing to offer the committee, and that to fail to elect his father-in-law was a piece of deliberate spite which would harm the village.

Two prominent village informal leaders—D. Fanos and Vourros deliberately avoided going to the elections. Both explained to me that they did not like a situation where an open show of hands in voting was needed, since this was embarrassing. Vourros recalled an election at which he had not voted for someone and the man next to him had shouted loudly at him, 'Come on—up with your hand. Vote for him.' He commented: 'The Texans are not afraid of New Yorkers—they are only afraid of other Texans.'[13] By this he meant, it turned out, that in spite of his education the Kalo people were not in awe of him in any way. He described himself as a 'New Yorker' in one sense because he is from the neighbouring village; in another sense because his education, wealth and urban background set him apart. In any case he chose to stay away.

The right leader Patris denied to me that there was any 'organization' or deliberate attempt to get out the leftists. Sklyros believed when he walked into the room and looked around that the people he saw there were evidence of organization. He calculated that he would easily be out-voted. Both men were sure that they could remember who voted for particular individuals.

Sklyros, on seeing the odds against him, decided that he would not stand for office and would thus avoid giving the right, and particularly Mangaras, the pleasure of openly defeating him; he added, however, that in view of the criticisms that had been made of the committee in the village, he had decided not to seek re-election. It is worth pointing out that in the 1962 Irrigation Committee elections, Patris had decided not to seek re-election, since he had been publicly criticized by a butcher that he had spent village money on irrigating his own land. It happens that the butcher's brother is married to a sister of Sklyros but I am unable to say if this played any part. The butcher is known as an independent, not to say uncontrollable trouble-maker, as will appear in his remarks in another context (p. 265). My point here is to note that leading personalities in village administration seem remarkably sensitive to public criticism, and may drop out of office for a few years, only to reappear later in the same job or another one.

There are several other points to be made about this election. First, the left leaders seem to have taken no effective steps to try to retain their position: they did not bring supporters or brief people to seek nomination; if they did, they did so in a manner well below their actual capability. Secondly, there was the belief of Sklyros that his half-sister's husband had organized a move to unseat him. The bad feeling between these men has been mentioned. Regardless of 'national policy' this election seems to have been conducted very much on personal lines for personal reasons, but the interest in getting an enemy out of office is all the sharper when he is also a 'natural' political opponent. The point here is not to reduce national politics to personal antagonisms, for one does not exclude the other. If Sklyros had chosen to rally leftist supporters and seriously contest the election, he could probably have done so. As has been earlier mentioned, this would have been the first step on a ladder of escalation which can end in a fully 'politicized' village, where left and right avoid each other.

If the national policy of the left had been other than the quietist one followed since 1959, Sklyros might have been called to task for his behaviour. Precisely because the national leadership adopt a 'low profile' over the issue of rights and representation, and continually accept less than their voting potential might suggest they deserve, Sklyros could afford to avoid a contest in the village, and still keep his status relatively intact. As it was, there were signs of mild dissatisfaction with his leadership during the period of my fieldwork. His increasing family responsibilities as his children approach the age of marriage, coupled with a heavy burden of debt, make it likely that younger, cooler-tempered men may step into his shoes in the near future.

1969–70 DISPUTE OVER THE CREDIT CO-OPERATIVE SECRETARYSHIP

In which the leftist Sklyros finds himself unexpectedly in alliance with the rightist, Patris, when they oppose the attempts of Fanos's children to prevent their father losing his job as secretary of the Credit Co-operative. Although both Sklyros and Patris have strong ties to the Fanos family, yet to avoid public criticism from other villagers, they are forced to ignore these ties. Inevitably the clash of public and private interests and the tensions of cross-cutting loyalties make for a bitter dispute in which farmers end up behaving like bureaucrats and bureaucrats behave like farmers.

The last case was a non-contest in formal political terms, in which all the tension took place off-stage. Thus we have seen cases where the right and the left opposed each other energetically, and later a case where they appeared to ignore each other. However, this account of disputes in the village would be seriously unrepresentative if it did not include the following case.

Old Fanos had for over thirty years been secretary of the Credit Co-operative. On its meagre wage he had successfully managed to educate his six children (pp. 71–4). Now at the age of sixty-seven he was very slow, and over the recent years a number of complaints had been made to the committee about this. However, the committee were in a very embarrassing situation. Sklyros is Old Fanos's wife's sister's son and has always been on very close terms with Old Fanos's children; he is fully aware of the fact that with one last child at university in Athens, and one unmarried daughter, Old Fanos needs every penny he can get. Patris is also a committeeman, but his situation is if anything worse, for his oldest daughter is married to the second son of Old Fanos, and the two men use the close affinal term '*sympétheros*' to each other. Moreover, Patris has never had a son of his own, and his relationship with his son-in-law D. Fanos has always been very warm. Over several years on a number of occasions Patris has tactfully mentioned the problem of the old man's retirement to his son-in-law, but always the reply has been, 'Just let the old man keep his job for another year or two and then he'll retire. Just until my sister gets married and my youngest brother finishes in Athens.'

By December 1969 Sklyros was asking the advice of his friend Vourros, as an educated man, on the problem. In July 1970 after repeated discussions the committee acted by calling in Old Fanos and telling him that they were going to advertise his job. He seemed to take it quietly, but later his children said that this was because he was stunned. The announcement went up in the coffee-shops the next day. Two sons of Fanos met Sklyros, and harsh words were exchanged. D. Fanos stopped talking to his wife's father, Patris. The whole Fanos family was united in fury against Sklyros and Patris. Another member of the committee, Akis, married to another sister of Fanos' wife, went and told the family that he had been against the decision and tried to talk the committee out of it. A fourth committee man did the same.

The bitterness continued for a number of weeks, and several people tried to mediate. The dispute was referred to the Department of Co-operatives, which refused to take action, arguing that it was for the village committee to decide. In view of the close ties between D. Fanos and the Commissioner this was a singularly impartial decision. When I left the field a compromise was being negotiated within the village: Old Fanos was to stay in his job, but was to take on an assistant, who was to be trained up to take over full responsibility in a short time.

The most striking thing about this dispute was the extent to which it cut across existing lines of political cleavage. Sklyros and Patris, who have been shown continuously opposed as left and right leaders, are here united, even at the cost of Patris's quarrel with his son-in-law D. Fanos. These two men had been very close both in politics and their personal relations for five years. Together they had moved from supporting Lyssarides to support Azinas; now they were seriously at odds. Akis, normally a staunch leftist who would support Sklyros, preferred to stress his kin ties to his wife's sister's family.

Kosmos had for years been regarded as a firm leftist and a supporter of Sklyros. But he is also the godchild of Old Fanos. During the 1970 election he had worked openly not for the left, but for the United Party, since he has become the political client of the powerful *múktar* of a nearby village who regularly employs him as bulldozer driver. Kosmos came to the Fanos household and promised them that he would get his patron, the *múktar*, to work on the problem, and that this man was so powerful that he could tell the powerful Commissioner of Co-operatives what to do and he would do it 'like a child'. He said that if necessary he would bring the *múktar* to the village the next night. He said many hard things against both Sklyros and Patris, that they were both very bad as committeemen, had no humanity, and that he would personally work to see them thrown out of the committee at the next election. He stressed his close connections with the United Party, through the *múktar*. For him the dispute was a chance both to deny his old leftist loyalties, and publicly to demonstrate his new ones by exalting the power of his patron.

This case is important since it shows Sklyros and Patris taking a stand over an administrative principle. Clearly, the pay-off for them is that they get the villagers 'off their heads' and thus retain their position as committeemen. This however is not their main motive, for the positions in themselves are not worth the cost of dispute. They take their duties as committeemen seriously, and have an internalized set of values about how the Co-operative should be run. It was quite clear to them that it would be a very touchy issue to replace Old Fanos, but they had counted on more sympathy from his educated children, at least two of whom were experienced civil servants, and had hoped that in spite of the obvious conflict with the self-interest of the Fanos family, some kind of technical objectivity would influence his sons. In this they were bitterly disappointed. However, it was noticeable that in the course of the dispute the sons of Fanos very soon abandoned the claim that their father was still fully capable of doing the job, and instead sought to maintain that it was the *method* the committee had employed which was so deplorable and which had made them so angry. 'They called our father in without warning, and told him they would advertise his job. They threw him into the street like you'd throw a dog. After the thirty years' service he'd given for a salary that was . . . sheer exploitation.' In this version they chose to ignore the many tactful overtures by Patris over several years in which he had tried to get them to act by themselves. Such is the rhetoric of disputes. Fanos's children saw they could not defend the issue of their father's technical ability, so they sought to turn it into one of 'common humanity' and presented a picture of the committee as ruthless technocrats.

The clash of norms is instructive. One side is a united kin group, and such supporters as they can rally among other kin and friends. On the other side are two men who are recognized political and administrative leaders of the village, although both of them have close ties to their opponents. One side charges a breach of kinship solidarity, but dresses this in the language of 'common humanity'. The other side insists that the issue is technical, that complaints in the village have reached a pitch which is unacceptable, and that even close kin must take heed of them. There can be no immediate reconciliation of these two views. Sklyros in the middle of the crisis said he would not attend the next committee meeting called to negotiate with Old Fanos and possibly with his sons. He was under the influence of the harsh words that A. Fanos had said to him, which included the words '*ise átimos*', 'you are without honour'; in addition he announced his intention of resigning from the committee. Patris who might under other circumstances have greeted his resignation with pleasure, said to him, 'If you do that, you are not up to much' (*dhén íse en dáxi*). He insisted in effect that he maintain solidarity with the rest of the committee, and that no easy way out for him as an individual was acceptable. For if Sklyros had resigned, it could have been interpreted as an action criticizing the committee. Patris was afraid of being left as the apparent initiator of the move. For once in his life he badly needed his antagonist Sklyros's support.

CONCLUSION

These six cases are not in any rigorous sense a sample of politics in the village. They are rather trouble cases; events which lay open salient features of political processes. Since during this same period the villagers have conducted numerous administrative meetings, elections, discussions and so forth without memorable dispute, in so far as it gives a picture of continuing strife the focus on the cases is misleading. Anthropologists, like novelists, do not normally devote much space to describing or analysing calm and uneventful social life, and this is perhaps a serious criticism of their methods; but it might be argued with equal force that from the viewpoint of capital and nation, the events I have described are trivial, and scarcely worth mention. The fact that both these views can be put forward equally strongly encourages me to think my approach may be fruitful.

It is worth noting that the first three cases all took place during the early years of independence, when the former EOKA activists were still highly influential throughout the island and when the issues raised by intercommunal violence were a matter of daily concern. These three cases all involved the implicit sanction of violence. In the first case a wealthy, educated city dweller is persuaded to give up his perfectly legal plans for a club to 'improve' the village, and lets the matter rest. In the second case the same man attempted to counter the autonomy of the self-appointed guardians of the village by bureaucratic control. They had felt the need of a broader base of support, since their authority had been slightly eroded. After the committee was formed the collection of money for arms was no longer sanctioned by the fear of force, nor did the use of the money go unsupervised by village representatives.

The third case, that of the Lyssarides *omádha*, again showed the threat of force as the final sanction. But this time, the threat was overt and self-defeating. The ensuing use of mediators, and the continuing struggle of each side to maintain its position during the mediation process show that the threat of force did not settle the issue or, in the short run, bring the active pursuit of political goals to a halt although the fact that the Lyssarides group lost support after this shows that most villagers set very definite limits to their participation. The threat of force however contributed to the decline in Moustachas's authority, for his would not have been the self-justifying use of force against a single individual who has insulted one's womenfolk or family, but force involving political groups, and thus spreading outward through the village; not only that but the motive would not have been the defence of household dependants, but the servicing of alignments outside the village, and outside the direct village status system. To the villagers there is all the difference between beating up a man for the justification of one's honour, and violence in the name of loyalty to a political matter outside the village. Both sides lost from this encounter. The gap between the tactics of elite politicians and village supporters was clearly illustrated by this case, for Lyssarides's call for vigilance ended up by losing him supporters, which strongly suggests he did not understand in one village at least what the consequences of his actions would be.

The first three cases were all to do with extraordinary facets of politics in the village—institutional innovation, emergency defence measures, and the clandestine organization of support for national political leaders; the other three cases are more run-of-the-mill matters. The Carrot Association elections were, it is true, the first elections for a new administrative unit in village affairs, but there was no novelty in the organizational principles involved. The critical feature of this case was the scope for manoeuvre within the overall framework of representational compromise between left and right. The case is settled by the selection of a compromise candidate, on one level, and by the introduction of new external resources on the other. The new resources are both the closer examination of the regulations laid down for committee roles, and the partisan appeal to the Commissioner of Co-operatives.

The fifth case is superficially similar, but here I was able to show the extent to which private animosities between close affines, were carried forward in their public political roles; for the leftist leader this could have been costly, had not national policy justified an avoidance of confrontation. The case also showed the extent to which villagers avoid making choices which will displease others, as shown by their voting behaviour, as well as by the deliberate boycott of the elections by two interested parties.

The last case showed certain protagonists usually at odds, now in alliance, to defend an administrative principle. The clash of norms—kinship obligations versus public service—produced an unusual dependence of rightist on leftist. Attempts to introduce powerful patrons did not succeed, and eventually, a compromise formula was found acceptable to all from within the village.

The Fanos family perhaps got a little more than their due, from the bureaucratic viewpoint; but what is more striking is that two committeemen (who could have avoided an uncomfortable confrontation by resigning from their unpaid jobs) should instead have chosen to brave the wrath of close kin. Perhaps their commitment to norms of public service stopped them from correctly predicting the storm they would raise. The children of Old Fanos, all gymnasium graduates or better, behaved in the more particularistic, traditionalist fashion, while the two committeemen, older and less educated, behaved more as rational bureaucrats.

It seems reasonable to suggest that this dispute was bitter for other reasons. Not only were close kinship ties being undervalued (from the point of view of the Fanos household), but farmers were exercising control over a family of educated men who from certain points of view, should through their education have received deference from the farmers. The committee's action was thus essentially unacceptable to the children of Old Fanos, precisely because it went against the normal transactions of prestige. Two of the Fanos children, as part of their regular jobs are in the position of checking on farmers and their committees in other villages, and as government employees with the interpretation of law and co-operative regulations in their hands, they are used to having their decisions taken very seriously. But in the Kalo situation the normal relations were completely reversed. As in the dispute over the proposed club, educated men were very far from having things their own way.

Each of these cases illustrates in a different way the potential or actual emergence of cleavage in the village political life, and what steps are taken to control the course of such cleavage. The actors are often to be heard claiming that their own policies will best preserve the peace of the village. By such a claim Moustachas was able to make legitimate his objection to the Graduates' Club, and by such a claim opposed political groups avoided the high costs of all-out electoral competition.

I shall restate what was salient in each of the six cases: The first case would have allowed a clear symbol of social differentiation in a village which otherwise had none, in the form of an institution open only to some villagers. Moustachas had enjoyed many years of unchallenged authority, due to his pre-eminence in EOKA but he would not have been eligible to join the club. In stopping it he did three different things at once: he re-established his authority, he asserted the equality of farmers with educated men, and according to his own right-wing views he kept (leftish) politics out of the village. This last was the most questionable achievement, since there was no necessary reason why such a club would become overtly political. Here we are dealing with village definitions of reality and competitions to define reality in certain ways.

The second case showed the efforts of two different kinds of village leaders to gain advantage. The militia leaders were in danger of losing village confidence, and were thus forced to include representatives of all shades of political opinion in a special *ad hoc* committee which immediately sought to assert bureaucratic control over the militia. The committee was meant by the militia to *symbolize* (and so induce) solidarity, but it was used by the educated Vourros and the leftist leaders to control the militia itself. Both sides insisted that they had the security of the village at heart.

The third case is very clearly about the rules for employing outside resources in the village arena. While only one *omádha* existed, village solidarity was apparently not threatened; but with the formation of the Lyssarides group, the rivalries of national politics are seen to be working in the village. Actions which in the capital or within the constitution may be unexceptionable (such as political meetings to discuss support for a leader) become very much more serious in the village, because some of the actors are working with very different ideas about power, and with control rules not devised to cope with such situations. The use by one side of novel political tactics (a newspaper article) could not be matched by the other side, who sought to define it as a serious breach of village control norms.

The fourth case was salient because neither left nor right in the village were prepared to allow control of an administrative committee to go to the other side. The controlled contest that resulted must be understood in terms of alignments with national parties— the village leaders are not prepared to let these alignments lapse, but at the same time, they do not allow them to take too great a part in everyday life. It is contests such as this one which actually keep local units alive; without them alignment has no meaning.

The fifth case shows how, under cover of political alignment, personal issues may be carried forward. This case does not allow us to decide that one interest dominates the other, but merely shows that they can both be present at the same time, and in the same issue. Once again, as voters the villagers are able to avoid the more divisive implications of electing a committee by giving public support to virtually *all* the candidates.

The sixth case shows norms of kinship in conflict with norms of public service, and educated men in conflict with farmers who control the key committee. the farmers, to retain their leadership positions, and to be consistent with their own values, were forced to initiate actions which brought them into serious breach with close kin and affines. The children of Fanos had relied too much on these ties, and had not calculated on the political autonomy of the farmers. The readjustment of interests was divisive for all concerned, and brought right and left leaders into an unusual alliance.

Finally, these cases illustrate the structural principles discussed in earlier chapters. All the cases bear on the solidarity of the village, on how far cleavage can be tolerated, on the notion of village membership and the village prestige system. Since all the persons featured are leaders or activists in the village, though for different sorts of reasons, the structure of participation has been revealed, by implication: it is a structure in which the leaders make *all* the running, the same men being prominent time and again. The use of force in supporting (and sometimes weakening) village leaders is shown in cases one, two and three, and the opposition between educated men and farmers appears in the same cases as well as in case six. The national alignments of right and left wing ideology appear in cases three to six although in different combinations and intensities, Patron-client relations are important in cases one, two, four, and six, and cases two, three, and four show the use of external resources as decisive. Finally, kinship and affinity can be seen to have very direct constraints on the actions of individuals in cases five and six, although in more diffuse ways their influence is present in all the cases.

NOTES

1. The first four cases are reconstructions, pieced together from accounts by a number of informants; the last two cases I observed.
2. Moustachas, as a former EOKA leader and rightist, was almost certainly involved in making reports on leftists either to the Ministry of the Interior, the police, or both. These agencies are also interested in the activities of anti-government extremists of the right wing.
3. 'But conflict between *social categories* of persons may be a matter of inference rather than of observation' Firth, (1964: 23).
4. The ultra-right nationalist newspaper *Patris* in April 1966 carried a series of articles which revealed in detail (though not fully) the AKRITAS plan. This was a contingency plan worked out by the group of Greek Cypriot leaders then close to President Makarios (including particularly Clerides, Yorgadjis), for how to advance the cause of *Enosis* as well as to make the Greek Cypriot majority appear as the sole legitimate government in the event of intercommunal conflict. *Patris*, a spokesman of the Grivas faction, seems to have published the plan to show how ill-prepared were Makarios's group, and how lacking in devotion to the *Enosis* ideal. The Turkish Cypriots have reprinted the *Patris* articles, with a foreword claiming that the plan reveals the bad faith with which Makarios and his supporters entered the early years of the republic.
5. The Committee consisted of the following people: Sklyros; Tangos; the *múktar*, Vourros, Patris, Patris's brother and four other men, of whom three are farmers, and one a truck driver. Thus, the committee had two leftists, one educated man, and full-time farmers are strongly represented, as was usual. Politically, it is a broad cross-section of village opinion. It also represents mature married men. The average age was about forty.
6. This item is different in form from the others, and the next item is unclear.

7. The same man was both EOKA district commander during the emergency, and militia commander in 1964. He comes from Market Town, is a professional man, and was also a Legislative Assembly Member for the electoral district. He later became a Minister in the Makarios government. He is personally known to many villagers.

8. Sklyros and Moustachas were 'childhood friends' and when Sklyros was about twenty-two he became the second wedding *koumpáros* of Moustachas. When he was twenty-seven, in 1950 Moustachas asked him to baptize his fourth child. Sklyros was by this time a leftist. Moustachas a few years later, about 1954 became the (right-wing) EOKA leader in the village. It is impossible to know just what effect on right–left relations in Kalo this tie of *koumpária* between men who became opposed leaders has had. During my fieldwork they did not seem to be close friends, but treated each other delicately, with caution and respect.

9. The notion of *omádha* was discussed in the last chapter. Here I shall use the terms *omádha* and 'group' interchangeably.

10. This gap has been discussed by many writers. See Bailey (1963). For a good review of the issues and recent literature, see Joan Vincent, 'Anthropology and political development' in (ed.) Leys, (1969).

11 The post of secretary was salaried, and so valuable, but the actual manoeuvres started over the composition of the two committees. There is no reason to think these were a 'blind' to secure the paid secretary-ship.

12. Campbell (1968: 99) reports how in 1868 mainland Greece adopted a voting system (borrowed from the Ionian islands) which allowed voters among other things to support all the candidates. In chapter ten, page 275 I describe how the 1970 national elections in Cyprus allowed the voters if they wished to support every *party*, or any combination of twelve candidates, distributed between the parties.

13. Kalo is known in the region, jokingly, as 'Little Texas' because its people supposedly have the same characteristics as Big Texas—recent new wealth, a certain rowdiness, proneness to carry pistols, and a love of the flamboyant gesture. The more lively Kalotes seem to go out of their way to publicize both the nickname and the qualities that go with it.

G

8
Dam

INTRODUCTION

The theme of this chapter is the attempt of certain Kalotes with men from the surrounding villages to speed up the construction of a dam, and the ensuing opposition from Market Towners. The next chapter describes how some villagers tried to intervene in the administration of the citrus co-operative, which was dominated by Market Town. In both cases, then, villages and Market Town are in opposition, and in both cases, government representatives play important roles. Both chapters will be concerned with the style of elite leadership, the underlying reasons for the structural opposition between villages and town and a number of other issues. But the reason for anticipating the next chapter at this point is precisely because the two issues are not merely similar but each must lend intensity to the other.[1] To make this clear, I shall sketch in the main issues of the two chapters.

Five villages, including Kalo, would benefit from the building of a recharge dam at Avla. Kalo would pay the lion's share from among the villages, but government funds would pay two-thirds of the total cost in any case. The dam has been discussed since the early years of independence. At the time of my fieldwork the issue was a lively one, and the problem hinged on the attempts of Market Towners through their Irrigation Committee, to block the dam, which they saw as threatening their own interests. During 1968 and 1969, the five villages through their own Irrigation Committees made a number of attempts to prod the government into favourable action, and prominent in all this was a Kalo-born lawyer Aglas who has large land holdings in the village, although he lives in the capital.[2] Later it emerged that his active campaigning over the dam was prelude to his attempts in 1970 to get elected to the Legislative Assembly, and certain astute villagers foresaw this during his activity over the dam, in which he organized a demonstration in the capital of men from the five villages. This was a major political innovation, and was followed by the additional innovation in Kalo of a short-lived Advisory Committee, in which another urban elite man (Vourros) figured prominently. This material then, raises a number of problems— the nature and style of rivalry between the villages and Market Town; the methods used by villagers to put pressure on the government; the reasons for the willingness of villagers to allow individuals who have risen into the urban elite to lead them in dealings with the government; the general question of relations between government and villagers, and how far these involve an awareness by villagers of their political rights.

To anticipate the material of chapter nine, Kalo is there again found in opposition to Market Town over the affairs of CITCOP, the citrus marketing co-operative whose central committee was, at the time of my fieldwork, dominated by Market Towners. Kalo and Kammari, both parties to the dam issue (see Figure 2) are

FIGURE 2

Common interests among the villages in two political issues with Market Town

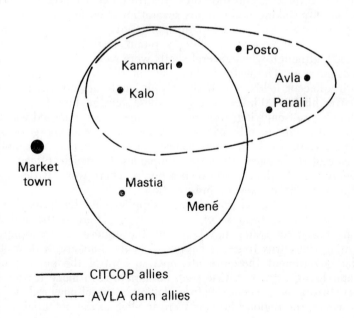

——————— CITCOP allies

— — — AVLA dam allies

again in alliance. Again elite leaders are prominent in the conduct of village affairs and play on village fears of Market Town particularism, to get themselves into positions of power. For reasons which will become obvious it is not possible to say just how far the animosity over the dam issue enlivened the animosity of villagers in CITCOP to the Market Towners on the committee: but the fact that the two issues had been going on for seven years, involving the more sophisticated and active people in the villages and in Market Town, make it obvious that they each fuelled the other. Therefore, the material presented in the next chapter is not simply added to that in this chapter; it ought retrospectively to deepen the insights provided, and in my concluding analysis to chapter nine I try to do this.

THE IMPORTANCE OF WATER IN THE REGION

The success of cash cropping in the Market Town region depends, as we have seen, on the supplies of underground water, which have been exploited more and more intensively since the 1920s. The 1950s saw the major development of water exploitation, and the concentration on citrus fruit, carrots, potatoes and melons. By sinking pump-shafts several hundred feet, and bringing up water with diesel pumps, perennial irrigation became possible. Drilling and installing a pump costs from £2,000 to £3,000, although when several shafts were sunk without success, costs increase. The water is then sold for 10/- an hour to people with adjacent fields, and if the supply continues an owner can recover his £3,000 investment from these sales in about five years while himself enjoying 'free' water. Farmers need pumped water for six to eight months of the year. In recent years the government has stopped granting licences to individual owners, and encouraged villagers to form companies in which fifteen or twenty shareholders jointly own a pump. There were two in the village in 1968 and several in formation.

In the region underground water supplies have for some years been decreasing because of over-pumping. There is the added danger that sea water may seep into the underground supplies, ruining the citrus trees, as happened in the Famagusta district. The government therefore attempts to control the amount of water being extracted. One such attempt was to make it necessary to obtain a licence before sinking a diesel-powered well. However, the region's farmers were so alive to the potential profits of irrigated cash-cropping, that many of them started 'illegal' pumps, that is, they proceeded to drill without licences. They argued that the government was showing partiality in the granting of licences and that it was giving them to persons who were not professional farmers while denying them to men without other means of support. The government was slow to act when the first illegal pumps were put down, so other people followed suit. Later the government took people to court, but often did not win its cases or the court imposed a modest penalty. However, the sinking of illegal pumps slowly stopped. In 1968 there were at least twenty-seven pumps operating in Kalo of which at least four had been started illegally.

As part of the overall plan to conserve water the government also initiated a policy of encouraging villages to build concrete water channels. In the region government pays a half of the cost and the village pays a half, which it raises by an irrigation tax of 10/- per government *donum* of land irrigated. The other strand of the government's attack on water conservation is the construction of recharge dams, to trap the winter runoff waters from the mountains which otherwise rush down into the sea. The recharge dams hold the runoff water until it seeps down into the underground water table. Several dams had already been built by the government in the Market Town region by 1968, but none which favoured the villages close to Kalo. The dams which were in existence directly benefited the Market Town farmers; and, some people pointed out, certain government officials who had bought land in the Market Town region. This point need not be stressed for there is little doubt that the Market Town farmers even without such support were politically in a better position to assert their interests between 1959–68 than were the surrounding villagers.

Between 1963 and 1968 a number of proposals were made to build a dam at a point on the Kari river near Avla village. This would be primarily a recharge dam, but would also provide some water for direct irrigation. Many of the proposals were made verbally, and because there were difficulties from the first stages, there were continual variations in what was actually proposed. The original proposals included four villages and Market Town, all of which would contribute to the costs of the dam, and would benefit both by recharge of the underground water available to them, and direct irrigation. A fifth village joined later.

By the middle of 1968 the villages were prepared to agree to the wording of a clause which allowed the Market Town dams to be filled once a year from the first water of the winter before any water went into the Avla dam, but after this first filling, they insisted that the Avla dam should then be filled. The Market Town people replied that they wanted a wording in which their dams would always be filled first, at any time of the year regardless of the condition of the Avla dam. This was roughly the situation at the time my fieldwork started. The Market Town Irrigation Committee seemed to be ready to block the construction of the dam altogether. The five villages were considering what to do next.

In early October of 1968 I watched the Irrigation Committees of Kalo, Kammari and Posto meet to raise the problem. A Kammari committee man, Varetos, had recently been to the relevant civil servant (a man known well to the inhabitants of all five villages since he had for many years been posted at the Market Town) who said the Market Town people had refused to sign the present form of agreement and the question was to be put in abeyance until the following March. The meeting of the three village committees was not satisfied with this position. They went over the ground again: that they had originally made a very important concession and a reasonable one by allowing Market Town to fill their own dam first, and now Market Town was trying to behave like the government of Cyprus. The money is ready, they said, and the government is supposed to be in favour of the dam, or why would they have found the money? Someone suggested they tell the government that they are ready to forego the Market Town contribution to the dam and find the extra money themselves. This point received no support and was not taken up. There was talk of contacting all the representatives in the Assembly and particularly the PEK M.P., Andreas Yangou. It was agreed that Patris from Kalo and Varetos from Kammari would try to get the Nicosia newspapers interested in the story. Just as the meeting was about to break-up the Kammari man, Yialyias, pointed out that the meeting had not resolved anything. 'All right,' said his fellow-villager Varetos, 'we agree on a statement that we demand from the government an explanation for the delay,' by which he meant the proposed delay until March for further consideration of the case.

A few months prior to this meeting, the old Kalo Irrigation Committee, which had the leftists Sklyros and Tangos on it,[3] had received a draft agreement from the government asking for their consent and Sklyros had drawn attention to the wording of Market Town's water rights, and whether their dams would always be filled before the Avla one, or simply once a year. He had suggested an alternative wording. Then as the dam question continued to drag on a Five Villages' Committee had been formed, which comprised the Irrigation Committees of the five villages concerned, with the Kalo-born lawyer, Aglas, as chairman. There is some doubt as to how the Five Village Committee came to be formed. In light of subsequent events many people were inclined to believe that lawyer Aglas had taken the initiative. Certainly the conversion of existing Irrigation Committees into the larger committee required nothing more than an afternoon's drive through the villages, each of which is within fifteen minutes' drive of the others, and a quick word with the committees concerned. Whoever took the first initiative, the urgency of the issue in the eyes of the Irrigation Committees was sufficient to produce rapid support as subsequent events soon showed.

About a week after this meeting, Varetos and Yialyias, from Kammari, with Patris and Aglas decided to see the Minister of Agriculture, a Market Town man.[4] The next morning they went to see him without an appointment. When they arrived at his office his secretary said, 'He is busy all day today and told me not to let him be disturbed.' They told her to tell him—and here the initiative came from the lawyer—that they were outside and that 'if he cannot see us, all right, we shall come back another day'. She gave this message to the minister who accordingly decided to see them. He told them that even as a simple representative he had always been in favour of the building of this dam and that it would be built. But the government could not go ahead without the agreement of the Market Town people, because Market Town could take the government to court and hold up the whole project at least for several years. Rather than waste everyone's time and money, the government's policy was to try to open the eyes of Market Town to its own self-interest, which was to agree to the dam. He also said he knew some people were murmuring that because he was a Market Town man, he was holding up the dam to help them fight off citrus competition from the villages. Everyone laughed.[5]

On October 13 several newspapers carried a simple news item which mentioned the visit of committee members to the minister and in which Aglas on behalf of the committee thanked the minister for his interest. When Patris heard of the newspaper piece, even though Aglas is his first cousin, he was most concerned that the wording should not imply that the initiatives were all coming from Aglas, but were a joint effort of the whole committee.

This needs a word of explanation, for in what follows there are frequent references to the possible 'politicization' of the dam issue. In chapter one (p. 18) I explained how until February 1969, there were effectively two organized political groupings in the Greek community, a unified left, and a broad coalition of right-wing 'nationalist' groups. Because of the fact that the elections due in 1965 for the Legislative Assembly were postponed, and because the Greeks wished to preserve some front of unity in the face of Turkish secession, there was little in the way of organized party life up to the end of 1968. However, there were continual rumours that President Makarios would encourage parties, and that the postponed elections would be held. Parties were permitted in February 1969, and elections held in May— June 1970. It was well known in Kalo that certain men, like the lawyer Aglas, were hopeful of being adopted as candidates for the Assembly by one party or another, and thus although for most of the material in this chapter, only the right/left distinction is relevant, there was the continual possibility that the right would regroup in a number of distinct parties; this took place in the spring of 1969.

During December 1968 the heaviest winter rains for at least twenty years carried away a number of bridges over the Kari river, including those at Ávla and Market Town. A lot of Kalo people who had trees planted along the river bank saw them uprooted and carried away. Most of the village men went to see the river in flood, and watched millions of gallons of potentially usable water flow away to the sea. This flooding and the way the villagers felt about it provided a dramatic impetus to the next phase of the Avla dam episode.

THE DEMONSTRATION

It was decided to organize a demonstration at the Presidential Palace. The lawyer, Aglas, was very active the evening before the demonstration, going around the villages giving people instructions on the wording of posters, and the time and place to assemble. He was repeatedly careful to prevent people lettering posters with direct comments against Market Town, for some people had suggested posters saying 'Who governs Cyprus— Market Town?' and 'Do only the Market Town farmers deserve water?' Those who were aware that the lawyer had ambitions to be adopted as a candidate for M.P. by PEK the right-wing farmers' association suggested his caution was closely related to his desire to keep the Market Town people friendly, for they are in the same electoral district as the five villages. They made very sarcastic comments about his motives for becoming involved in the dam problem. 'Obviously', they said, 'his large land holdings in Kalo would justify his interest, but if he really wanted to help his village, he would tell the truth about the Market Town people. He wants to be representative, that's it.'

The next morning buses from the five villages carried men into the capital. There had been some mild discussion of whether to bring women and children to make the event more dramatic but this idea had not been adopted although it might have been very effective. A column of farmers formed up near Metaxas Square; carrying posters which complained about the water flowing into the sea, and some stating simply 'Water is our life'; they started to march to the Presidential Palace. It is hard to say how many people went on the march; my own estimate is about 300, but it could be low by 150. The column marched three abreast in a cheerful and orderly fashion, with a police escort, through the streets of Nicosia. The lawyer was in the front, and several representatives of PEK were also there by his side. There were no official representatives of EKA, the leftist farmers' association but a number of Kalo leftists took part. Retrospectively, some Kalo leftists argued that from the start it had been clear that the whole series of meetings about the dam were of an anti-government nature designed to further the candidacy of Aglas and to embarrass the government, and that since the left has a broad and steady policy of support for the government, it chose to ignore the demonstration. However, it seems equally likely that the left leadership in Nicosia did not know about the demonstration until it had practically finished, and that at the village level the left leaders saw that the initiative had come from the right and decided that rather than risk being snubbed if they made a formal offer to associate themselves with the march, they would ignore it officially, but participate quietly. Certainly for several days after the demonstration I heard discussion in the coffee-shops between leftists and rightists about the situation, but it was mostly at the level of jokes which went, 'You deliberately didn't ask us to come because you don't want us.' 'No, you deliberately stayed away because you were jealous that we had done

something good.' In any event the left were not formally represented on the demonstration and the right were, through PEK.
As with many other political events in the villages, the most elusive facts are those concerned with where actions and policies
originate.

When the column of march reached the Presidential Palace, it
started to bunch up around the outer gate. The police guards
shut the gate in an almost ceremonial way, leaving the marchers
outside and the police inside. 'All we'll get now is promises,'
someone grumbled. The lawyer and some of the committee men
started to confer. An off-duty Kalo policeman wandered up to
the gate, and was allowed inside where he stood chatting to his
fellow policemen. Presently a Kalo man called out to him, 'Hey,
Yiorkos, you come out here or we'll cut your trees down. They
need water too.' A few minutes later he came out, even though
the remark appeared to be a joke. The general mood of the
marchers was amused, but uncertain. People kept making suggestions about what to do next. After a while, when a message
had been sent up to the Presidential Palace, it was decided to
admit the *múktars* of each village, and the Irrigation Committee
members. The whole purpose of the march was to lay the problem of the dam at the feet of President Makarios. Many people
said throughout the march that it was the only thing to do. The
implication was that Makarios was the only man above the personal ambitions and interests of the rest of the society: even
though people were aware—or believed that they knew—of many
examples of Makarios's particularism.[6]

After a while the committee came out again, but not before
some of the marchers had started to drift off. Aglas started to
address the now somewhat dispersed crowd. To those who could
hear him, which could only have been a small fraction, he said,
'Today we have won a great victory . . .' The meat of his statement was that he had not succeeded in seeing Makarios but had
then insisted on seeing the Minister of Agriculture who happened
to be in the Palace on business. The Minister had made a statement to the effect that when a few minor technical problems had
been solved the dam would go ahead very quickly. Aglas emphasized that he had confidence in the word of the Minister and that
as far as he was concerned the demonstration had succeeded.

At one point a Kalotis called out, 'We've come to see our father
(priest) and not to see our cousin,' which meant, 'We've come to
see Makarios, and not the Minister.'[7] The meeting now became

rather confused, largely because there was no system of communication organized by the leaders of the march. People stood about in knots discussing what they had understood to have occurred, while Aglas rushed about from group to group, giving instructions, changing his mind and contradicting himself. He had the impression that all that had to be done now was for the Irrigation Committee members to go and sign some papers in the office of the District Commissioner and the dam would practically be under way. He seemed to be in some doubt as to what to do with the demonstrators. Finally, he decided to dismiss them, while the leaders would go and see about the papers. But one old Kammari man—Yialyias—shouted to him, 'All right, but if you've been cheated this time, don't think we'll come with you again on a demonstration.' Yialyias was one of those who had wanted the demonstrators to stay outside the Palace 'fasting if necessary' until Makarios agreed to see them. The demonstration marched back through the city to the buses in an orderly column, with the lawyer standing on the opposite side of the road, a few hundred yards below the Presidential Palace making dismissive signs with his arms reminiscent of a rookie traffic policeman but undoubtedly meant rather to convey the impression of a general taking a victorious march past. I do not think that most of the marchers regarded themselves as being formally under his orders, but then again they were not under anyone else's, and no one seemed seriously to be challenging the suggestion that they should disperse. On the way down the hill towards the centre of town, somebody had the bright idea of sticking the placard he was carrying in an empty house site. As the other marchers passed his placard, they followed suit, so that further on the purpose of the returning march would have been quite invisible to any curious passer-by unless he took the trouble to ask. But on the empty house site, the marchers had left some details of their story.

On Sunday, 12 January 1969, Patris and I went to see Varetos in Kammari; it turned out that since the demonstration he had been several times to see Tambis, the senior civil servant to whom the villagers referred on the questions regarding the dam (when they were not dealing directly with ministers!). The last time Varetos had been to see him, Tambis had told him that on Monday, 13 January he would telephone the Minister of Agriculture and get the whole situation clarified. Patris and Varetos now decided that they would get together some other committee members and visit Tambis, in the morning. They suggested arriving at 9.30. At this point I made the suggestion (an unfortunate one as it turned out) that since there was no formal appointment it might be better to go early, when the office opened, rather than later, when the secretary might be in a stronger position to say that the civil servant's diary was full and it would be impossible to see him.[8]

The next morning, a Monday, two Kalo committee men, three from Kammari and myself arrived in Tambis's waiting-room at 8 a.m. A few moments after we arrived, Tambis himself came and on seeing the room filled with waiting people turned on one, the Kammari man Yialyias and shouted loudly and angrily, 'So you think you've come here early to check on me, to see if I'm doing my job . . .' and disappeared into his office. The committee people were taken aback by this display and angry in turn. Patris suggested that it was completely improper for a civil servant to address village committee men in that way and that we should all leave the office and go either to the Minister of the Interior or the Minister of Agriculture. Patris, like many other people, believed that Tambis was against the dam being built and favoured the Market Town people over those of the villages. This view was even shared at times by people as sophisticated as Vourros who had had some recent dealings with Tambis and found him rude. However, now the Kammari people told Patris we should not leave and that they knew the real reason for the outburst. At this point the assistant to Tambis came by having obviously heard a version of the outburst. 'It's *very* early,' he said in a remonstrative tone.

The secretary came out and said that Tambis would see two men from the Kammari committee. Varetos and Yialyias went in. Patris was a little put out by this, one reason being that Kalo often pays large sums of money for co-operative projects, and on the dam was certainly scheduled to pay the lion's share among the villages; Kalo should therefore be represented in any discussion of events. Now a uniformed porter arrived and offered us drinks. The remaining Kammari man and I ordered coffee. But Patris and the other Kalo committee man said firmly that they did not want anything. 'You can't not have anything,' said the porter, and then ran through a list of all the available drinks. When he got no response from them he said he would bring them lemonades, and off he went. When he was away they discussed whether perhaps the office had an arrangement with the man running the canteen and was not in fact offering them hospitality on behalf of Tambis. They were quite explicit that after the treatment they had received from the senior civil servant they would not accept his hospitality. Evidently they decided the porter was acting on his own initiative for when he returned with the lemonade they drank it.

The two men were with Tambis for about forty minutes; when they came out all three were smiling and Tambis said in a jocular voice loud enough for the rest to hear, 'And don't you come checking on me at 8 a.m. again.' As it turned out one of the two men had deliberately used the fact of an observer's presence (mine) to chide the civil servant, who was now making quite sure that the episode would appear in a new and more favourable light. 'There was an educated man outside, who has been following village affairs for some time, and it must certainly have made a poor impression on him,' Varetos had said. He had not of course discussed this tactic with me.

We left the office and the Kammari men explained what had happened. First, they said, they had thrashed the whole thing out and had arranged another meeting with the civil servant for 11 a.m. Patris now complained that it was not right of Tambis to have seen only the Kammari people, but he was persuaded that in view of the new meeting, and certain additional facts, no harm had been done. The additional facts were that Yialyias had some months before sent Tambis a letter which was probably libellous, about the running sore of the Kammari pump licence which the government continued to block.[9] In this letter he said among other things that Tambis viewed the villagers of Kammari *san mávrous* which means 'as blacks' or 'as slaves', people to whom he could do and say what he liked. In the eyes of the Kammari people this letter was the real explanation for the early-morning outburst. Patris was now somewhat mollified.

At 11 a.m. all returned to the office, and once seated, some banter passed between Tambis and Yialyias. The civil servant said, 'Why did you people go to all that trouble and expense to keep the pump issue going? You acted quite illegally into the bargain ...' 'Oh, yes, that we admit,' said Yialyias, 'but we've had our water there for many years.' The discussion continued, and during it Tambis referred to the offer the government had made of another licence in another site, and to the frequent charges made by the Kammari people that certain persons had received their licences who shouldn't have done so, and why should not Kammari preserve its traditional water rights?

After these preliminaries, Tambis got down to business. He put in a call to the Minister of Agriculture. 'We haven't yet spoken this year so allow me to wish you a Happy New Year, Minister. Now I have here in my office some of those gentlemen who were carrying placards outside the Presidential Palace the other day, and I wish to get it entirely clear, from you yourself, what you did and did not promise them.' He then took down a statement in writing during which he repeatedly said, 'Yes .. I see ... ah, that's it ...' and as he wrote down the words of the statement he emphasized in repeating them out loud all the points which apparently the Minister now wished to stress. The statement stressed that *when* all the necessary technical obstacles had been removed, and *when* all other problems had been solved, *then and only then* would work begin on the dam. The statement sounded highly conditional. When he had finished taking down the statement he thanked the Minister and said goodbye. He made no attempt to keep the Minister on the telephone in case the committee people had anything to say. Both during the statement and after it the villagers looked somewhat stunned and when the telephone finally clicked back into place, Yialyias said, 'What he said now and what he said the other day are as different as day and night,' and the room hummed with agreement to this. I was not able to obtain copies of either the statement made at the Presidential Palace or the one made over the telephone. My impression was that the same words were used and that mere differences in spoken emphasis and tone were enough to change the perceived meaning from a highly optimistic 'the dam is practically under way ... to the highly problematic 'as soon as the technical problems are solved the dam will be under way'.[10]

Once the villagers had got over the initial shock, Tambis made a little speech. If they really wanted to argue with officials, then they must get things down in writing. In view of the Minister's statement, this was ironic, yet still practical advice. Perhaps Tambis was indirectly criticizing the Minister. In contrast to the rather deferential tone he used to the Minister, he used a paternal manner with the villagers, and often emphasized his own white hairs, age, experience, how much he had seen of life. The problems were (i) the consent of Market Town (ii) some minor technical problems related to siting, compensation and so forth.

Now if Market Town wished to block the government in the courts they could do so. Someone asked, what about the new law that people had been making so much of, which would allow the government to go ahead without the consent of Market Town? That law was not as clear as it might be, said Tambis, and might well have to go to the Attorney General for interpretation. In the case of either the court or the Attorney General being involved, he hoped the gentlemen present appreciated that the delay could be *years*. 'And if we go to court, who gains? No one except the lawyers. I hope you are not studying law, not that I have any objections to lawyers, my own son is studying law, but in this case ... So the government's policy has been to try to persuade the Market Towners and win them over. This would cost less time and money in the long run.'

At this point the committeemen said that they understood more or less, but that he should understand the kind of things that were being said in the coffee-shops, and that just as he had them at his head over the question, so they had the men who had elected them in the villages at *their* heads. 'And', added Varetos, 'it's all very well telling us that if we clash with the government and are legally in the wrong, then we shall lose, but look at it this way: I am a father. If my daughters ask me for a few *groschia* to buy sweets and I refuse them, why naturally, they will turn to stealing. And that's the way it is with us in the villages ...'

The meeting ended on what from the villager's point of view was an inconclusive note. The civil servants were to arrange a new meeting with the Market Town people in the very near future to see if they would change their position. However, they were not prepared to give any kind of a timetable on results of this, or of a general meeting of those government officials involved (which he set up in front of the villagers) or even of new information on the project. He warned them that these things move slowly. He was gentle but firm about it and at this point no one demurred.

It was clear the meeting was at an end. As the villagers rose to go one man said, 'We've gone back ten steps today,' while old Yialyias said quite loudly enough for Tambis to hear, 'The word of a Market Towner ...' He left the sentence uncompleted but the implication was clear—the Minister was not to be relied on. The expression 'The word of a Market Towner' has almost the status of a proverb in the surrounding villages. Tambis ignored this. Instead he turned to me and said in English, 'I do not get angry easily but this gentleman', nodding at Yialyias 'found the way to do it.'

Outside the office there was a brief discussion of what to do next among the villagers. Someone suggested using the news-papers to convey the results of the morning's meeting; Varetos was keen on the idea of sending a telegram to the government on the day of the administrative meeting. They decided to go and see the lawyer, Aglas, and tell him what had happened. But when they got to his house he was out.

A NEW COMMITTEE

A few days after this meeting, events took a new turn in Kalo. Patris apparently suggested to a number of people, about twenty in all, that some sort of a meeting on the various water problems would be in order. Now subsequently various people in the village, particularly Aglas, Sklyros and Vourros were all puzzled about where the real initiative for this meeting came from. Patris took the line that a meeting was advisable in the natural course of events, and that no outside person had suggested it to him. It is probable that there was in fact no more to it than that. My point here is that several of the more politically alert people in the village were not willing to accept such a simple explana-tion, and were immediately looking for the hand of an organiza-tion, outside instructions or long-term plans behind the simple suggestion of Patris that a meeting should be called.

Twenty of the more substantial and respected farmers, as well as several teachers, spanning all shades of political opinion, met for two hours, in the card-playing room of one of the coffee-shops. Several other people dropped in on realizing that there was a meeting going on, and as is usual in such meetings where no formal committee is operating, virtually everyone who arrived was welcomed and sat down. Young unmarried men do not usually try to come in. People spoke in an impromptu way about a number of issues related to water. The rural constable said that if M.P.s and doctors kept getting licences to plant citrus trees or sink water pumps, then he would go ahead and plant trees anyway and if the government moved against him he would take the case to the Constitutional Court and fight for his rights. People discussed the new regulations about planting certain kinds of vegetables among citrus trees, and the rules about fit-

Kalo village from the east

Water from underground

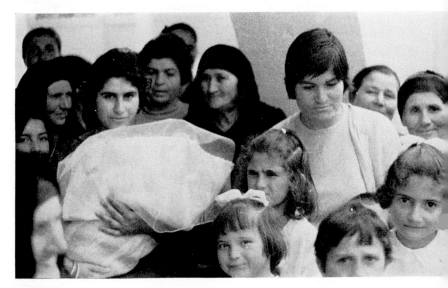

Baptism

Festivities after a baptism

offee shop

rds

Checking Electoral Lists, February 1968

Not what to vote, but how to vote

traditional mudbrick house

d houses, new bricks

The village, from a tall house

ting meters to water pumps, and the number of hours one might water and the best methods of irrigation.

Patris gave a brief report to the meeting of how the meeting with Tambis had fared, and then suggested the possibility of a new demonstration on the date of the administrative meeting. This then opened up a general discussion of tactics regarding the dam problem and the need to put the problems to a more general village meeting was stressed. I am not sure exactly who opened up this issue, but traditionally it is something the left and centre people always tend to support as an inherently good practice. At various times various people, particularly D. Fanos, tried to get the meeting to follow an orderly procedure, with one person speaking at a time, and so forth, but this did not happen. Village meetings without a strong chairman often tend to comprise several smaller sub-meetings, with several people talking at once to their own immediate group of listeners. Among the main speakers at this meeting were Kellis, a teacher, Tangos and Dhaskalos, who made the point that the Irrigation Committee had not had an appointment when they went to see Tambis. The meeting also discussed at some length the new water regulations and the general atmosphere was a cheerful consensus that the rules were not acceptable in their present form, and the government was not going to find the law being obeyed. Some of the leftists, Tangos included, spoke clearly in support of the government's *general* policy of water control and conservation but emphasized that this particular plan was back-to-front and impractical. By this he meant that norms of water consumption had been laid down before any provision had been made for meeting them.

This meeting was followed a week later on 24 January 1969 by a much larger one to which in theory the whole village was invited. It was attended by between 150 and 200 men, which was a very large turn-out in village terms. There had been no formal programme except that a full village meeting would discuss the problems debated by the smaller group in the previous meeting. When Vourros arrived someone, probably the teacher Kellis, suggested he should take the chair and there was general agreement for this. Vourros then announced that if he took the chair he would want the meeting to follow an efficient pattern, that is that people should only speak one at a time, and that what everyone wanted was new ideas, not that people endlessly repeat the same thing that others had said.

There seemed to be a sort of speaker's desk around Vourros—one side of him sat Dhaskalos and on the other Kellis. All three men are teachers and between them span a wide political spectrum. This was not any kind of official grouping but proved symbolically important in view of later events. Vourros soon ran into difficulty with the rule of one person speaking at a time, and when one particular man interrupted several times and would not heed the chair, Vourros got irritated and said, 'If you won't keep order I shall leave the meeting.' The farmer (who had been on several village committees because he is not identified strongly with either right or left and therefore gets elected not for his ability but for his moderation) was instantly repentant 'Sorry, was I out of order in some way, Mr. Vourros?' 'No, no, that's all right,' Vourros replied.

This farmer went on to explain that in his view the relationship between the village and the government was like that between a child and its mother, 'If the child doesn't cry, the mother doesn't feed it.' This saying had been used by the lawyer Aglas in one of his meetings about the dam. The meeting now settled down to a discussion of the new water regulations. The farmer continued: 'The real mistake was to put the water meters on the pumps in the first place. The Market Town people should never have started putting them on.' At this point a series of speakers all spoke in favour of putting on the meters, including Dhaskalos, Tangos and Vourros. They made points critical of the government's administration of the policy but stood by the point that this method of water control was both inevitable and necessary.

During this stage of the debate Vourros from the chair occasionally clarified a point for someone who had not understood. It would be quite obvious that people had not understood something, for after a point had been made the very next question might ask the substance of the lost point. There was a tendency for the more frequent speakers to speak a modified form of *Demotiki* while occasional speakers making minor points used village dialect.

It is worth noting that Vourros had been invited to chair a meeting in Kalo although he was not either a full-time resident of the village or born in it. Another man who spoke on several occasions at the meeting was a senior civil servant. He had been born in Kalo but his career had taken him away from the village for many years and he was only rarely there. Nevertheless, his presence at the meeting was regarded as both natural and desirable and no one showed any sign of thinking that as a senior civil servant he might be representing the government in his views. He said at one point with reference to the Kammari dam that he firmly believed the government was sincere and wanted to see it built.

The discussion of water problems began to turn into a discussion of tactics. Vourros said he hoped the village would decide to have regular monthly family meetings. He chose the phrase quite deliberately. So when a little later the meeting started to discuss the advisability of producing a new committee, called an Advisory Committee, the ground had to some extent already been prepared by his suggestion. Those who thought the new committee a good idea argued that there were special problems facing the village at the moment, particularly to do with water, which the existing committees were probably too busy to handle by themselves. A teacher said he thought the committee was not a good idea because it would undoubtedly politicize the village. At this Vourros immediately called out from the chair, 'Is there likely to be a misunderstanding that this Advisory Committee would have a political colour?' at which a number of people said things like, 'No, we don't do things like that here.' His point was carried.

Part of the debate became the question of whether the Advisory Committee would have any legal basis. The *múktar*, whom some people said was asleep for most of the meeting was asked what he thought; he said he thought there was no need of such a committee even in a purely advisory capacity. He also was understood to express some anxiety about it producing tension between left and right. Sklyros also said he could see no need for such a committee. The civil servant then emphasized that there was no legal problem about a purely *advisory* committee. Another man said if the village was going to be organized properly it was essential the opinions of everyone should be regularly heard, the opinion of the secondary school teacher, the primary school teacher, the shepherd and the camel-driver.[11] A leftist said that monthly meetings like this would keep the other village committees on their toes.

When it looked as if discussion of the need for the new committee would get bogged down, Vourros said that there was no reason why anything had to be decided today—it could all be put off for a month if need be. The civil servant said that while they could always elect a committee at the next meeting, it would be a pity not to take advantage of the present large turn-out to do something. There was some discussion of this. Some felt that the best thing was to call another meeting for the very next day but those who wanted the meeting called for a week's time, a Saturday again, carried the day. They argued that it would be better attended because better advertised by word-of-mouth and possibly a notice. It was said that there were not really enough men present to take any major decisions, and this argument had some force since on a number of occasions during the meeting people had made the point that, in future, village committees should not take major decisions like signing agreements with the government without a meeting and discussion with the whole village. The two outgoing leftist members of the Irrigation Committee had some time before been complaining that although consultation was their policy, the new committee had ignored it and gone ahead and signed a form of agreement over the Avla dam without consulting the village. The new committee, they claimed, influenced by Patris, had asked a few prominent men in the village and left it at that. During this meeting people repeatedly used an expression which means 'the whole village' (*to horkó olóklyro*) and the way in which it was used had a moral force, endorsing the desirability of full consultation.

Vourros now tried a new tactic. He said that the test of the need for the Advisory Committee was whether or not the Irrigation Committee thought it needed advice to carry out its work. He would put it to them. He asked the five members by name, around the room. They each said 'yes' and then Vourros said, 'So the Irrigation Committee itself agrees that an Advisory Committee would have some purpose.' This move effectively stopped further discussion of whether or not the new committee was needed.

The discussion now turned to composition of the new committee. Dhaskalos said it should be ten people. The civil servant said five, and it should be temporary only.

Finally, the meeting broke up after having lasted over two hours. The owner of the coffee-shop seemed quite annoyed, possibly at the amount of business he felt he had lost, and went around telling people, 'It's all over now.' People went on sitting around talking quite excitedly on some of the matters that had come up. A group of young unmarried boys said among themselves, 'Nothing happened. Nothing will come of it,' but this was

not the general mood. Vourros in particular was very pleased
with the way it had gone, and the promise it held for the future.

One week later the meeting took place. When Vourros arrived
he found a certain vagueness about the programme, and there
seemed to be a certain hesitancy on the part of the people he
asked to give him any details. He kept saying he would go if
nothing was going to happen. It is probable that this atmosphere
was created on the one hand by his nervousness, and on the other
by his feeling that the meeting might in some way have been
'got at' in advance. He was perhaps thinking of the Graduates'
Club fiasco. However, people started to arrive until there were
finally about 120 present, fewer than the week before but still a
fair turn-out. Vourros took the chair and said, 'Dear fellow-
villagers: let us talk about the dam first, and vote for the committee when more people get here.' A right-wing teacher got up
and said that the Irrigation Committee was doing a good job but
the issues of the dam and the meters required a separate committee. Vourros now stressed that an independent committee
would have no government recognition, it would merely be an
advisory one, helping the existing legal ones. The right-wing
teacher then said that surely since the new committee would
represent the *whole* community it would have a legal basis?
Tangos said that since the Irrigation Committee had formally
accepted the need for advice from this committee perhaps it
would have a legal basis. Dhaskalos then made a short speech
which bridged the apparent gap produced by the last two
speeches. Vourros now stressed that the Advisory Committee was
to be entirely without political colour. He viewed its functions
as being to meet regularly and to seek and express the opinions
of the villagers on current problems. Here Tangos added that
it was in general a good thing to seek many opinions. Dhaskalos
now said that the Advisory Committee should handle both large
and small problems. Sklyros and Tangos both disagreed and said
for large problems only, and the latter said it should meet every
three months, but more often if needed.

At this point Vourros emphasized that in doing business with
the government it was quite essential to make written submissions
and to seek written replies. The same point that Commissioner
Tambis had made to the discomfited Irrigation Committee a few
days previously. He mentioned that one possible solution to the
dam problem would be to by-pass Market Town, the villagers
themselves paying the share of costs that it would have paid.

He said that so far this year fourteen dams full of water had flowed into the sea. That he believed the government in the final analysis favoured the dam. Dhaskalos now said that there had been a number of committees, a number of meetings with the government and many conflicting answers and changes of policy. A farmer then said that ever since Aglas had been Chairman of the Five Villages' Committee he had kept a written record of all the meetings, letters exchanged and so forth. Patris then pointed out that Aglas is chairman of the Five Villages' Committee. (Patris and Aglas, first cousins, were both PEK supporters.) Tangos said that the Advisory Committee should study Aglas's file and discuss it.

Vourros from the chair now asked what tactics should be adopted on the dam? A new demonstration? More telegrams? He suggested that they write a letter which would necessitate an answer. He thought the government wanted to build the dam but at the same time wanted to avoid conflict. Someone said, 'We should go and see our Papás (priest)' by which he meant Makarios. A discussion now started about a letter the government had sent to Aglas, in answer to his telegram, in which they made a reply that the dam would be built, when conditions permitted. There was some discussion about exactly when this letter arrived, the day of the demonstration or before or after. Vourros then said that in any case the letter was ambiguous.

Now a leftist suggested among other things an interview with Makarios should be requested. Vourros added that the record of the interview should be sought *in writing*. Sklyros said that they should get the M.P.s, their representatives to raise these questions in the House. Tangos asked, one particular M.P.? Dhaskalos said, no, all of them. There was then some discussion of what the role of the *múktar* should be in these matters. He was in any case absent, which is often in the villages a sign of disapproval of an event. A leftist now said that both the left (EKA) and right (PEK) farmers association M.P.s should be asked to take up the issue.

Vourros now raised the question of the committee's size, and suggested also a written ballot, to ensure secrecy. The general feeling in the room was against this. One man said, 'If we take three from here and two from there, there will be trouble,' which meant, the right-left cleavage would become active. Without any vote being taken, the meeting bypassed the notion of a written ballot, and decided that five would be the right number of members. Vourros now made a major speech: he asked them to make some use of the educated men in the village. 'You have plenty of educated men in the village. I myself am willing to help at any time. But of course I do *not* mean by this that you should overlook and under-estimate the uneducated men, for there are a lot of men here who have not had the chance to go to secondary school but still know how to handle affairs . . . but in the last analysis people who have had the chance of education should be ready to serve the community.' He also stressed that the essential written work of such a committee needed at least one educated man to handle it.

Following on his speech, he was immediately nominated for the committee. He tried very hard to back out, but people quoted straight back at him the statements he had just been making. He then called out for D. Fanos to be nominated, who said 'this will make a lot of trouble for me' because he was a civil servant, but Vourros went on urging him until he accepted. Then Vourros turned to a teacher and said 'Are you ready to serve your community?'—a question to which it would have been extremely hard to have answered no. Someone then nominated another quietly leftish teacher, Kellis, who tried extremely hard to get out of the nomination on the grounds of being a civil servant. A farmer said to him, 'But you ought to be on the Advisory Committee—you have a lot of land.' Another farmer said, 'We should not force people who don't want to.' Someone else said, 'The government doesn't check up on things like this,' by which he meant that the Civil Service Law did not apply to things like the Advisory Committee.

At one point in this bout of nominations it seems that five names had been put forward: Vourros; D. Fanos; Tangos; Patris's brother Oligos; and Kellis, the teacher. Other names had been shouted out but had apparently not got the mysterious support of the meeting. (It is possible that whoever decided to recite the list of names put in or left out those names they thought fit or unfit). However, when this list of five names was recited, Tangos said, 'We have two uneducated men on this committee, myself and Oligos,' and suggested that this was not right. In the ensuing confusion of discussion several teacher's names were put forward to replace one of the uneducated men. The result was that Oligos was replaced by a teacher.

The five names were accepted by the meeting in an informal way. There was no show of hands and no one suggested that any more formal method was needed. Once this was over the main meeting ended and the committee decided to meet. A member of the Irrigation Committee, Mangaras, also came along, which it turned out was his privilege under the current interpretation of the relation between the two committees. Kellis and D. Fanos discussed whether they were allowed to participate or not, under the civil service law. Kellis said he was there 'practically by force', and that his trade union on top of everything else had laid down limits to the sort of extra-curricular activities teachers should have to take part in, and if any of the meetings turned out to have a political aspect then he would just not turn up.

Tangos said only an educated man could follow the paperwork. Vourros said that one of the things this committee could do would be to look into the problem of the students in the village gambling. At this point Vasilakis came in, and was welcomed and asked to sit down and join in. What did he think were the village's problems? In his view *the* community problem was the problem of our young people. Then someone said, 'What about people shooting off guns?' which referred to a recent incident where a drunken man had fired a pistol in one of the drinking shops. Vasilakis said this was undoubtedly wrong. Then someone said, what about the problem of the slaughter house. The next suggestion was for a club, but it was then suggested that a club would inevitably get coloured (politicized). Vourros said that a club such as they had in Market Town of orchard-cultivators (*kypourón*) would be all right but Vasilakis said that even this would get coloured too.[12] Someone pointed out that Kammari has a club and Mastia village has one in formation. Vasilakis now got up to go as a friend had called for him, he said.

On this note the committee adjourned. Vourros said he would telephone the lawyer Aglas in the morning for a discussion. He went off to eat with Sklyros and myself. Both men discussed the possibility that the original initiative for the first pilot meeting had come from PEK, the right-wing farmers union, for which Patris is the Kalo representative. However, they were unable to make up their minds one way or another. Sklyros was asked why last week he had joined the *múktar* in saying that he did not think the village needed an Advisory Committee and he said that at that point he had been fairly certain the whole impetus was coming from PEK and had therefore opposed it. Part of his reason for being suspicious that it was a PEK manoeuvre was that he had heard that the village of Mastia, which has no interest in the dam was forming such a committee, and this would have made it appear part of a larger scheme, and not a local initiative.[13]

The next day the lawyer Aglas came to the village and sat in the coffee-shop and made a tape recording of some of the villagers' complaints and problems, and among other things said, 'Vourros should not think that I am less interested than him in the problems of the village.' People said that he made this remark with a good deal of heat and generally seemed both surprised and irritated by what he heard of the previous day's meeting.

As far as I can ascertain the Advisory Committee never met again. A month after the meeting at which the committee were chosen, no meeting had been called, and at that time Kellis said, 'We exist to advise the Irrigation Committee. If they don't ask for our advice there is nothing we can do. They never asked, so we did nothing.' When I returned to the village both in December 1969 and again in June 1970 I asked committee members if they had ever had another meeting and they said 'no'. When asked why, they said that the heat went out of the dam issue.

During my fieldwork there was one more piece of activity about the dam issue which is highly revealing. In late March 1969 the Kalo *múktar* told a member of the Kalo Irrigation Committee to be ready to go to Nicosia the next day. He did not want to, but the *múktar* said it was essential he go. About twenty men from the five villages went, and he noticed that they were nearly all supporters of the man who had recently resigned as Minister of the Interior, Polykarpos Yorgadjis. The group reached Yorgadjis's house where they were given coffee. Yorgadjis then telephoned the Minister of Agriculture, and explained that he had been visited by a group of men who were concerned about the dam issue, and could they come and see him? A District M.P., both a close friend of Yorgadjis, and well known to the Minister, now took them to the Minister's office, where he promised that the dam would be built whether the Market Town people agreed or not. My informant was very certain that this whole meeting had been conducted in order to create political support for Yorgadjis, who a month beforehand had, in harness with Glafkos Clerides announced the formation of the United Party, the first party off the mark once Makarios had given his formal approval to the idea of parties and elections. I asked the Kalo *múktar* why the group of men had gone to Yorgadjis about the dam since he after all was no longer the Minister. The rural constable, who was sitting with the *múktar* said, 'Well, he is and he isn't... really there's a sense in which he still is...' and a number of other remarks which added up to the idea that Yorgadjis was still very powerful.[14]

By June 1970 no work had been started on the dam, but some people in the village now believed it *would* be built in the next few years and that the government would go ahead no matter how much the Market Town people were against it. They also thought that the demonstration and the events which accompanied it were very closely related to the desire of lawyer Aglas to be adopted as a candidate by the PEK group. However, hindsight in such matters is always rather clearer than vision during the actual events. One must point out that Aglas's candidacy was a simple and satisfying explanation for villagers, but it also had as a logical consequence the shifting of the responsibility for the failure or success of the demonstration from their own shoulders to those of Aglas. Furthermore, if they were correct then at the very least they accepted his leadership, and when a device was created—the Advisory Committee—which might have served as an alternative channel for the expression of their views, they did not make use of it.

By 1970 the government had decided to waive Market Town's contribution because of their objections, and the proposal became the following: the dam would cost £380,000 of which the government would pay two thirds, and lend the four remaining villages the remaining third, to be paid back at 4 per cent over fifteen to twenty years. The four villages were assessed according to the number of *donums* estimated to benefit from the dam, in the following way: Kalo, £85,000; Posto, £28,000; Avea, £13,000; Kammari, £9,000. Posto was trying to get its assessment reduced to £18,000. Parali, which cannot irrigate (but will benefit from enrichment) was not assessed. In 1971 the government finally started building the dam.

DISCUSSION

The preceding material has been concerned with the behaviour of the villagers in relation to government. The villagers do not experience government agencies as impersonal institutions carrying out reasoned policies, nor do they in fact *consciously* see themselves for what they are—an interest-group which can steadily and effectively exert pressure on the government. However, once having said this, it must be stressed that both tendencies are emerging, and the last ten years have seen a greatly increased experience of dealing with government by villagers.

The villagers cannot be expected to see the government as impersonal, since they have had many years' experience of contact with some of the most prominent officials in the dam issue—particularly Tambis and his assistant. They know for example that the assistant owns substantial citrus land in the Market Town area, and often talk as if they think this explains his actions, which they interpret as favouring the Market Town people. I believe they are often wrong in their assessments but they are also—in other situations—often right about the ways in which personal interests affect the impartiality of official decisions. Here, of course, as elsewhere in this book the question of scale comes to the fore. By most standards Cyprus is a small-scale state. The dam demonstration was feasible because it only took the villagers an hour to reach the capital. Their local knowledge of which powerful people have land in what place, or links to whom, are facilitated by this factor of scale. The information which cannot ever be available to the villagers—and indeed which is extremely hard to obtain under the best of circumstances—concerns exactly when a person or a policy is free of special considerations, and when not. The only evidence of impartiality which is at the present moment acceptable to villagers is in fact evidence of *partiality* towards and favouring policies desired by the village itself. That is, while the government gives the village what it wants it may be seen as acting honestly, impartially; when it fails to do so, the commonest explanation is that someone with powerful connections and self-interest opposed to the village is wielding influence in the situation. Thus when during the floods the bridge at Avla was swept away by the waters, the explanation most villagers favoured was not a technical one, such as a poor design, a miscalculation about the possible force of flood water, a decision that it was cheaper to build a cheap bridge every so often than an expensive one once. They chose as explanation the notion that the contractor responsible for the bridge put less of the appropriate materials into it than he had been paid to do. I heard no actual evidence for this, so cannot even have an opinion as to whether they were right or not. However, I know of similar cases where such an explanation would have been correct.

The tendency to see issues in terms of persons and partiality is also reflected in the way village committees approach the government officials. They very rarely write or telephone for an appointment. They decide to go, and simply turn up. If the man they wish to see is not there, they either see his assistant or go away. They do not take notes or keep records of discussions, nor do they ask officials to send them a written account of the discussions which take place. The more educated men of the village—the teachers and civil servants—often tell them that the approach is wrong, and I have cited a situation where a senior civil servant reminded them of the need to have things in writing after the Minister's statement had been so ill received. It is significant in this context that one of the issues in the setting up of the Advisory Committee was the place of educated men; the initiative for this came from an educated man, Vourros, but there was wide acceptance of the idea from the floor. The reasons why most educated men are reluctant to take on administrative responsibilities have already been discussed (p. 113) but it is clear that this reluctance only slows down any possible change in the relations between village and government. Charitably, one assumes this is an *unintended* consequence of the relevant Civil Service Laws.

This last point is closely connected to the problem of the villager's need for and reliance on, leaders. The village puts its own best men forward for work on committees. But these men are usually substantial farmers, too busy and too unsophisticated to deal with government in anything but a frontal way. For more indirect approaches, the village committees call on those men who are born into or married into the village but are now resident in town. Vourros, Aglas and the Kammari Inspector of Education, Kefiros, have all been involved in village encounters with government this way.[15] The villagers co-opt such men for at least two distinct kinds of reasons: firstly their level of education makes them able to see the legal complexities of government proposals, and suggest appropriate amendments. This is in fact something that a number of the villagers are quite capable of doing for themselves, but they feel happier when a more highly educated person has looked into it. Secondly, the men they co-opt are likely to have closer contact with members of the elite in normal city life, and may thus obtain inside information about the government's intentions, or may be able to exercise special pressure behind the scenes.

There is also a more hard-headed reason for the ordinary villagers to favour elite leadership. Quite simply, it is safer. To approach officials or politicians—whom many villagers simply group together, in a single class of 'powerful men'—with requests or demands is regarded by many villagers as risky. Perhaps names will be taken, files opened, future benefits withheld. It is always safer to keep one's head down, to remain anonymous. The whole situation has been succinctly expressed by Michael Attalides when he writes (n.d.):

> In other words rights seem to be rather an obscure and arbitrarily granted phenomenon that are always linked to the bestower.

He explains that villagers' and many urban Cypriots' notions of citizenship rights are scarcely developed, and all their relations with authority suggest the need for personal propitiation. Such a view explains why in matters relating to external authorities, villagers are content to see educated men out in front, while they are less willing to accord them recognition in matters within the village, where no threatening authorities are involved.

To have said that villagers favour or permit elite leadership is not to say that they are satisfied with it. But the choice is between doing little or nothing themselves, and allowing others to do something—however little—for them. The latter course is usually preferred.

Such reliance on urban elite leaders from their own village has certain consequences. It led for example to the situation in which Aglas could create or capture the Five Village Committee; a number of people in the village believed he was doing it for personal political reasons and were quietly hostile to him, but since there was no alternative person prepared to take action he won by a walk-over. When Vourros accepted a prominent place in the Advisory Committee it immediately aroused Aglas's antagonism, and revealed the extent to which the dam campaign was linked to his aspirations to become a Representative.

If Aglas manipulated the Dam Committee to suit his own ends, then this was at least obvious to a number of the villagers. However, when Vourros became Chairman of the meeting to discuss formation of the Advisory Committee, his forms of manipulation were more subtle. For example, when it looked as if the very question of the Committee's formation was likely to be shelved, he successfully reopened it by putting the question to the Irrigation Committee—did they feel in need of additional advice? Had they answered 'no' to this, they would have laid themselves open to several charges: one, that they thought they knew everything, which was obviously presumptuous since they had no educated men among them; two, that they had been too proud to put the welfare of the village first. There would in addition have been the implication that they were able to solve the problem of the dam by themselves. None of the committee were rash enough to answer that they did not need advice, so Vourros was simultaneously able to reopen the issue, and to have appeared to marshall considerable support from the Irrigation Committee itself. The technique he used was a rather subtle one. He has for many years been active on committees in the capital so he has had ample opportunity to pick up special skills. The villagers' reliance on educated leadership lays them open to such forms of manipulation.

However, the leaders themselves face two ways. There are a number of important cleavages in Cypriot society, the urban/ rural, the educated/uneducated, the rich/poor; these may or may not overlap, and thus give rise to a number of possibilities for differences of status. The feature completely absent from Cyprus is that of a traditional titled aristocracy, based on a feudal estate system. Loyalty to the village of birth and one's kin there cuts across achievements in education, wealth and urban residence. Thus mobile people become special resources available to their natal village in encounters with government or the elite. The tie with the village is usually greatly reinforced by the likelihood that a man will own property there. Vourros and Aglas both have substantial property in their villages. In order to have this property successfully managed it is essential for them to keep up good relations with at least some villagers. It would be unfortunate in the extreme if they became seen as men who wished only to take things out of the village and not to put anything back.[16] Furthermore, their ties are reinforced by the fact that their property gives them—in certain situations—common interests with the villagers.

It was clear at a number of points during the dam campaign that the villagers were anxious about the possible politicization of the issue. On a number of occasions they said things which suggested that they wished to treat the dam as a simple problem of administration, and that issues of political alignment should be kept out, since they would inevitably break the solidarity of the villages. The villagers were only partly successful in this desire. For one thing, the left were not officially present on the demonstration to the Presidential Palace. While not sure of the reasons for this, I can say it is entirely consistent with the attitude of the left national leadership to avoid any action which might appear to be anti-governmental. The absence of the left, and the presence of the PEK leaders were both signs that national politics could not be 'kept out'.

During the formation of the Advisory Committee the matter of possible politicization was again overtly raised, and nearly all those present rejected the idea that the new committee would be thought to have a political flavour. This expressed attitude, it will be readily seen, is a form of social control: by saying that something will not happen, one makes it less acceptable and less likely. Since the position (or lack of position) of all village leaders is known, there is a sense in which it is impossible for the village to put up a committee which is without a political complexion. The only thing to be done is to produce a committee and to put it on its honour to avoid behaving in a party political fashion. This, I suggest, was why the villagers were against Vourros's suggestion of the formal secret ballot for the committee. For if, as eventually happened, the new committee was produced in a fairly confused fashion but by acclamation, it would be nearly impossible for any single group to control the course of events, without being seen to be so doing. However, in a secret ballot all sorts of things could go on which would result in a political committee: a group could secretly vote for several people and afterwards deny that they had acted in an organized fashion. The 'secret ballot' which in another culture or situation would be a way of ensuring open selection, here had a quite different meaning, and Vourros did not show himself to be fully in touch with village thinking when he tried to press for it.

However, in spite of the expressed wishes of the village to keep the dam issue non-political in the party sense, the ambitions of the lawyer, Aglas, were clear evidence that this was impossible. Furthermore, the villagers saw themselves—realistically as it happened—as involved in a power struggle with the citizens of Market Town. They frequently asked each other, 'Do they think they are the Government of Cyprus?' and their considerable mistrust of the Minister was rooted in the thought that because of his origins he would be bound secretly to support the town.

They announced their intention to make sure that at the next elections, he would be made to feel their wrath. This intention was thwarted since he did not stand for office in June 1970, having been guaranteed further government office, by the President.

The anxiety about politicization of the issue was displayed by the behaviour of Sklyros. When he first attended a meeting to discuss the Advisory Committee he took the line—along with the *múktar*—that such a committee was not necessary. This he did because he did not know who was behind the idea, and was afraid it was a right-wing initiative. Later when he had convinced himself that there was no outside grouping behind the idea, he was prepared to support it.

Vourros was impressed by the atmosphere in the village at the time of the creation of the Advisory Committee. He then immediately reopened one of his pet projects, the possibility of forming a club in the village. The man who opposed this, Vasilakis, was a man who had already been involved in disputes with Vourros before as I described in the previous chapter, and whose uncle had been instrumental in stopping his earlier attempts to start a club. Thus we see a continuity in the alignments and oppositions among the village leaders over nearly ten years, and the same reason being used by the less educated to the more educated for rejecting a formal institution based on educational difference. 'It would politicize the village.' However, if there is continuity, there is also change. For Dhaskalos the teacher who had remained neutral over the Graduates' Club five years earlier, now stands openly with Vourros as well as with leftists like Tangos over the need to control water use and to form a new committee. This is in spite of the fact that he remains a passionate right-nationalist.

The Advisory Committee came to nothing in the end. Since in fact the Committee had no formal legal existence, and thus no teeth, it is not surprising that without explicit requests from the Irrigation Committee nothing came out of it. It is always possible that the Irrigation Committee *deliberately* avoided calling it. Some of the people on the Irrigation Committee—Patris for example—were supporting the candidacy of Aglas in national politics. They would thus have had a good reason to avoid calling a committee which threatened to take some of the steam out of Aglas's role as champion of the dam. But the fact that at roughly the same time a new move to launch a Graduates' Club was again thwarted 'to avoid politicizing the village' throws the issue into sharper relief: for the Advisory Committee was once again a committee of educated men, and the Graduates' Club was also for the educated: their influence would have been considerable in internal village affairs, would have symbolically taken an institutional form, and would have threatened some of the prominent nationalists in the village. It is one thing to allow educated men to take the lead in something as external, uncertain and hazardous as a demonstration; but it is quite another to allow them a permanent position of authority within the village itself.

Other reasons for the failure of the Advisory Committee must include the fact that such thorough-going participation seems to be the wrong style for village administration. Inertia is inevitable, unless there is a continual crisis, or clear danger. In this sense the early readiness of the villagers to attend the first meetings can be seen as expressing their anxiety, and the act of choosing a committee released their tension. Having selected a committee, many of them saw their affairs as in safe hands. The memory of the flood water and the demonstration passed, and with them, the will of individual villagers to pursue the matter. These are not structural features of village life, but more cultural, and historical. One cannot ultimately explain the reluctance to make the committee work without mentioning the political culture of the village. There is no need to invoke such notions as 'amoral familism' to explain this behaviour; it is simpler to say that the villagers are not used to keeping up constant pressure on their representatives, and it requires effort they are generally unwilling to make. They do things in the mood of a moment that they will not do on a day-to-day basis.

Yet another reason for the demise of the committee was the climate of incipient elections, rife with party manoeuvre, which meant that the committee was inevitably overtaken by politics, even though I shall argue in the concluding chapter that the committee was also an attempt by villagers to control possible divisions produced by politics. The forces of the larger society, in this instance proved too strong. When a number of villagers, clients of powerful patrons, showed a readiness to work for the dam through these patrons the committee and such village-wide initiatives were doomed. In the event, after the 1970 elections several political parties took up the dam issue and the villagers did not preserve their local unity sufficiently to forestall this politicization. Not that it would have been easy[17] for them to do this,

H

since it would have meant influencing the perceptions and interests of party leaders in a way that few villagers have yet learned to do.

An historical note of some interest concerns the role of Moustachas. In none of the events described in this chapter did he appear to play any part at all. He did not turn up at Advisory Committee meetings, and no one put forward his name. The days when he 'did what he liked in the village' had gone for good, although his nephew Vasilakis was still able to put his weight against the proposed citrus grower's club.

In the next chapter I discuss a number of villagers in conflict with a number of Market Town people over the conduct of CITCOP, the citrus co-operative; by the end of the discussion it should be clear that this issue and the dam issue which covered the same period of time were mutually intensifying.

NOTES

1. Dahrendorf (1959: 213) has described what he calls the super-imposition of conflicts, in industrial society. Although he is specifically concerned with class conflict, the distinction is a useful one, which deserves wider currency.
2. He is not a lawyer in real life.
3. In the previous chapter I described how these two men came to lose their positions on this committee.
4. This man has already appeared, in the previous chapter, (p. 155) as the district militia commander to whom village militia problems were to be referred. As individuals advance through the structures of government, their value as people personally known to villagers increases.
5. Although they laughed, this was sheer nervous politeness, and unease, for many villagers had been saying—and showed every sign of believing—that the Minister was guilty of precisely this form of partiality.
6. Davis (1969) has spoken of the willingness of the Pisticcesi to become state clients. Something similar is going on when villagers claim that Makarios is 'above' particular interests. They say in other situations that they know he looks after his kin and co-villagers. They really mean that they hope he will show his impartiality by favouring them. They express their readiness to become his clients by saying that he is 'above' such things.
7. The statement has other levels of meaning, or ambiguity: since the minister comes from Market Town, there is a real though improbable sense in which he literally is a cousin to some Kalotes. The sentence must then be rendered, We've come to see our priest (remote and inaccessible) and not our cousin (close related and available). Makarios is of course both Archbishop and President.

8. I was not usually in the habit of offering advice, for obvious reasons. But as an 'educated man' I was often asked to give an opinion on courses of action and although I had no illusions about the chances of my advice being either useful or heeded, it seemed both over-cautious and ungrateful to refuse on all occasions.

9. This was a case where the village of Kammari wished for a licence to turn a traditional well into a bore-hole. The government refused this, and the Kammarites went ahead anyway. They were taken to court by the government on a number of occasions. On one occasion I accompanied them on a visit to President Makarios, in which they asked him to intervene in their favour, claiming that others had been unjustly favoured, while their traditional rights were being ignored. A Water Department official described their case to me as 'a put-up job', and suggested that the villagers were cunningly misrepresenting the situation.

10. The reader may care to try saying this last sentence over to himself with differing emphases.

11. The reference to camel-drivers in the case of Kalo is an anachronism. Less than a dozen camels existed in Cyprus at the time of my fieldwork, none of them in Kalo.

12. The resemblance of the positions taken here by Vourros and Vasilakis to those taken by Vourros and Moustachas over the Graduates' Club is striking. (pp. 140–3.)

13. Sklyros' argument here was not sound, since Mastia had, like Kalo, also got the issue of meters for water pumps to deal with.

14. Later still in 1970 the dam became an openly party-political matter, when the United and Progressive Parties both tried to monopolize the high-ground of agitating on the farmer's behalf for the dam. This explains in part the delegation to Yorgadjis earlier.

15. A Water Department official, describing Kefiros's efforts to help his fellow villagers in their attempts to get their (illegal) pump licensed said to me, 'Kefiros used to come into my office from the Ministry of Education a hundred times a day about it. I always had him at my head'. He did not suggest Kefiros was doing his duty to his fellow villagers. Kefiros also managed to get elected to the Legislative Assembly in July 1970, so his efforts were amply rewarded, and his campaign in Kalo will be discussed in chapter ten.

16. On pages 91–2 I described how an outsider who bought a water pump in the village, and tried to get villagers to pay their debts, suffered damage to his water pipes. Such sanctions could equally easily be employed against a fellow-villager who forgot to live up to his obligations. Vourros, at least, is very careful to make no enemies in the village if he can help it, and he refers to just such incidents as the reason for his caution.

17. Again, the fact that Cyprus is so small in scale makes such links between 'local' and 'national' issues inevitable. For a survey of problems related to smallness, see (ed.) Benedict (1967).

9
Co-operative

Certain crises arose in the administration of CITCOP, the citrus wholesale co-operative whose plant is near Market Town. In 1968–70 only about thirty Kalotes were members of CITCOP, so it is necessary to offer some justification for what might at first sight seem a digression. The affairs of CITCOP involve certain leading figures from the Kalo political arena, and involve other actors and issues in the village's several political fields. The villagers are watching the progress of CITCOP closely. If in their eyes it seems to fail, they will feel they have been right not to join hastily; if it succeeds others will join it, or similar organizations. CITCOP will be a test case for the acceptance of future co-operative enterprises.

In terms of the more general arguments advanced here, there will be a further exploration of the prominence of elite personnel in village politics, revealing the nature of the political calculation which must be employed when conflict is muffled; it will show how individuals with conflicting loyalties attempt to avoid action which will antagonize friends, kin or allies.

The CITCOP issues are to some extent superimposed on those of the dam campaign and each fuels and intensifies the other. The material presented here not only adds new data but also makes clearer the story of the dam campaign.

BACKGROUND FACTORS

CITCOP was founded in 1964, with 271 members. By 1969 it had just over 900 members, and handled about 50 per cent of the district's citrus production. In 1969/70 CITCOP handled 150 million pieces of fruit worth £1,622,000. Three quarters of the members are from Market Town, and the rest from the surrounding villages—Kalo, Kammari, Mastia and Mené being the most important. In Kalo at least, a very large majority of those who had citrus trees producing fruit in 1969 were still selling through private merchants. Members of CITCOP had to put up £50 *per donum* share capital to enter the organization. They were then bound by its rules to sell their entire citrus produce through the organization. All members received the same price per 1,000 for saleable fruit cut, and this was an average price, finally settled at the end of the season, based on an average price from all oranges sold throughout the season.

The features which attracted both Market Town and some village growers to join CITCOP were the safe and normally high average price; the ability to obtain loans in advance on their standing fruit; and the certainty that they would be paid on time. In contrast those who sold through a private middleman could hold back their fruit until getting a favourable price, or could try to sell at the start of the season, when the price was also high, but they were always gambling. Prices were unpredictable, and fluctuated widely during a season. If a man borrowed money from a merchant in advance, he would then be committed to selling his fruit to him, which made him feel vulnerable in a bargaining situation; finally, each season at least one of the five major merchants got into difficulties over payments, and farmers after signing a contract of sale were often kept waiting for their money for months, or even a year. Villagers with very small numbers of fruit to sell (either because they had little land, or because their trees were still very young) did not join CITCOP because the entry fee was simply too much to make it worth their while. Men heavily indebted also did not join, since they could not raise the share capital.

There were of course other reasons for selling privately; those with close kin-ties to a middleman might be inclined to sell through him. It is possible that those persons who favour Co-operatives will tend to join while their produce is still relatively small, and those who do not greatly favour Co-operatives will remain outside even when their produce is large. But attitudes to Co-operatives are not a simple matter of party political views (which are in any case strongly held by relatively few villagers) but seen as a separate largely economic issue. Men who are strong right-wing nationalists, like the school-teacher Dhaskalos, nevertheless favour Co-operatives. He joined in the 1966–7 season and in 1967 sold 120,000 fruit through CITCOP at an average price of £5.15.0 per 1,000. But Tangos, a strong leftist, was still selling privately in 1968, when he cut 160,000. He laughingly describes himself as 'a crook, since as a leftist I should believe in Co-operation but I'm not practising what I preach, I'm waiting to see how CITCOP goes, and until I have more fruit... At the moment I can do better outside.' Finally, as I shall later show, there has been some agreement to define the Co-operatives as 'outside' party politics, at least temporarily. Joining or not joining is not currently interpreted by villagers as an indicator of expressive political action.

At the time of my fieldwork one thing which seemed to deter a number of people from joining CITCOP was the idea that since it was dominated by Market Towners, the interests of villagers would tend to come a poor second. Villagers pointed out that nearly all the twelve committee members were from the town, (table 13, p. 229) and that the Market Town people were 'all interrelated'. Thus, they argued, over a number of issues they would support their own kin and friends. Among these issues was a grower's position in each of the schedules for first, second and third cutting of citrus during the season. This was important for two reasons. First, it is widely believed that if fruit stay late on the tree, they take from the tree nourishment needed for flowers and ultimately for the next year's crop of fruit.[1] Secondly, the longer that ripe fruit stay on the tree the greater the chance of large numbers being spoiled by disease, over-ripeness, weather damage, etc. Another issue which exercised the growers was the grading of fruit: if a man produced too many fruit which were graded by CITCOP's checkers as *skárta* (reject class), and thus not up to export standard, he would lose money. It was said that how one's fruit was graded sometimes depended on how well one was connected in Market Town. There were a number of other minor complaints about the way the Co-operative was run, and often these were expressed by villagers in terms of Market Town people running the organization to their own advantage.

It is important not to overstate the degree of hostility between the villagers and the townspeople. There are only three miles between them, and many villagers have relatives in the town, make frequent trips there, have friends there and business contacts. The town and the CITCOP plant provide a small number of jobs for villagers, particularly young women who work at the CITCOP factory packing fruit.

But on the debit side there were issues of economic rivalry, independent of the dam or CITCOP as such. For example, the Kalo Truck Drivers' Association in 1968 held the CITCOP contract to truck fruit to the coast port of Famagusta. But in 1969, under the competitive bidding system, Kalo drivers lost the contract, and it went to Mastia village drivers. A specific group of Kalotes were angry with the CITCOP officials over this.

There was no need for any articulate corporate policy in the village about CITCOP since relatively few villagers were members, on the one hand, and on the other, membership was a matter for private decision and in no way linked to other village memberships. But the general question of how CITCOP was running and whether or not it was worth joining was frequently debated in the coffee-shops, and since Kalotes inevitably come together more with each other, and are already prone to believe their interests are opposed to those of Market Towners, they tended to speak as if Kalotes ought to have a collective position on CITCOP.

Vourros had watched the proposals for the foundation of CITCOP, joined early in 1963, and his entry as one of the larger growers in the region as well as the second or third largest in Kalo was important, given that he is widely thought to be a progressive man. After the committee's first three-year term of office was over in 1966, Vourros, like a number of other people, was not altogether happy about the way they were behaving. At the A.G.M., however, he listened to the speech made by the Commissioner of Co-operative Development, Andreas Azinas, who appealed for the committee to be given a second three-year term of office unopposed, both to give their experience a chance to work *for* the new organization, and since the general political climate of the island was unsettled, so in the interests of keeping unity within the Greek community, elections of all kinds were being avoided. Vourros complied with the Commissioner's request, but by the end of 1968 he was openly dissatisfied.

JANUARY 1969—A.G.M.

On 18 January 1969 the A.G.M. of CITCOP took place. Before the meeting Vourros spoke to a number of the Kalo members in the village coffee-house, and suggested to them that they put specific questions about the running of the Co-operative at the A.G.M. Most of them agreed to do so. When the actual meeting took place, most of the Kalo people sat in a group in the large Market Town cinema hired for the purpose.

The A.G.M. took over five hours to get through its business.

There were a very large number of issues raised, only some of which will be mentioned here. Vourros played a prominent role, although it had been his intention to avoid this, and it was partly for this reason that he had tried to arrange for other people he knew to ask questions. He was careful to preface his first questions with a statement about the need for unity in the organization, the need for the committee to understand that points raised in criticism were not meant as *personal* criticism, but were meant as criticism of the running of the organization. He pointed out that all his personal estate was committed to the organization so that in criticizing its running he was not acting in a spiteful spirit, but merely protecting his self-interest.

One issue he raised was the loss of 600 boxes of fruit which had gone bad in a deep freeze unit. This loss had not appeared in the accounts, and he had only found out about it by accident. One of his sources of information had been a Kalo truck driver, a member of the village Truckers' Association, which had failed to get its contract with CITCOP renewed.

Another issue he raised was the question of the construction of a juice extraction plant. Vourros was highly critical of the committee for having asked for tenders from a number of European firms without having done proper background research on the desirability of the plant itself. Members of the committee had also been abroad on trips to inspect extraction plants. This, he implied, was not helpful, since the men who had gone on these trips did not have the expertise to come to any useful conclusions.

Soon after the start of the meeting he asked whether minutes were being taken, and when it appeared they were not being taken, requested that they should be. This was agreed by Azinas, but he said they would not be sent out to each member but would be available for inspection in the organization's building.[2]

A Kalo teacher, Dhaskalos, raised a question about the costs of boxing the members' fruit, since he had heard that it could be done more cheaply privately. Were costs fully competitive? From the chair, Azinas said he would not release the actual figures in public, because there were guests present and it would be inhospitable to ask them to leave (a reference to myself and a journalist), but he added there were no secrets in the Co-operative movement and the details could be released to members. It would not be in the Co-operative's interest, however, for the private merchants to learn the costs.

At one point a man got up who had the same surname as

Vourros, and when he gave his name Azinas asked him if he were a brother of Vourros. 'No, no relation . . .' the man replied. It is highly likely that the simple fact that members were asked to stand up and state their names when asking questions was sufficient to put some people off.

Later in the meeting some suggestions of minor irregularities were made from the floor, particularly involving allegations that some people managed to get fruit cut ahead of their strict position in the queue. Whereas people were ready to shout out 'yes' to the question 'Do some people put their own relatives first?' there was far less readiness to name names. For even though there were possibly seven or eight hundred people in the room, people would have been able to identify each other by means of only a few quick questions to their neighbours. If you can first locate the village a man is from, it is then an easy matter to find someone you know from that village and ask him, 'Who was it from your village who asked the question about bribing the checkers?'

As the meeting went on Vourros continued to play a prominent part. Since he had been thinking about the affairs of the Co-operative systematically for some time, he had come to the meeting with a number of questions to raise. Although he had tried to get people he knew to raise some of these questions, he saw that they were not speaking, and so he raised some of them himself.

The teacher Dhaskalos was a man who during previous years in village affairs had often found himself on the opposite side to Vourros (pp. 140–3). Now he was one of the few villagers who consistently raised questions from the floor. For example, he asked whether the system of deciding cutting order could not be decentralized, and each village have a committee which would arrange the cutting order for its own members. In this way, since at the village level everyone knew the special needs and problems of the other, allowances could be made, and a watch could be kept on the just execution of the queue order. From the Chair, Azinas replied that he was against this proposal: 'I cannot accept that—you'd all quarrel among yourselves.'

Dhaskalos replied spiritedly, 'No, we wouldn't.'

'Not in your village, perhaps,' Azinas conceded, but he did not alter his rejection of the proposal.

The idea of village-level control arose also in a suggestion from Vourros, that each village have an Advisory Committee, which would function to keep the main CITCOP Committee informed of village-level complaints and problems. Azinas, from the Chair, showed himself against this too. Being a skilful chairman he was able to turn down certain suggestions by the simple expression of an authoritative opinion. Since Vourros and Dhaskalos had not organized support in the meeting for such specific suggestions, and apparently had no appetite for turning them from the floor into substantive issues, they were forgotten as soon as Azinas had spoken against them. It would have taken a far greater investment of time and effort to bring such proposals to the level of issues to be formally voted on by the members of the Co-operative. Thus, the lack of conscious organization kept the criticisms of the CITCOP management on the level of the *ad hoc* ventilation of grievances.[3]

The most difficult decision facing Vourros during the meeting was over the question of the acounts; the fact that 600 boxes of fruit had been lost, yet the loss not recorded in the accounts, troubled him. He at one point suggested that the meeting should not accept the accounts as rendered. Azinas quietly pointed out that never in the history of the Co-operative Movement had this happened, and it would create a very bad impression were it to happen now on the strangers (non-members) present.[4] Vourros asked if the Commissioner would appoint a committee of inquiry to examine the accounts, composed of qualified members but picked from members not on the main committee. Azinas agreed to appoint an investigative audit committee, and said he would make a note of Vourros's wishes on the composition of this committee, but did not promise to stand by them. Vourros felt, following Azinas's appeal and his readiness to appoint a committee, that he should not press the non-acceptance of the accounts. He also thought it unlikely he would obtain sufficient votes (51 per cent) from among those present, since he believed the majority of members were from Market Town and would be inclined to vote against something they would interpret as an attack on 'their' committee. He had noticed that the several Market Town people he had asked to raise issues had refrained from doing so. In this way the accounts came to be approved.

The meeting, then, appeared to be dominated by Vourros and a number of other critics, most of whom were not from Market Town. The potentially critical issue—the approval of the accounts—did not produce cleavage. Commissioner Azinas in his summing-up speech took up a number of the points raised from the floor and discussed them, which gave members the impression that their comments and grievances were taken seriously. He particularly asked the members to make use of his office, which cost the tax payers a large sum of money, to make their complaints felt. That, he insisted, was what he and his staff were there for, but little or no use had previously been made of them. The A.G.M. was not the place to raise such issues; it was better to raise them as they occurred. They should also take matters to the manager of the organization.

At the end of the meeting Vourros deliberately rushed up to the rostrum and shook hands one by one with each member of the Committee, to show them that his criticisms were in the interests of technical efficiency and not in the nature of personal attacks. Later he visited the Market Town Orchard Owners' Club and made a point of chatting with a number of prominent growers for the same reason.

On some issues Vourros was disappointed with the way the meeting had gone. He had for example, asked Patris to raise some questions, but although Patris had come to the meeting he had not opened his mouth. Vourros apparently did not understand this.

However, an analysis of some of the network relations between Patris and Azinas suggests why he failed to raise the issues. First, Patris's son-in-law, D. Fanos, is related to Azinas in several ways. He is an employee in the Department of Co-operatives. In recent years he has moved from active national political support for Dr. Lyssarides, to support for Azinas (pp. 156–7). Azinas, as is well known throughout the island, is the unofficial leader of PEK, the National Farmers' Union. Thus, D. Fanos is both employee and political client of Commissioner Azinas.

But Patris is also linked to Azinas in other ways. First, he has for many years been a local representative of PEK, which although it has been somewhat quiescent in village affairs, was at the time of my fieldwork undergoing a revival. Secondly, Patris's wife's brother was at university with Azinas, and with a third man, Orphanos, who holds an important position in PEK. The close friendship of these three men and their common political views are still well known to Patris. He thus has two links to Azinas through affines as well as his own formal political link.

Patris's relation to Vourros is one of relative warmth and friendship. But whereas Vourros is economically independent, Patris sees himself (in spite of his very large land holding) as a man with a limited range of options. His seven daughters are an ever-present burden: in his own view it would have been irresponsible of him to appear openly to criticize a man as powerful and well-disposed to him as Azinas.

To Vourros, criticism of the way CITCOP is run does not constitute either an attack on Azinas or disloyalty to him. Vourros's view of the norms of bureaucratic efficiency demand the use of open criticism. But to Patris the criticism was likely to be interpreted by Azinas as ingratitude. To the extent that Vourros failed to foresee the view Patris would take, he had misread the situation.

1969—VOURROS'S CAMPAIGN FOR SUPPORT

Three months after this meeting I left the island and did not return until December 1969. I was thus not able to see how far the villagers continued to be interested in or critical of the running of the Co-operative. However, from my inquiries on returning it did not appear that the affairs of CITCOP had been in the forefront of the villagers' minds, and this is not surprising since, as has been said earlier, relatively few of them are directly affected by it. In addition, the competing attractions of the continuing national political campaigns added an interest to life usually lacking. However, towards the end of 1969 Vourros had been elected to the committee of the Kalo Co-operative Retail Shop, a responsibility he was taking up with some enthusiasm. It became apparent that his appetite was increasing for involvement in the affairs of the community in which so much of his economic interests were tied up. The Co-operative Shop has an annual turnover of £50,000 (an annual average household expenditure on consumption of nearly £170 a year) and thus requires skilful management.

Shortly after my return I attended a meeting of this committee, which Vourros was chairing. Also present on the committee was Patris, and during the course of the meeting Patris's son-in-law, D. Fanos, arrived and informally sat in on the meeting. This illustrates the extent to which in village affairs everyone is living in everyone else's pockets. Vourros knows that D. Fanos is an employee of Azinas, and that there thus exists a possible flow of information back to the Commissioner on the relative efficiency of Vourros on the Co-op Shop Committee. D. Fanos has no formal right to attend these meetings but the world of the village is not a formal world, and since D. Fanos is closely related to nearly every member of the committee by kinship, affinity or friendship, and is also an influential person in village affairs in his own right, it was extremely unlikely that anyone would have suggested he leave.

There had been a number of events during 1969 which, while they had not attracted much attention in Kalo, had involved Vourros. The most important of these was his realization that in Market Town there was pronounced hostility on the part of a number of large growers in the Market Town Citrus Growers' Club to the idea of a Citrus Marketing Board. There are successful marketing boards for both potatoes and carrots, and in the view of certain experts the greatest weakness in citrus marketing in Cyprus is its failure to produce one, in contrast to most other major citrus-producing countries. Vourros was aware of these views, and felt that the issue was not getting a proper hearing. It was clear that one consequence of such a Board would be greatly to diminish the personal power of Commissioner Azinas, as well as a number of people who regard themselves as his political clients. In some quarters it was thought likely that Azinas had encouraged the criticisms of the Marketing Board proposal which were being voiced in Market Town.

Vourros tried to get the matter openly debated in an extraordinary general meeting; he easily obtained the 25 signatures he needed to call such a meeting, by visiting the villages, but only 150 people turned up to the meeting. Since constitutionally the meeting needed 25 per cent of the 900 members to pass any resolutions binding on the members, Vourros was at least 100 people short of his target. The meeting did not even officially discuss the issue of a Marketing Board. Vourros's initiative was, then, a failure. It made it clear to Azinas that Vourros was likely to have strong views on the Marketing Board issue.

Of course the issues behind a decision to set up or not to set up such a Board are not normally decided on the village level. It is reasonable to suppose that the major departments of government will have differing interests on such a proposal. However, it is fairly obvious that the Board would have had far less chance of coming into existence if it could have been plausibly shown that a majority of citrus producers were themselves opposed to the idea.

The Minister of Commerce was certainly interested in the creation of such a Board. It was pointed out to him by Vourros in a chance meeting that a number of smaller producers had not understood the draft proposal for the Board that the Minister had tabled, and that they thought the Board was against small producers. It would thus be advisable for the Minister to send someone to explain the position. The Minister agreed with alacrity. He said he would send someone to the extraordinary general meeting called by Vourros. However, no one appeared from his Ministry, and it is possible that Azinas took administrative steps to insure that he was unavailable to give permission to the Commerce Ministry official to attend the meeting.

The other major issue in CITCOP during 1969 was the resignation from the Co-operative of a number of major producers. Some of these men were very large businessmen who have diverse interests, and thus do not depend on citrus. Others were more specialized. But it was estimated that some ten producers, between them producing some 8,000,000 fruit a year, had withdrawn from the Co-operative, on the general grounds that it was not being efficiently enough run to suit their interests. There was some discussion among other members, particularly in the village of Mastia, whether or not to do the same. One proposal was to form a series of smaller co-operatives, perhaps based on villages. Vourros in some moods saw the issue as having implications for the actual *survival* of CITCOP, for if enough people left the organization would collapse. But at other times he saw it more as a question of shaking up the committee.

The week before the December 1969 A.G.M. he visited Mastia village. The village, large and prosperous, on the main Market Town–Nicosia road, has a Graduates' Club. Here he stopped, to discuss the forthcoming meeting with various friends and acquaintances who were members of the Co-operative. In this discussion two themes evolved. One was of the common hostility to a Market Town-dominated administration; the other which was closely linked with it, was that more competent educated men were needed on any future committee. Vourros and another teacher, a Mastia man called Chilos, who had been prominent on the floor in the previous A.G.M., were now fairly openly canvassing support. They agreed that it would be a good idea to divide up the key questions to be raised at the A.G.M., between the villages and between different individuals. The topics raised at this discussion included problems about sales; problems of favouritism and inefficiency in the packing factory; the issue of whether in the future fruit should be sold by weight or by numbers; the problem of inadequate technical research on problems such as the creation of the juice extraction plant; the problem of the resignation of important members; and the feeling of Market Town domination. This meeting broke up having agreed to have separate village meetings to plan tactics in a few days.

This informal discussion made it clear to me that Vourros was not by any means a lone voice in being critical of the CITCOP administration, although he was a particularly articulate one. A number of other educated villagers in other villages had criticisms to make and they were prepared to organize informally to put across their point of view.

During the next week he mentioned the importance of attending the A.G.M. to a number of Kalotes, and was active in the region generally. He was able to discuss details of the CITCOP accounts informally with D. Fanos, who had been promoted during 1969 in the Co-operative Development Department, and was one of the key persons to carry out the CITCOP audit on which the accounts were based.

Vourros had suggested a village meeting, and on the day agreed a number of key persons were waiting in the coffee-shop for him to turn up. When he arrived, D. Fanos said to him jokingly, in his role as a CITCOP official, 'You'll cut us into little bits, I'm afraid. . . .' But no one suggested that D. Fanos might have a conflict of interest, and should be asked to leave. Vourros started to go through a list of Kalo people who could be relied on to ask crucial questions. Someone mentioned The Lion, a tough and fairly independent-minded farmer with a solid land holding. But he was ruled out, since he occasionally took temporary work as a checker for CITCOP, 'and he'd have to think about his future'. The Lute-Player was suggested, one of a number of leftish brothers. But he was ruled out for the same reason—he occasionally worked as a checker. Vourros started to get irritated. 'I don't want it to be like last year, when several people said they would ask questions, and then didn't,' he grumbled. D. Fanos had already said it was better for the questions to be spread, and not all to come from Vourros.

There were some sixteen CITCOP members at this village meeting, most of whom were solid land holders. Vourros took the initiative, somewhat to the irritation of Dhaskalos, and started to bring up topics which should be raised. Vourros mentioned that a man who was a brother of a committee member had managed to get all his fruit cut before April, and that this should be raised. D. Fanos made a mollifying remark, and then Vourros said to him, 'Don't mention this to the committee, will you?'

D. Fanos said, 'Maybe I shouldn't be here now?' A number of people all said, 'No, no', meaning that is was perfectly acceptable for him to be there. The implication was that he was thoroughly trusted. 'Well', D. Fanos added, 'I'll be at CITCOP tomorrow but I won't mention it. . . .'

Vourros now made a little speech, 'We've got to break up the family alliances down there at CITCOP. We've got to show them we know they're running it as a *family* business. . . .'

At this point D. Fanos got up and said, 'Look, I'm going for many reasons. You understand—I'm in a delicate position. . . .' There were murmurs of assent on all sides. He left. The meeting went on. Vourros briefed people on a number of questions, but also on some issues, such as the desirability of adopting a shift system, instead of allowing women to work overtime up to a twelve hour stint, when their efficiency would be greatly reduced.

Then he started fishing for more ammunition to use against the committee. He himself cited the fact that when producers brought in quantities of reject fruit, to be sold very cheaply for juicing, they were not given receipts. This meant that there was an opportunity for sharp practice. He then turned to a man known to have done a lot of work for CITCOP and asked him to give other examples. 'I haven't seen anything,' he answered sheepishly. 'Come off it,' Vourros said. 'Well, then, there was the case of Andreas . . .' he mentioned the name of a senior civil servant. 'Ah ha, now you're talking,' said Vourros. 'There are lots of cases come to think of it,' he said. Vourros now told the meeting that if at the A.G.M. people were asked to give examples of queue-jumping or other favours, they should name names. D. Fanos's brother, A. Fanos, who was still present at the meeting, said, 'But Vourros, that's a bit hard since if someone told you something in confidence and then you use it, he will know.' Vourros agreed that this was tricky, but said they could get a third party to supply the details in such cases. He continued to press the man for more details.

He asked a youngish, unsophisticated farmer to ask about the builder on the Committee who had received the contract to build the main factory. He wanted the farmer to ask about the fact that the building contract stipulated £700 of iron which was missing from the building. When it was objected that on a question like this source and evidence would certainly be asked for, Vourros said, 'Refer to me. I know that the architect in question resigned from CITCOP over this and is ready to go to court about it.'

Now Vourros had been in possession of this information for a long time, and had not seen fit to raise it himself. Had it been raised, it would have caused a major uproar, and he was not unaware of this. The builder in fact had from the podium (where he sat with the other committeemen) blustered fiercely at Vourros at the last A.G.M., but later Azinas had made it clear to him that he had better control his tongue, since Vourros knew quite enough about his affairs to make life hot for him. How far Vourros had now considered the wisdom of asking a young farmer to raise this issue is not clear. In the event, the farmer did not ask this question, and it is not surprising that he didn't. But nor did Vourros.

THE 1970 A.G.M.

After the Kalo discussion, some seventeen Kalotes attended the A.G.M., and most of them had been present at the village meeting. Vourros himself made a poor start with a somewhat rambling speech but after he sat down questions from the floor came briskly. The range of topics raised was wide. One questioner asked why the men who had looked into the operation of juice extraction plants abroad had not included someone technically qualified; another asked why some members had been paid for their produce after long delays, and this man received strong support from the floor there were heated exchanges over problems of doing business with the Soviet Union, and only strong intervention from the chair kept some of the more politically partisan members from injecting party political views into the situation.

Vourros recovered from his weak start with a very searching question which involved names, dates, and exact prices of members, produce sold in the U.K. He had in fact got his information on a trip to Britain for other purposes, but it was in any case a bold and detailed question which most members had neither the opportunity nor the self-confidence to ask. The chairman acknowledged the force of Vourros's question.

Lawyer Aglas made two attempts to speak neither of which were impressive. The first time, Azinas jokingly put him in his place, implying that he was trying to teach the chairman his own business; the second time, he appeared to a number of members to be fairly blatantly seeking votes in his role as candidate for a national political party, the Progressive Front.

There were searching questions from the floor about the committee's attitude to a proposed Citrus Marketing Board, and here Azinas came to the committee's defence. There were then a series of sharp questions from the floor in which members claimed that the manager of CITCOP and his office staff had been unresponsive to members' complaints and difficulties. Here Azinas replied that an A.G.M. was not the proper place to take up such issues, which should properly be brought to his office, the Department of Co-operatives, if satisfaction was not gained locally. He returned to this in his summing-up speech[5] urging members to think about large issues, and not to pick on small ones, to make more use of his supervisory office, which had a legal obligation to investigate all complaints. He acknowledged Vourros's opening point, that certain important members had been lost. He reminded members that the give-and-take of criticism and self-criticism were essential to the health of the organization. He hoped 1970 would be a better year.

After this meeting the committee, and a number of notables including Vourros and Aglas, went off to a meal at the CITCOP factory. The atmosphere was jocular, with much joking between Vourros and certain committee members about Vourros's critical role. He was going out of his way to show the committee that his criticisms were not 'personal' and that his aims were nothing more than the protection of his own economic interests through the Co-op success.

He was in fact pleased with the way the meeting had gone. Although his own early performance had been poor, the fruits of his organizational work had been plentiful, in the volume and acuity of questions from the floor. Certain villagers told me that in the early years of CITCOP most people had been most unwilling to ask questions. They said that members were now learning to take a more positive interest in the way their organization was run.

It is clear from the activities of Vourros that members relied on elite persons to take the main initiatives and needed to be encouraged to participate themselves more actively. Certain remarks of the Commissioner suggest that the wish to see members participate more fully and in a more bureaucratically sophisticated fashion is not a monopoly of the village school-teachers. However, it is not clear that Vourros, Azinas and other educated people fully understand why villagers find participation difficult. Vourros claimed to be puzzled after this A.G.M. that the question he had suggested to the young farmer about the builder had not been asked. He had in the same way been puzzled over Patris's failure to ask a question. But whereas Patris's failure could be explained not so much by the content of the question but by the *act* of questioning persons to whom he owes loyalty and support, in the case of the young farmer the content of the question in itself is reason enough. Villagers do not deliberately make enemies in such a public way. They do not separate the performance of a bureaucratic role from the person of the per-former, and thus any attack is seen by them as a *personal* attack. Vourros himself, although he makes such distinctions, is still sufficiently cautious to avoid a direct confrontation either with Azinas or the CITCOP Committee over critical issues which privately, and on the verbal level, he feels very strongly about. He can be said to operate the same political culture from a position of greater personal security than the young farmer and with more subtlety. But it is still in its essence the *same* political culture and the same public cautiousness.

SUBSEQUENT DEVELOPMENTS: THE SUMMER 1970 E.G.M. AND AFTER

I was not in Cyprus from January to May, 1970. When I returned, it was to face a new development. An Extraordinary General Meeting had been called for June 27 to discuss serious losses which had taken place. Consignments of members' fruit had been sold in the U.K. at give-away prices, and an estimated loss of £120,000 on one consignment had occurred. More members had withdrawn, feeling was running high, and once again Vourros was in doubt about what line he should take since he claimed to fear the imminent dissolution of the organization.

Azinas opened the meeting by asking how many of those pre-sent were from the villages, as opposed to Market Town. On my impressionistic count, about three-quarters of those present were villagers. Azinas then proceeded to a somewhat edited statement of the circumstances of the major loss. These had been, in brief, that the sales representatives had taken a decision not to sell at 22/- a box, and thereafter the price had continued to fall. To gain time, the fruit already docked in London had been put at great expense into cold storage, where it had quickly rotted. It had then been sold at knock-down prices, and the bills for the cold storage also had to be met. The result pleased no one.

Members started rapidly to fire questions at Azinas and the committee members. Vourros then rose to make a major speech in which he mentioned many themes from his speeches in previous meetings. He was interrupted a number of times by the committee from the platform, and in response he offered to give up the microphone. When he looked like being stopped there were shouts from all over the hall of *ás milísi* (let him speak). Then a senior official said sarcastically from the podium 'Perhaps Mr. Vourros wishes to become an M.P.?' a remark which was thought by many people to be highly insulting. Vourros riposted and went on with his speech. The gist of this was that many mistakes had been made through over-confidence, lack of attention to detail, to scientific and technical knowledge, and he included here an oblique reference to the lack of iron in the factory, but that now they were confronted with the seriousness of the mistakes it was the time for unity, for critical analysis, and a new course.

Later in the E.G.M. a member called for the resignation of the committee. Vourros, however, rose to say that nothing would be served by demanding their resignation now. They only had four months to go, and they should stay till then. But later he pressed Azinas for the technical details of the elections for a new committee. Later still he strongly endorsed the idea that when the time came for new elections, some of the committee should remain since their experience would be valuable. He stressed, however, that the committee badly needed new blood of specialists, economists and scientists. 'When I asked three years ago why we didn't have an economist on the committee and suggested that we get one, not one of these gentlemen' (here he indicated the committee above and behind him on the podium) 'offered to resign in order to put in an economist. And I myself, with a university degree would never have done what the committee did—start inviting bids for the juice extraction plant without having the relevant research done.'

The four main speakers at the E.G.M. were all teachers, including one from Market Town. A young man stated his own readiness as a trained economist to aid the committee in any way possible, and Commissioner Azinas made a note of his name; the leftists in the meeting were extremely restrained in their criticism of the committee.

In the main the keynote of this meeting was the admission of serious errors, and the need for a change. The fact that the Manager was not present but still in the U.K. was taken by many people to mean that he was unable to face the criticism, the brunt of which would inevitably have been laid to his charge, and it appeared from his summing-up speech that Azinas took this view too. There was even a question from the floor about the health of the Manager, since there were numerous rumours during 1969 that he had a heart condition. This was strongly denied from the platform.[6]

The final event which must put this protracted narrative into perspective, occurred in the winter of 1970.[7] Elections were held for the CITCOP committee, and after much behind-the-scenes manoeuvring on all sides, both Vourros and the Mastia teacher Chilos were elected to the important executive committee of CITCOP. They are both village-born university graduates, who are, as yet, trusted by villagers to represent village interests as well as for their efficiency. They replaced two Market Town farmers, each of whom had had primary education only. As villagers they could be relied on to see that Market Townsmen didn't have things all their own way. Vourros, born in Kammari and married to a Kalo girl from a large kindred, could in any case rely on solid support from these two villages. The election did not go to a vote, but was more a 'feeling of the meeting' approach. Azinas was heard to remark that now the teachers would 'eat' the organization (meaning, would dominate it). He was probably not entirely serious in saying this, but word of it got back to Vourros who then and there threatened to resign; diplomatic mediation by D. Fanos, on Azinas's instructions, brought Vourros back into active co-operation; he had made his point at the start.

Before this election, Kalo opinion had been divided over the simple problem of whether or not Market Town people would be ready to vote an outsider man onto the committee, and whether they would support Vourros or not. Some people maintained that the townspeople would only vote for their own. Others said that after the mismanagement and losses in CITCOP, and after the public energy of Vourros on these matters, townspeople would vote him in just to get things run better. Although I was not

present for the election and thus cannot be sure just what processes were at work, the outcome favours the view of those who
thought that bureaucratic values and long-term self-interest would
prevail over the more particularist ones and a shorter-term self-
interest. In each case the growers were interested in the good
management of their affairs. The issue was one of their perceptions and values about which method of committee selection
would best satisfy their needs. One Kalo teacher put it in simple
terms when he said, 'When Vourros first started criticizing the
CITCOP committee the townspeople used to get angry with him.
Now they've understood him a bit better.'

CONCLUSION

At the start of the previous chapter I looked forward to the
CITCOP material, and suggested in a general way that the dam
issue affected the co-operative issue, and vice versa. Now I shall
make more explicit the points of comparison and the relation
between them.

In both situations there is a basic cleavage between Market
Town and the interests of a number of villages. The villages are
not the same in both cases since, for example, Mastia and Mené
are not required to contribute to the proposed Dam, but they do
provide a large number of CITCOP members. Avla and Posto
have little citrus produce, and hardly figure in the Co-operative's
affairs. But both Kammari and Kalo are prominent and have important economic interests in both situations. Both CITCOP and
the Dam have been issues since the early 1960s. The traditional
rivalry of the villages with the town received a particular impetus
from the dramatic economic boom enjoyed by the town through
its entry into citrus production earlier and more intensively than
the villages. Little Market Town land is now used for anything
else but citrus, whereas the villages still have substantial land
in less profitable activities. Many town houses are strikingly
more luxurious than most village houses. Market Town is *not*
a village any longer, and has pretensions to urbanity. All these
factors are present alongside the economic interests of CITCOP
and the Dam, and they have been in continuous process for over
seven years.

In both situations ordinary villagers depend on more educated
men to take initiatives and provide leadership in conflicts outside

TABLE 13

CITCOP Management Committee 1963–70

Old Executive Committee	New Members 1970
(1) from Market Town secondary education white-collar	(1) continued in office
(2) from Market Town primary education farmer	(2) continued in office
(3) from Market Town primary education farmer	(3) Vourros, from Kalo village university degree teacher
(4) from Market Town secondary education white collar	(4) from Market Town primary education builder (formerly no. 7 on old committee)
(5) from Market Town secondary education white collar	(5) Chilos, from Mastia village university education teacher

Old Supervisory Committee	
(6) from Market Town secondary education white collar	(6) from Market Town secondary education white collar (formerly no. 4 on old committee)
(7) from Market Town primary education builder	(7) from Market Town secondary education retired teacher
(8) from Market Town primary education farmer	(8) from Market Town secondary education teacher
(9) from Nicosia secondary education farmer	(9) continued in office
(10) from village ? education white collar	(10) continued in office

the village. For practical reasons this tends to have a basis in the
superior abilities of men like Aglas and Vourros to handle the
details of bureaucracy—the interpretation of laws, constitutions,
minutes; all the paraphernalia of literacy and administration in
complex organizations. But although higher education often
confers advantage in such matters, it is neither a necessary nor
sufficient condition for competence. A number of men of little
formal education, such as Sklyros (and many leftists, who in the
words of D. Fanos, 'read a lot') have mastered such matters.
The other reason then that villagers are so dependent on elite
leaders stems from the status values of the society, and its tendency to equate high status with power. To be a villager, in
most situations, is not only to be less able in administration but
also to be of lower status and weaker in terms of power. Also, it is
always *safer* for villagers if they are pushing educated men ahead
of them, since this does not expose them as individuals to great
risk. It is not necessary for this argument's validity that villagers
should be heard consciously discussing the desirability of avoiding risk by sheltering behind educated, wealthy men, in their
attempts to crack the nut of Market Town particularism. Their
motives have been inferred from a more general understanding of
village values and behaviour.

Material from other societies, including several accounts of
Indian villages, suggests a greater distance between villagers and
elite members is common, and that the way in which this gap
is bridged (however ambiguously) is by brokers and middlemen;
Bailey suggests that 'peasant conservatism' is directly related
to this gap, to the failure of modernizing administrators to explain to peasants in comprehensible terms the advantages, real or
supposed, of new policies.

My data are somewhat different. Both Aglas and Vourros
although urban residents are sons of the village. However high
their status, they are essentially village boys made good. Their
families were both large landowners, but their fathers were both
peasant farmers and thus manual workers, their mothers illiterate.
They both have important land holdings in the village, and thus
realistically present themselves as politically active not from any
desire to run other people's affairs or get to positions of power,
but because they literally have a stake in the issues. The readiness
with which most villagers accept their leadership stems from a
reservoir of trust accorded to sons of the village in its external
affairs, to which is added an additional trust based on the obvious

and acceptable activism of able men with economic interests to defend. I have already spoken of the value of *synféron*, self-interest, with which almost all actions in Cyprus must be ultimately justified. It is acceptable to villagers that Aglas and Vourros work hard at certain village affairs out of *synféron*.

This situation suggests, perhaps, why notions such as Banfield's 'amoral familism' add little to our understanding of peasant political behaviour. On the level of their statements about values, Cypriot villagers with their perpetual appeals to *synféron* are as amoral familists as any to be found. Yet they enter into co-operative organizations, and take corporate action under the direction of their educated men, to further their interests. Self-interest may be pursued collectively, and leaders may be trusted, when certain interests are common to all and when membership in a common moral community provides some actors with instruments of social control over others. This will always be a matter of context and perceptions.

The fact that sons of the village start out with this much credit does not mean they are granted infinite licence. As soon as some of the sharp-eyed people in the village realized that Aglas was using the Dam campaign as a political springboard, they withdrew some of their previous goodwill towards him. Also, when the CITCOP committee man interrupted Vourros's eloquence with the thought that perhaps he had his eye on the House of Representatives, this was a serious insult, and he in fact explicitly rejected it when he replied, 'I am not trying to become an M.P. because I know I wouldn't be up to it.' The substance of this charge is that one is mixing oil and water, the national arena with local affairs, and hints at the possibility of the betrayal of primordial ties for 'outside' interests.

These, then, were some of the similarities between the course of the Dam Campaign, and the course of CITCOP administration. But there are important differences. First, the issue of the Avla Dam is in an obvious way many-sided, to take even a narrow view. The parties are the villages, the town and the Civil Service assorted Ministers, even the President. In the later stages, when the political parties took up the Dam issue, the issue became more complex. Extraordinary political action, both the demonstration and the Advisory Committee, contributed elements of innovation in village politics, and even in national political life. The issue remained for many years outside the scope of national politics, but soon after the emergence of political parties the

Dam became a party issue, and in my last visit to the area during the summer of 1970 two of the nationalist parties were competing to monopolize the issue: each tried to seem pre-eminent in putting pressure on the government.

To achieve their goal the villages must have the specialist opinion of government experts on their side (or force their hand politically) and must also deal with problems of constitutional law if Market Town continues its obstruction. The Constitution thus becomes a resource which is more useful to one side than the other. But, in this case, it is balanced by the opinions of government experts, a resource which favours the villagers over the townspeople.

Aglas was unable to achieve his more personal goal, since his electoral success was tied to the regional performance of his party to be described in the next chapter. His election results in the immediate villages were excellent. But his aggregate results in the region were not strong enough to overcome the regional defeat of his party (although in theory he could have been elected however badly his party did). The rewards of being an M.P. are considerable—a salary of £200 a month; this is a vast gilt-edged security for even a professional man like the lawyer, as well as carrying high national status.

The Kalo CITCOP members had no more clearly defined corporate interest than their wish not to come second-best to Market Town. This is a diffuse goal, which could be satisfied in a number of ways. On one level it was satisfied by getting up at CITCOP meetings and expressing general or particular dissatisfactions. In this they were following a cultural rule which suggests a man must not be taken advantage of by another without reacting. To accuse the committee of partiality is to show that one is alive to one's rights, and to shame and slightly dishonour those who seek to erode or trample on those rights. I do not mean to imply that the villagers have no interest in the material improvement of their situation, but to point to the similarity with the formation in the heat of the moment, of the Advisory Committee, which was then allowed to lapse, and the voicing of impromptu criticisms at the A.G.M.s, while in each case leaving the hard thinking and organizing to the educated. The meaning of voicing criticisms for ordinary villagers may be expressive of their view that Market Towners are no better than they themselves, and are nothing but jumped-up villagers whose impudence must be challenged or countered. To men like Vourros, the same action is seen as an instrumental attack on an organizational problem. He is shrewd enough and at home enough in the village actively to employ the villagers' feelings that the townspeople must not be allowed to 'do what they like', but implicitly, the villagers are shrewd enough to let him take the major risks. There is some suggestion in my material that villagers are getting more inclined to stand up for their rights; perhaps what started as a direct response may, in time with practice and self-confidence, become a habit and a reflex.

NOTES

1. Citrus fruit can remain on the trees while flowers bloom for the next season's crop. Old fruit may stay on a tree alongside new fruit.
2. Later when Vourros went to CITCOP offices and asked to see the minutes the manager said he would have to get special permission from the Commissioner.
3. At the end of the last chapter I suggested that this was one of the things the Kalo Advisory Committee had done; and that this release of tension may have served to insure that the Committee itself would do nothing, for in its *formation* was its true purpose.
4. I have already described in the last chapter how my presence with a village committee in the office of a civil servant was used by both sides in their manoeuvres against the other. This illustrates the conventional difficulty when the simple fact of the observer's presence modifies the situation he wishes to observe, but it also underlines the self-conscious political culture of Cypriot society and perhaps suggests why I have often adopted an oblique approach to dealings with higher officials and politicians.
5. Under the co-operative law, the Commissioner has important powers of intervention, veto or final decision in the running of any co-operative. In the meetings described here, the CITCOP manager and the committee constantly deferred to the Commissioner, and he constantly interrupted them if he thought they were handling issues improperly or incompetently. In each meeting I attended he always ended with a summing-up speech, given with great clarity and authority. He constantly put people right on points of co-operative law, and just what they could and could not do in a meeting.
6. The manager died of a heart attack six months later; his condition was certainly known to some senior co-op officials.
7. Most of the material used in this chapter comes from my observations at two CITCOP A.G.M.s, and one Extraordinary General Meeting. The period covered is from January 1969 to June 1970, during which eighteen months I spent eight months in Cyprus, the end of my main fieldwork period, and two later short trips, each of which happily coincided with a CITCOP meeting. It is worth pointing out that after the first A.G.M. certain committee members thought I should not be allowed

to be present again since I had seen them in dispute 'and this would give a bad impression'. I hastened to reassure these men (a) that I regarded such disputes as normal and useful to the organization and (b) that I would not use real names.

10
Election

INTRODUCTION

In July 1970 elections for the Legislative Assembly took place for the first time in ten years, and most of this chapter will be concerned with them. The general political background has already been outlined (pp. 18–22, 132–4) but the particular events which led up to the elections are now described, particularly the emergence of formal political parties; then certain local events, linked to underground groups operating elsewhere in Cyprus, are described. The most striking cleavage in Kalo was between two nationalist parties, and this is traced to the murder of a young villager in 1963, and the way in which this murder has since then altered factional alignments to national political leaders, who themselves have changed in their alignments.

From there, I turn to the specific campaigns in the locality of these two parties, and analyse in detail the election appeals of party leaders, and the response to these appeals of village activists. These responses involved a number of incidents which brought opposed activists into opposition in the village, and threatened to breach village solidarity. How these incidents were handled, and how the norm of solidarity was invoked to do this, lead to analysis of village voting behaviour, and the linking of local to national themes in electoral appeals.[1]

NEW PARTIES EMERGE

In 1960, at the start of Independence, there was political compromise among the Greek community, in order to start the new status on the most favourable terms. AKEL, the communist party, agreed to accept 5 out of the 35 Greek seats in the Legislative Assembly, which was almost certainly many less than they might have won in full contest. The other 30 seats went to a loose coalition of 'nationalist' elements, the Patriotic Front which was less a party than an alliance of individuals. Fifteen seats, and the office of Vice-President went to the Turkish community.

The Turkish secession of 1963–4 did much to keep Greek political leaders in loose unity, but the enmity between Makarios, and the former EOKA commander Grivas was a continual feature of political life; most Greek leaders decided to support President Makarios, his cabinet, and the *status quo*. But there were occasional alarms and excursions which looked like altering the main balance of power between Makarios and Grivas. Then, too, the atmosphere of armed confrontation with the Turks, of paranoid security precautions, as well as the presence of numerous foreign embassies pursuing different cold war policies, all added to the intrigue and uncertainty. New alliances, threats, spying rumours and coup plots were the daily stuff of Greek Cypriot newspapers during the independence decade. Relations between the main Greek political leaders were constantly shifting, or looking as if they might shift. If these leaders were patrons of village clients, then stones cast into the waters of Nicosia politics often produced disturbing ripples in villages far from the centre.

But after five years of 'crisis government' (1963–8) the unity of Greek politicians was beginning to wear a little thin, and one response to this emerged in the problem of the postponed elections to the Assembly. These should have taken place in July–August 1965, but were continually postponed since they would, it was argued, have promoted disunity among the Greeks, and thus furthered Turkish interests.

Throughout 1968 there was discussion in the press as to whether or not there would be organized party life and elections. Those papers which were against the government wanted elections because they hoped to gain ground; those which supported the government hoped that elections would strengthen the government's mandate. Under the Cypriot system, the President is elected, and then appoints his ministers who need not be Representatives, or be approved by the Legislative Assembly. The Assembly itself has the right to vote for or against ministerial budgets. Under certain conditions it can also initiate legislation. So the legitimacy of the government does not depend directly on the existence of parties or on the composition of the Assembly. However, under normal circumstances the Assembly would have played a more sharply critical role in its relation to the government. The exceptional inter-communal issues of 1963 onwards made it possible for the Assembly to avoid this responsibility in the name of national solidarity and support for the President. The other factor which contributed to this was the personal prestige of Makarios himself coupled with his not inconsiderable powers of patronage. The Assembly became so identified with support for the government that only new elections could make clear how much support the policies of Makarios enjoyed.

When in February 1969 Makarios gave his formal approval for the formation of political parties the first men off the mark were the English-trained barrister Glafkos Clerides and the former Interior Minister, Yorgadjis, who together formed the United Party (UP). I have already sketched in the events which led to the resignation of Yorgadjis from the ministry (pp. 21, 133) There was therefore widespread surprise at the alliance of these two men since it might have been thought that the area of Clerides' strongest support—the urban bourgeoisie—would be precisely the area of greatest antipathy to Yorgadjis, an upwardly-mobile village-born ex-EOKA fighter of great power but little formal education. It looked at first sight like an alliance in which Clerides would have to lose more than he gained. But Yorgadjis's rural organization of village groups was strong enough to provide a skeletal electoral machine, something which Clerides completely lacked. Three-fifths of the island's electorate are village residents, and Clerides could not afford to neglect this.

Yorgadjis in turn stood to gain increased respectability, and a share of the otherwise disaffected urban bourgeois vote. People who would never have voted for him by himself, since they regarded him as a semi-literate upstart, could not avoid voting for Clerides. Whatever their personal antipathy to Yorgadjis, they could not support Clerides' party without also supporting Yorgadjis. In terms of policy UP claimed to be a nationalist party, to be open to all nationalists, to support the tactic of intercommunal talks, to represent the interests of all classes as opposed to those of a single class; to support private enterprise, but also to favour improvements in subsidized education, medical care and other benefits. UP is widely believed to be a pro-Nato party.

Very soon after the formation of the United Party, Makarios's personal physician Dr. Vassos Lyssarides announced the formation of his own party, EDEK. This was also a nationalist party, but of a democratic-socialist and populist cast (pp. 150–1). Then Nikos Sampson announced the formation of his own Progressive

Party. Takis Evdokas, the only public opponent of Makarios was already at the head of DEK, a party which had first been formed by John Clerides (the father of Glafkos Clerides) in 1959 and always a nodal point for the most fanatic Enosists. The two right-nationalist associations, PEK and SEK, were both vertically split, since some members wanted to support the UP, and others did not. They were not political parties, but rather politicized interest groups, representing right-nationalist farmers and workers respectively. Furthermore, it was not clear how strong PEK was in organizational terms.[2] AKEL's primacy in party political experience can be judged by the fact that its main election slogan was to be '45 years in the service of the people' whereas its closest competitor in organized party terms, DEK, was just coming up to its tenth disorganized year.

From February to April 1969 the first organized party initiatives started to affect the village. The activists in the village started to discuss what sort of electoral alliances might take place between the parties which had so far officially formed. Even at this time it was clear that two possible kinds of alliance were favoured and likely; either that all the self-styled nationalist parties would form some sort of grouping against AKEL; or that several nationalist parties would combine against the UP which was seen to be a party of the 'ins'. In the early spring of 1969 both Lyssarides (EDEK) and Sampson (Progressive) made formal political speeches in Kalo, which was certainly one of the first villages in the island to attract the attention of party leaders. Both speakers drew large audiences and both meetings passed without serious incident. Lyssarides seemed to get the bigger audience, including a number of women who watched from a distance. But Sampson was carried into the villages on the shoulders of a group of unmarried men, chanting his name. Among them were a number of young relatives and former friends of the deceased Levendis. When in his speech Sampson referred to the murderers of EOKA fighters, one young man called out, 'Let us shoot them,' but Sampson immediately replied, 'No, let us bring them to justice.' There was a certain amount of tension between the supporters of the two parties over the hanging of banners and use of coffee-shop facilities: the best coffee-shop for speeches and for hanging banners happened to belong to a firm Sampson supporter, and for some time it seemed that the Lyssarides people were to be denied this facility. In the end the Sampson supporters relented. This tension was undoubtedly aggravated by the fact that some of

PARTY	AKEL Ezekias Papaioannou and central committee	EDEK Dr. Vassos Lyssarides and Takis HadjiDimitriou	PROGRESSIVE FRONT (PF) Nikos Sampson and Odysseus Ioannides	UNITED PARTY (UP) Glafkos Clerides and Polykarpos Yorgadjis (killed, March 1970)	DEK Dr. Takis Evdokas
Main leaders					
Formal attitude to Enosis (Union with Greece)	Currently favours independence for Cyprus; would consider *Enosis* with a democratic Greece	pro-*Enosis* but intensely anti-Junta; actual line close to AKEL's	pro-*Enosis* with the existing Greek government	pro-*Enosis* with the existing Greek government	very strongly pro-*Enosis*, preferably with a Right-wing Greece
Attitude to President Makarios	Strongly supports	Strongly supports	Strongly supports	Supports	Strongly critical
Main political line	Communist; pro-USSR, anti-NATO; rejects a 'right-wing monopoly of patriotism'; opposes present Greek regime	Social democrat; Greek nationalist; anti-NATO, pro-unaligned bloc, pro-Arab	Free-wheeling populist with social democratic tinge; Greek nationalist	Private enterprise anti-communist, Greek nationalist, pro-Western Europe. Popularly regarded as a pro-NATO party	Extremely anti-communist and millenarian Greek nationalist. Pro-Grivas
Probable electoral base	Manual workers of all kinds, through trade unions; some rural people; some urban intellectuals	White collar workers, and intellectuals; some rural people	Dissatisfied former EOKA militants 'wild' young men; mobile people of Greek education, hostile to the dominance of English language. Some rural people	Business and merchant interests; urban middle class; urban elite; some rural people	Deeply dissatisfied elements of a right-wing or nationalist complexion; persons hostile to Makarios; passionate believers in *Enosis now*. Pro-Greek Junta elements; some rural people
Other comments	Cautious, law-abiding low-profile, still handicapped by its exclusion from EOKA's campaign. Normally very close to Moscow. No obvious pro-Chinese faction. Some patronage power though own organisations and links to socialist bloc	Resembles the centre-left position of Andreas Papandreou in Greece, pre-1967. Strong critique of *status quo*. Little patronage power	Potentially radical, but most supporters probably have no well-developed critique of *status quo*; party for people ready to become the 'ins'. Some patronage power in armed forces	Party of the 'ins'—those who are more or less satisfied; because of Yorgadjis' years as Interior Minister has many clients in government jobs, and the strongest stock of general patronage	Never looks like gaining much ground, and very limited patronage powers

the present Sampson supporters had been involved in the episode in 1965 when the Lyssarides group meeting was harrassed (p. 153).

DISTURBANCES BEFORE THE ELECTIONS

I have already described (pp. 20–1) how the two years preceding the 1970 elections were marked by instability, some terrorism, attempted coups and murders. These events had their counterparts in the village and the surrounding district, which must be briefly mentioned.

On 1 March 1969 the chief of the Cyprus police was shot and seriously hurt in an orange grove near Market Town. A number of Kalo villagers were arrested and subsequently released without being charged. They were, it was asserted, all either enemies of Interior Minister Yorgadjis, or strong right-wing nationalists or both.

Later in 1969 two village boys were arrested for having been seen distributing leaflets in a nearby village for the *Éthnikon Metópon* (EM) the illegal organization which had just appeared pledged to the speedy achievement of *Enosis*. I was told that some of the witnesses were intimidated, that a prominent mainland Greek Army officer interceded for the arrested youths, and after a few days in prison they were released.

A third incident involved the villagers. Still later in 1969, a group of masked men carrying sub-machine guns walked into a coffee-shop in a near-by village and told everyone to put their hands up. They then gave the *múktar* of the village, an ex-EOKA fighter who had come out strongly for the UP, a rather close haircut. Six men from Kalo village were arrested for this, some of whom had also been arrested at the time of the shooting of the policeman. The police then virtually occupied the village for three days, and searched a large number of houses. Once again, after some days in prison, the six men were released. They denied that they had cut the *múktar*'s hair; but it was widely believed in the village that they had done so. Once again, their common characteristics were that they were right-wing nationalists, hostile to Yorgadjis and the UP.

Shortly after the haircut episode, came the dramatic national events mentioned earlier (p. 21) an attempt to capture Limassol police station by offshoots of the EM; many arrests and arms searches; then in March 1970 the attempted killing of President Makarios; a few days later the murder of former Interior Minister

Yorgadjis. During this period there were also continued rumours of threatened coups, and most people doubted that elections would be held at all.

I cannot say what the links were between these three village-based incidents, and the disturbances in the capital and Limassol. It is widely believed in the village that there was a strong EM cell there. One villager—an extreme right-wing nationalist closely linked to Greek army officers of similar views—was said to have been called to the Presidential Palace, and personally reprimanded by Makarios. My own view is that the village harboured a strong EM unit, which may have acted more or less autonomously. There is no point in guessing at other connections. Since the failure of the Limassol raid, people with EM connections have had good reason to be extremely cautious.

It is worth stressing again that Cypriot politics have two distinct levels: one is the formal level of public debate, newspaper articles, speeches in the Assembly and so forth; the other is the underground level of clandestine *omádhes*, secret arms dumps, involuntary haircuts, beatings and threats, midnight leaflet scattering and endless intelligence trafficking. An individual may be active at both levels, and pursue different goals with different alliances and different techniques at each level. Such a man might maintain loyalties with several national politicians, and added to this is the problem that certain groups are penetrated by people in fact loyal to other groups, playing the double game of espionage. Makarios's agents were said to have been told to join the illegal EM *omádha* for this very reason, although other people in Cyprus believed that Makarios himself had given his support to the formation of the EM for his own reasons, one of which would have been to protect himself against hostile groups.

Given the possible complexity of individual motives which such events suggest, it is not surprising that although people are very quick to invent explanations of other's motives, they readily admit when pressed that the motives of most others remain opaque, that secrecy and double-bluff men are facts of life, and this they express in the common reply to questions about where a man stands: '*piós porí na to xéri?*' 'Who can possibly know?'

THE DEATH WHICH STRUCTURED FACTIONS

Tables 15 and 16 show clearly that the election results for Nicosia district are very different from those in Kalo village. In

TABLE 15

The 1970 Legislative Assembly Elections: Kalo and Kammari

KALO VILLAGE

registered voters: 740   votes cast: 710   spoiled ballots: 36

AKEL (Communist)	DEK (Extreme Right-Nationalist)	EDEK (Left-Nationalist)	ENIÆON (UP) (United Party Nationalist)	PROÖDEFTIKI PARATAXIS(PF) Progressive Front (Populist-Nationalist)	INDEPENDENTS
(1) 238	(1) 34	(1) 208	(1) 187	(1) 339	(1) 59
(2) 231	(2) 20	(2) 107	(2) 125	(2) 310	(2) 13
	(3) 15	(3) 93	(3) 111	(3) 284	(3) 2
	(4) 13	(4) 124	(4) 121	(4) 305	(4) 2
	(5) 14	(5) 91	(5) 108	(5) 305	
	(6) 13	(6) 103	(6) 99	(6) 287	
		(7) 147	(7) 103	(7) 289	
		(8) 156	(8) 114	(8) 282	
		(9) 160	(9) 99	(9) 277	
		(10) 166	(10) 97	(10) 396	
			(11) 101	(11) 266	
			(12) 97	(12) 264	

KAMMARI VILLAGE

registered voters: 776   votes cast: 732   spoiled ballots: 16

(1) 227	(1) 38	(1) 318	(1) 280	(1) 224	(1) 55
(2) 221	(2) 22	(2) 159	(2) 268	(2) 148	(2) 25
	(3) 19	(3) 150	(3) 196	(3) 103	(3) 3
	(4) 18	(4) 472	(4) 250	(4) 123	(4) 1
	(5) 19	(5) 147	(5) 225	(5) 134	
	(6) 17	(6) 152	(6) 212	(6) 113	
		(7) 195	(7) 214	(7) 112	
		(8) 209	(8) 426	(8) 103	
		(9) 230	(9) 211	(9) 110	
		(10) 217	(10) 201	(10) 233	
			(11) 271	(11) 81	
			(12) 189	(12) 79	

1 Each voter could vote for up to 12 candidates, distributed among the parties in any combination.
2 Numbers in brackets refer to candidates.

the district, the UP won roughly three times as many votes as the PF; in Kalo the result was the reverse. There are two different sorts of reasons for this but both are grounded in village values and political culture. One which I discuss more fully later (pp. 275–7) is that lawyer Aglas, a Kalotis resident in the capital, was a PF candidate and many people voted for him because they knew him, and he was a prominent 'son of the village' who had been active over the dam campaign. The other reason is to do with the murder of another Kalotis, a former EOKA militant, Levendis (The Handsome) Tangos, and the way in which the PF leader and former EOKA militant, Sampson, took up the issue of this murder in his election campaign. To appreciate this, we must consider some details leading to the death of Levendis Tangos.

During the 1955–9 EOKA struggle, the Kalo EOKA group included two of the older Tangos brothers, Levendis, and H. Tangos, who was captured and spent six months in prison-camp. Levendis was not captured. During this period Kalo was used to hide EOKA militants on the run, and one of these was the Famagusta leader, Sampson. He became friendly with several Kalotes, and felt a sense of obligation to the village for protecting him. He baptized a child of the village EOKA leader Moustachas, and at least one other Kalo child. One of his close friends and drinking companions was Levendis Tangos, who used to visit him after 1960, at his newspaper in the capital.

In 1963 Levendis was shot and killed outside a night-club in Famagusta. A man was arrested and charged with two offences but later released after trial in the criminal court. When Levendis's family and friends first heard of his death they wanted to go into the capital with placards and banners, to hold a demonstration demanding that the killer of their brother be brought to justice. As the story is now told, they wished even then to bring certain accusations against the Minister of the Interior, Yorgadjis, who is also said to have heard of this and had the roads blocked by police units. In any case, Moustachas tried to persuade them not to do it, saying he was against it.[3]

There are now at least two conflicting accounts of the life and death of Levendis, current in the village; these accounts tend to reflect among other things the relationships of the speaker to the dead man, and/or to either Yorgadjis, his friends and the UP on one hand, or Sampson and the PF on the other.

The anti-Levendis version, which friends of Yorgadjis favour, is that although he was a courageous EOKA fighter, he was so

TABLE 16

The 1970 Legislative Assembly Election: Nicosia District

registered voters: 96,820   votes cast: 72,617   spoiled ballots: 1,781

AKEL	DEK	EDEK	ENIÆON (UP)	PROÖDEFTIKI PARATAXIS (PF)	INDEPENDENTS
(1) 27,288	(1) 10,862	(1) 23,918	(1) 27,982	(1) 14,543	(1) 9,290
(2) 27,206	(2) 7,210	(2) 10,536	(2) 26,294	(2) 10,410	(2) 1,372
	(3) 6,979	(3) 9,301	(3) 24,939	(3) 8,811	(3) 2,197
	(4) 6,710	(4) 10,040	(4) 24,638	(4) 9,309	(4) 1,449
	(5) 6,443	(5) 8,701	(5) 24,075	(5) 9,555	
	(6) 6,174	(6) 8,936	(6) 22,648	(6) 8,728	
		(7) 16,001	(7) 22,510	(7) 9,004	
		(8) 17,099	(8) 22,785	(8) 8,373	
		(9) 19,672	(9) 22,629	(9) 8,043	
		(10) 17,411	(10) 22,036	(10) 8,761	
			(11) 22,080	(11) 7,275	
			(12) 21,739	(12) 7,604	

National Results in Seats

AKEL	9
DEK	0
EDEK	2
ENIÆON (UP)	15
PROÖDEFTIKI (PF)	7
INDEPENDENTS	2

Nationally registered voters: 263,857
Votes cast: 200,141 = 75·8% turnout

praised that it tended to go to his head. His reputation attracted bad characters to him, and he became involved in robberies, and even killings for gain. He kept company with bar-girls, from whom he took money. He was feared rather than loved. He grew too big for his boots, threw his weight about just once too often and got killed in a sordid row over a woman.

The pro-Levendis version, which his close kin and other supporters of Sampson and the PF tend to maintain is that he was a courageous EOKA fighter, who was loved and admired by all. He was a high-spirited, fun-loving young man, who in his friendship with other distinguished EOKA fighters enjoyed a drink or two. He was attractive to women, but never took money from them. Any part he played in robberies was not for gain but either for EOKA funds or to help his friends. If he was involved in killings, then it was the killing of scoundrels, and money was not involved.

The pro-Levendis version then describes his killing as an act of politics which arose in the following way: Not only was he once friends with Sampson, but also with Yorgadjis. At first these two national political figures were themselves on good terms, but with the growth of rivalries between the former EOKA leaders (p. 133) they grew increasingly hostile. Levendis tried to remain on good terms with both but it became impossible. The simplest version of this is almost a morality play, on the impossibility of serving two masters, or having powerful friends at loggerheads. A more subtle version, told by close relations of the dead man is that Sampson was arrested for a killing in Kyrenia on the orders of Yorgadjis. At the time of the killing however he had been drinking in the village with Levendis, who immediately went to Yorgadjis and demanded the release of his innocent friend. Later he fired a pistol outside the home of Yorgadjis and threatened him. This challenge was not ignored, and when an opportunity arose, a client of Yorgadjis took it.

There are many variants of these two versions. In one a pamphlet war went on between Sampson and Yorgadjis. In another the killer of Levendis acted for private reasons, but Yorgadjis was his friend, and so he got off because Yorgadjis was not displeased with the result. These stories in their various forms are well known throughout the island.

There are some facts, however. Sampson, for example, gave the killing, the funeral, and the trial very full coverage in his tabloid newspaper. He attended the funeral himself, as the newspaper photographs showed, weeping openly and calling the dead man 'my brother'. He ran an editorial in his paper demanding that the 'political killings' should stop, and calling for the trial and execution of the killer. He printed a statement by the Minister of the Interior which criticized the paper for the assumption that the killing was political, when the matter was *sub judice*, to which Sampson replied. Whatever Sampson himself believed, he was far too aware of the laws of libel and other dangers to make any accusations against the Minister himself, and confined himself to calls for action by the police and justice departments.

Sampson's support in his paper for the dead man and his subsequent election speeches—which will be discussed later—made it a matter of honour for Levendis Tangos's close kin and friends to support Sampson in politics. (There is one exception, a leftist brother, Y. Tangos, who believes that Sampson merely exploits the issue. Y. Tangos voted only for the two AKEL candidates 'on principle'.) Since 1963 this has meant that numbers of villagers who otherwise would have become or remained clients of Yorgadjis and his associates have either avoided open commitment, or have come over to Sampson. I cannot give numbers, since in many cases positions in 1963 were unclear, and people are also concerned to cover their tracks. At the very least it has made it difficult for people who might out of inertia have supported the UP (originally headed jointly by Yorgadjis and Clerides) to do so in a casual spirit; and has forced them either to keep their opinions quiet, or to take the line that Sampson's supporters are in the main youngsters, would-be tough guys, whose heads have been turned by stories about Levendis, EOKA and so forth. However, when the content of Sampson's election speeches is discussed, it will appear that there was a most convenient fit between his attacks on the UP as monopolizers of patronage, and as betrayers of EOKA goals and Hellenic aspirations. His chief appeal was to those who felt themselves to be relatively powerless in the society, and so effective was this appeal that by the end of the campaign his followers believed that they would win because their cause was just; the death of Levendis, the sins of the UP and the moral rightness of the PF cause became linked symbols of intoxicating power.

THE PF CAMPAIGN IN THE DISTRICT

The most important development at the national level was the

announcement on 25 June that the Progressive *Front*, headed by
the mayor of Nicosia, Odysseus Ioannides had merged with the
Progressive *Party* of Nikos Sampson. The new grouping was to
be called the 'Progressive Front of Change and Power' (PF) and
Sampson was now called the General Organizer of the new party.
Some of his Kalo supporters were concerned that in the merger
his slate of candidates had been too greatly reduced in favour of
the other partner, and indeed the next day bitter articles appeared
in *Agon* (the UP newspaper) by some of the men Sampson left
behind,—i.e. who had failed to be adopted as candidates in the
new party—calling him 'Judas' and other choice names. The
general effect of the merger in Kalo was to hearten the members
of both former parties, since obviously under the prevailing
electoral system neither had stood much chance alone. Both
parties appealed to those strong nationalists who felt the Makarios
government had been too soft in prosecuting *Enosis* with Greece,
and in both parties were to be found a number of people who
felt that they were excluded from the monopoly of power and
privilege enjoyed by some UP supporters, and who were suspicious that the main impetus of Greek Cypriot society was
towards Britain and away from Greece.

The other important event which was announced on the same
day though in much smaller print was that the illegal *Éthnikon
Metópon* in Paphos had sent a letter to Makarios announcing its
dissolution and pledging support to him. A few days later the
Limassol branch and its dissident offshoot, the Holy Brigade,
(which between them had been responsible for the daring raid
on the Limassol Central Police Station) made similar announcements. Their move was less effective since many of them were
already prisoners of the government, but these announcements
had the effect of telling the electorate that, whatever the alarms
and tribulations of the previous eighteen months, there was unlikely to now be an important armed disruption of the electoral
process.

On 26 June Nikos Sampson was due to speak in near-by Kammari. According to Pavlos, who had been chosen as one of
Sampson's thirty-five district organizers, his presence in the
district, a district in which he was not himself standing, was a
personal favour stemming from his concern for the deceased
Levendis and his desire to help his friends. For several days
before the 26th Pavlos worked hard in the surrounding villages
to organize attendance by PF supporters at the meeting. One of

Sampson's staunchest supporters in Kalo owns a bus and a taxi, and he himself states that his commercial 'T' licence was due to a personal intervention by Sampson in the administrative process, when others including Yorgadjis had failed to do anything. This man was to be seen throughout the pre-election period continually putting his vehicles to work in support of PF meetings around the district, and loudly telling the world why he was doing so.

An hour before Sampson came, buses and cars started to arrive in Kammari, there was an excited atmosphere as old friends, and particularly old EOKA associates recognized each other and their common purpose in arriving. The excitement was intensified by Sampson's brother: every few minutes he would bellow through the highly effective amplification system some of the slogans that Sampson had been hammering home in his newspapers, his speeches and his posters: *Axiokratía*; *Allaghí*; *Káto i favlokrátes*; Rule by the Worthy; Change; Down with the Corrupt. He would also say, 'In a few minutes will arrive the General Organizer of the Progressive Front of Power and Change; will arrive the renowned EOKA Fighter, the man who brings us the Wind of Change and the Message of Victory, NIKOS SAMPSON.' Then the amplification system would play stirring martial music until the next announcement. Such tactics were calculated to excite the faithful; but to the UP supporters sitting at another coffee-shop within earshot of the amplifier, they seemed like precisely the crude demagogic techniques which they always associated with Sampson. They were also depressed by the very large crowd which was gathering to hear him and by the obvious signs of his party's energetic organization.

Finally Sampson himself arrived. A number of candidates for PF were introduced to the crowd. They were all standing for the Nicosia District and each felt constrained to make a short speech. Among them was the Kalo lawyer, Aglas.[4] Then Sampson himself started to speak. He spoke in a markedly more simple, direct and emotional style to any of the previous orators, all of whom were concerned to show their mastery, as educated men of the higher levels of the Greek language, where *Demotikí* turns towards *Katharévousa*; Sampson, it is often said even by his own supporters, 'doesn't know how to speak' by which they mean two things: one is that when he speaks his own emotions come across in an uninhibited way, and he can be close to weeping when he speaks of dead friends or social injustice; the second is that his style is simple, eschews the classical structures of formal rhetoric, and relies on such techniques as repeating 'And we ask ... they do not answer ... And we have seen ... Who are the men who? ... *we* are not the men who ...' In spite of the comment that he does not know how to speak, large crowds listen to his speeches with close attention and show no sign of boredom even after an hour and a half of anecdotes. Anecdotes are a potent weapon in his speeches and he was to use a good many on this evening.

He began with memories of the EOKA struggle, names of those who had fallen, reminding the audience of the cause, and the heroism of the dead fighters. Then he went on to a list of names of those fighters who had died *after* the end of the struggle, and whose killers had not been brought to justice. He mentioned the man from Kalo, a village where he himself had been in hiding as a wanted man, a man whose name they all knew, the hero Levendis. For ten whole years such murders had gone on, as they all knew, and men were walking around in the streets who should at least have been in prison.

He moved on to other themes, to corruption in high and secret places, the arrogance of the rich and their indifference to the poor. He spoke of government officials 'with their fat salaries' and their harsh treatment of poor farmers with no regular income at all. He told a number of stories about how many had given their life or limbs at various phases of the national struggle in the last fifteen years, and how when they or their families had turned to the government for some sort of compensation they had been shabbily treated.[5] He told a story of a widow with four children whose husband had died fighting the Turks and who was ready to start begging in the streets to feed her family; when she had asked a government official what she should do he had answered 'marry again'—a patent absurdity in contemporary Cyprus, and one which drew an angry, incredulous gasp from the crowd.

He told a story about their children in the army being entitled to three quarters of a loaf of bread a day and tax money going to pay for this amount of bread, and the lads actually gettting only a quarter of a loaf, because of corruption.

By the use of simple rhetorical devices he attacked the UP as if it were responsible for the mistakes of the government over the last ten years. This was a favourite line of all PF speakers throughout the campaign. The Presidential system of government means that there need be no connection between government ministers and any political party. Furthermore, Makarios had persuaded the representatives both in 1960 and subsequently that national unity was the most important issue of the hour, so that the House had rarely made use of its powers either of budget veto, or of outspoken criticism of government policies. Thus, when PF speakers attacked the government and/or the representatives for inaction, there was a real sense in which they could be said to be attacking the President. But this they were careful never to do.[6] All the main political parties, while hitting out at their rivals, contrived to imply that they themselves were *closer* to the President and enjoyed more of his support than anyone else, and that people in other parties were only *pretending* to be pro-Makarios and pretending to enjoy his confidence and favour. Since Glafkos Clerides, as UP leader, also enjoyed Makarios's confidence to the point of being in charge of the intercommunal talks with his Turkish counterpart Raouf Denktash, the PF speakers had somehow to imply that Clerides was pulling the wool over Makarios's eyes, seeming to obey him, while pursuing other plans.[7] Their supporters in private conversations took this sort of point much further, and since the other UP leader, the now-deceased Yorgadjis, had been deeply implicated in the assassination attempt on the President before himself being assassinated, they had plenty of ammunition. In PF mouths the UP was a party of thieves, liars, murderers and plotters. Although it had only been in existence for a year, they claimed it was also responsible for everything wrong with Cyprus since 1960. The evidence for this was that 'the same old clique' who had organized the Patriotic Front in 1960 and later taken ministerial jobs were now running the United Party.

The major flaw in this chain of reasoning should have been the apparent gullibility of President Makarios. Since nearly everyone claimed to believe that Makarios was the wisest man on the island, the man who still really controlled everything and everyone, who knew all about whatever was happening, and so forth, this would have clashed with any notion of his gullibility. The only way to save the argument logically was to insist on the satanic brilliance in deception of the UP leaders and this of course PF people did whenever they could. Logic aside, at various times it suited their case to blur distinctions between government ministers, the Representatives, and the United Party. They could point to three living persons and one dead (Yorgadjis) in the

United Party who had been either ministers or representatives and this was enough to justify the charge of 'the same old clique and their friends'; that their own party contained several men who through PEK or other means had been representatives they chose to ignore. They numbered no ex-ministers in their ranks.

In his speech Sampson introduced many of his charges by indirect methods, speaking of 'those who for ten whole years have fooled the people, cheated the people, betrayed the people'. As a practising journalist who has also successfully brought libel actions against several newspapers, he was far too astute to make crude connections between 'those who . . .' and the United Party. But it was his plain intention. It was further evidence that both as a speaker and a politician he has far more wit than his opponents like to pretend. He now turned his attentions to nationalism, genuine and false. True Greeks wanted *Enosis* with Mother Greece and he was sure everyone in his audience agreed with him about that. He would explain what he meant by true Greekness. Greekness did not include leaving one's daughter unbaptized, or worshipping Buddha, nor did it include saying he was ashamed to be Greek or that Greek army officers in Cyprus were illegal. He had on numerous occasions asked Clerides publicly whether or not his daughter was baptized and he as yet received no answer. How could Clerides say he stood for the family and the Church, when this meant having un-baptized daughters? How dare Clerides go around giving speeches with the Greek flag in front of him singing the Greek National Anthem when everyone knew what sort of man he really was?

The men who were responsible for the Green Line, the Zurich Agreements which had led to the Green Line, and who were now carrying the island towards Partition . . . everyone knew what sort of men they were. How could Clerides claim to stand for law and order when he failed to collect the guns which had shot down former EOKA fighters like Levendis, had failed to collect the thousand odd guns recently discovered in a storehouse in Nicosia, which had belonged to the man who had organized an assassination attempt on President Makarios? He could not say that the United Party were completely without ability—they were cunning enough to see that when Lellos Dimitriades had had the gall to say 'Cyprus for the Cypriots' they could no longer afford to have him as a candidate in their party, because they wished to fool the people into believing that as a party they stood for *Enosis*, and they realized that people would not be taken in by this. There was, however, only one party that really wanted *Enosis* with Mother Greece, that was a truly Greek party, a party concerned with rule by the worthy, with change, with an improvement in life for the poor, with cleaning up corruption, and that was the Progressive Front . . . He brought his speech to a close.

Sampson's speech raised a number of issues which most of the PF speakers were to stress; it also was to be repeated back to me by Sampson's supporters fervently and with great conviction for three weeks, with the very examples he had produced and the anecdotes he had recounted with the exact choice of words being repeated by young men as if they themselves had been eye-witnesses to the events, and the events themselves recorded and established by the most impartial tribunals in the world. The most striking fact both about Sampson's speech, the repetitions of his supporters, and the conduct of the whole election in and around Kalo was the intensity of opposition between the UP and the PF; while most of the current flowed from the latter to the former, there was a reciprocal flow which is hardly surprising in view of the PF attacks. For all practical purposes the communists (AKEL) and the EDEK party of Lyssarides need not have existed, for all the attention that PF speakers paid to them. There was in fact a bitter electoral struggle being conducted between Lyssarides and Clerides but in the main PF supporters took the position that 'the enemy of my enemy is my friend' and were vastly more sympathetic to Lyssarides than to Clerides. This raises the issue of the dimensions of party cleavage: whereas in conventional European terms, Lyssarides as some sort of democratic socialist should have been further away from PF than the more 'centralist' United Party, PF supporters believed that in spite of his leftism Lyssarides was a more genuine nationalist, and more genuinely pro-Makarios than the leaders of the United Party. The PF supporters believed that they had most to fear from the UP, given the political patronage system. UP leaders had command of patronage, and could buy off potential PF supporters. PF, like EDEK, was a party of 'outs'—of people out in the cold. In addition, if EDEK took votes from anywhere, the PF people argued, it would be from AKEL, and not from UP.[8]

There were few questions after Sampson's speech, and he soon went off with some of the other PF candidates to supper at the house of one of his leading supporters in the village. This he had done the year before after his Kalo speech, and the house visited was that of the wealthiest of Levendis's brothers. This man and Pavlos now joined the Sampson supper in Kammari. The atmosphere was relatively relaxed, but the tension soon mounted: Sampson, like other PF people, believed that a 'landslide' had begun, of former UP supporters coming over to the PF. He suddenly turned on one young man, a former EOKA stalwart who was sitting at the long table. 'Look at him,' said Sampson, loud enough for all to hear, 'when the UP was formed he joined straight away; he became one of their top activists and organizers in this district. And look at him now—now he's come over to us ... because he knows we will win.' The young man hung his head and said nothing in reply. A little later and possibly to take the sting out of Sampson's treatment of this man, Pavlos explained to me in front of Sampson that when the UP got organized they sent people out all over the island to get villagers to register as members. 'Pachulos, the *múktar* of Themo, you know is a *koumpáros* of my father. My father doesn't know much about politics so when Pachulos asked him to sign up in the UP, he signed. Now do you think I'd let my father vote for the UP? There are lots of cases like that, and they must have seriously over-estimated their strength if they take seriously all those bits of paper. . . .'[9]

Sampson had however a moderating influence on some of his supporters. When for example someone at the table asserted that Clerides and the Turkish leader were affines because their wives were cousins, Sampson said this was wrong. (The logic behind this astonishing notion was that Clerides's wife was a foreign woman, and assumed not to be a Christian. From there it is still a rather large jump to making her a kinswoman of Denktash's wife.)

Later Pavlos said he had been pleased with the turn-out, it had been a good meeting. Sampson leaped on this, harshly. 'Oh no, it *wasn't* a good meeting—I'm not at all satisfied. There should have been a much bigger crowd. You must all work much harder,' he told them. They looked suitably chastened. Next day Pavlos was repeating Sampson's words to his Kalo team, with similar inflections and similar results.

When nearly everyone had left an incident took place which was highly characteristic of politics in the villages. Our host, with two Kalo men and myself were at the table, as well as an uncle of the host's wife. He was a staunch leftist and very much the worse for drink. He had been jolly before, but now was approaching a sort of privileged, challenging belligerence. He got to his feet and said 'I'll tell you about *Enosis*. We don't want *Enosis* of a *poushtissima*[10] sort. We want real *Enosis* . . .' The effect of the way he spoke was to leave the whole issue delightfully vague. But what he was continuously doing, which was an embarrassment to the others present, was to shout out the beginning of the sentence, 'We don't want *Enosis* . . .'. What he meant by 'genuine *Enosis*' I cannot say, but it would probably involve union with a democratic Greece. Now for half an hour everyone in the room went on drinking and trying to humour him and he went on trying to get a rise out of them. At one point Pavlos said 'Uncle, I can see only guns will make you change your views.' 'Guns? Never . . .' replied the old man rolling his eyes. Someone else said, 'We're going to have to take you for a long ride in the mountains on election day and tie you up among the pines . . .' The point of this anecdote is that kinship norms and those restraining political conflict within the village meant that no-one was allowed to get angry with the very provocative old man. However, since all had been drinking, the sort of jokes which were made about violence between right and left suggests some anxiety in the village over how to manifest solidarity.

Sampson's Kammari speech took place on the first day of the merger of his party with that of Ioannides. From this point on in Kalo this produced close co-operation between the activists of the two former groupings. A number of planning meetings were held in which Patris as the representative of the PEK-Azinas-Ioannides group worked with Pavlos, the PF representative, in going through the electoral list marking down those among the 740 Kalo voters whom it was thought worth attempting to win over. After two long evenings' work the first canvass reached a rough verdict of 50 sure votes for AKEL; 20 for EDEK; 50 for UP; 200 for PF and 400 *adiáphori* (indifferent; uncommitted). In calculating the number of uncommitted voters the usual rule was anyone who was not known to be a staunch supporter of a party was marked as uncommitted. In the case of a wife or sister, it was assumed that she could be approached if there existed a strong tie with someone in the PF camp. Old people were often marked down as uncommitted. It was clear to all that the voting system (p. 275) would allow many people who felt themselves to be under cross-pressures to give a few votes to a party merely to

satisfy an importunate friend of kinsman, and that therefore it
was worth trying to cadge the odd vote or two from any but the
most intransigent activists.

The first meeting of the new party in the village numbered
about twenty-five men and youths; the atmosphere was excited,
and a number of highly partisan remarks were made by some of
the more hot-headed supporters. For example, while the lists
were being checked, on several occasions a voter was revealed to
be a UP supporter, whereas some people present had imagined
he was with them. There was some swearing, then the man who
had read the welcoming speech to Sampson when he came to
Kalo to speak said, 'I always said we should stop the sale of
Agón in this village'—*Agón* being the UP newspaper.

Such remarks as this became a regular feature of the talk of the
younger PF supporters. It was noticeable that PF attracted far
more boys in their late teens and early twenties than did other
groupings. These boys would sit around the main PF coffee-shop
ready to hold forth to any listener on the government and the
UP's sins over 'ten whole years'. I heard several discussions about
the need for them to give anyone looking for trouble as good
as they got, to prevent the UP's meeting taking place in Kalo,
or at the very least to disrupt it. Whenever Pavlos heard such
remarks he swiftly clamped down on them, and said that they did
not want that sort of trouble, and they were to do nothing of the
sort without consulting him. He was continually cooling them
down. Much that the younger men said can be seen as the typical
'tough talk' of young men anywhere, *but there was none to be
heard from the other parties.* Indeed, whenever the other party
activists wished to denigrate Sampson and his following they
said, 'Who supports Sampson? Just a bunch of kids trying to be
tough, and if you look around you'll find that in every village
in Cyprus, the kids who like him are the bad ones, the ones who
don't work, who fight, gamble, carry guns. So much for his
supporters. . . .'

It was clear during the examination of the electoral lists that
although the villagers insist that they know 'everyone' in the
village they cannot always identify them from the formal names
written down for official purposes. There were long discussions
of what person was designated by a particular name (p. 96) there
is no doubt that most adult persons in the village could identify
all other adults on sight, but they would not be able to do this
formally. The time spent over the lists and the difficulties they

produced stressed the gap between the official world of electoral lists and the face-to-face village world.

Since later in the campaign many village PF supporters were to feel and to suggest that the government officials conducting the elections were biased in favour of the UP, it is important that at the earlier stage they took the electoral lists seriously, as valid, and made little attempt to check them systematically. I did hear people discuss ways in which one could fraudulently get oneself on to two lists and thus vote twice, but there was no UP collusion suggested in this, rather an individual initiative equally open to supporters of all parties. However PF supporters did discuss, with a degree of seriousness, the power of *múktars* to help the UP get extra votes but they did not suggest it would happen in Kalo, where the *múktar* was weak.

It should not be thought that the PF village leaders looked on their slate of twelve candidates in the Nicosia district as men of high calibre for whom it was morally essential to work. Two of the most prominent Kalo PF activists expressed themselves quite differently. One said sometimes he got thoroughly sick of politics, and disillusioned and wanted no part of it. I asked him why. 'When I think that Aglas the lawyer, who is a fool, is a candidate and may become an M.P., and I know how much better I am than he is. But when Azinas was looking for good men to be candidates for the party, he went after them with a candle—there were none....' The speaker suffered under the additional handicap of not being ideologically committed to the PF group but being unable for career reasons to follow any other course. But even men heavily committed to PF told me, 'The men we have as candidates in this election don't impress me. Most of them are simply ambitious and would stand for any party. They are after a steady £200 a month and the prestige and opportunities to make a bit on the side. To build a party organization and get experience we must use them in this election. But in five years time we'll have better men.' Such impressions were confirmed from other sources. One candidate standing for the EDEK party admitted to an informant that he would have stood in any party except the communists. Ideologically the EDEK candidates spanned a very wide range; some of them would not accept the words 'democratic socialist' to describe the party, while others would accept no other title. In such a small party this is suggestive.

Villagers are not unsophisticated about the motives of the candidates. Their frequent comment, 'They're all out to line their pockets,' was not wildly inaccurate: For many of the candidates £200 a month is a very useful sum. When I commented to one villager that some of the election photographs of the candidates seemed to have been taken a long time ago when the men were younger, he said, 'Oh they do that to make themselves appear *fresh*,' using a word that is usually applied to the condition of meat or vegetables.

This detachment was even present in comments on Sampson by his own close supporters. Several of them told me that even though he spoke strongly and said things which needed saying, he did not speak *well* and did not have the 'capabilities' to be President of the Republic or a senior minister. They added that his behaviour was sometimes unpredictable and harmful.

Such views did not stop Pavlos as Sampson's district agent from working very hard for him. He made sure that every night a busload of Kalo PF supporters went off to wherever a PF speaker was having a meeting. Some of these trips were not un-eventful. On 28 June, the lawyer Aglas went to near-by Themo village to speak. The Themo *múktar*, rich and powerful, is a strong UP supporter. That year one of his grandchildren had been baptized by Yorgadjis, and he himself had thrown a huge party for the occasion. Aglas, in his speech attacked Clerides, and some UP supporters in the audience heckled him. He replied that he was not attacking Clerides as a man, but on the record of his party. A little later a fight broke out between UP and PF people, from which the Kalo PF contingent remained aloof. In the melée, the lawyers's car tyres got slashed.

The same evening in Kalo there was a fight, on the same lines. Yorgadjis had a *koumpáros*, K. Karas from Kalo, with certain canteen concessions in Yorgadjis's offices in the capital.[11] It was often said to me that this man was kept near the Minister so he could inform him of any possible moves by the kin of the mur-dered Levendis, against the Minister. Karas's younger brother, P. Karas, is one of the most active UP supporters in Kalo. He is also, as it happens a first cousin of the dead Levendis. Levendis's brother R. Tangos, and P. Karas got into a fight about whether or not a UP election poster could be hung up. R. Tangos threatened to tear it in pieces if P. Karas stuck it on the wall. At one point P. Karas said the words 'your poove of a boss is *better*?' (*o poúshtis o mástros sou 'en kallítera*?) and the two young men had come to blows. The fact that first cousins were fighting, though deplorable enough soon worsened, for now another tough young man, Pyrgos, joined in against P. Karas, enraged by the slight on his friend Sampson. Pyrgos is married to P. Karas's sister[12] and so their relations are *gambrós/kounyiádos* (sister's husband/wife's brother); this fight then involved three young men closely related by kinship and affinity. It was to lead to further repercussions a few days later.

THE UP CAMPAIGN AND PF'S RESPONSE

The next important incident to take place concerned the speech by United Party leader Clerides in Market Town. On this evening a busload of young Kalo PF supporters went there. Before the bus—driven by R. Tangos the youngest brother of the deceased Levendis—set out, Pavlos murmured something to him. R. Tangos told the young men in the bus, 'I don't want any fooling about, and mind those things in the back.' I saw a few pieces of cardboard piled one on the other and thinking it was something to do with the bus-driver thought no more of it. The bus drove down into the town which was full of people, and went below the main square where Clerides was to speak. The boys in the bus were in a state of considerable excitement, but I still did not know why and finding their company exhausting decided to go and listen to the speech with some older people from Kalo I had seen in the crowd.

Clerides arrived and was clapped and started his speech. He was about seven minutes in, facing the packed square in the artificial light when there was a faint disturbance from the far side. Something was clearly happening, and in a few moments everyone could see what it was: slowly across the square like carnival floats moved a line of posters, held high in the air by eight young Kalo PF supporters. The lettering was crude and cramped, which made what then happened all the more pointed. A very large number of the people in the crowd who were facing Clerides to listen to his speech turned round to read the posters. Clerides was confronted with several hundred inattentive backs. Once the crowd had managed to decipher the posters (which took some time) they then had to ponder their messages:

1. The president of mother Greece condemned the moral instigator of the assassination attempt against him. What party did the instigator belong to?
2. One party leader has in the study of his home a picture of the Queen of England. Do you know who he is?

3. Were the guns which killed the fighters handed over to the police?
4. Who broke the fifth commandment—that is, who swore at his own father from the balcony in public?
5. Who said the Greek officers were illegal?
6. Makarios condemned the moral instigator of the assassination attempt on him. What party did he belong to?
7. One party leader from earliest days has been a spy for the Intelligence Service. Do you know who?
8. In the centre of Nicosia a warehouse was discovered with a thousand illegal weapons. To what party did they belong and what was the purpose of that party?

I shall not here explain the background to each poster; it is enough to say that in each case they referred (obliquely enough to escape libel action) to certain charges and events which Sampson in his newspaper *Máchi* has continuously used as ammunition against Clerides and the UP. Some of them refer in particular to the role thought to have been played by the deceased Yorgadjis in two unsuccessful assassination attempts on heads of state, Papadopoulos and Makarios.

Clerides lost no time in facing up to the challenge of the posters. He badly needed to regain his position as the focal point of the meeting. He said he could see placards before him (shouts of 'shame to them' from the crowd) and did not propose to answer such questions except to say that the Greek Government and Archbishop Makarios clearly had full confidence in him which was why he was entrusted with the conduct of the inter-communal talks; that he did not worship Buddha and that he was, as everyone present knew, a Christian. That he was not however a POLITICAL WINDMILL (a quick jab at Sampson's many ideological shifts which brought applause from UP supporters) . . . 'and that he believed . . .' But at this point a man in the crowd shouted out, 'You believe only in *money*.' This man was not from Kalo or standing near the placard-bearers, and he shouted loudly enough for most people in the crowd not to find out what it was Clerides believed in. A number of people started to move down in a threatening way towards the man who had shouted, and the police moved down too and Clerides said from the rostrum, 'Don't do anything to them . . .' For some minutes there was a continual mild disturbance in the crowd, and it seemed as if a brawl would take place, but the moment passed.

Clerides spoke for a much shorter period than when I heard him speak two weeks before in the village of Klirou, and he did not accept any questions, which was also a departure from his usual practice. But since eight fairly unpleasant questions were staring him in the face through most of his speech, this is hardly surprising. He departed and the crowd started to disperse. Clerides then in fact went to Parali village and is reported as having spoken for a long time and taken on questions including some like those on the placards. Since there had been a strong and rather tense PF election speech in Parali a few days previously, where a young man apparently representing the United Party had persistently questioned the main speaker, Clerides's move was not without tactical value.

The Kalo PF supporters got back into their bus and set out for the village three miles away. They were jubilant. They felt they had really defeated Clerides, that his failure to answer the questions was a clear moral defeat. Since they had not seen him speak elsewhere they were actually unaware of the real scope of their 'victory'. Afterwards it was reported to me that Clerides had feared there might be a disturbance and had deliberately curtailed his speech. But the young PF supporters did not have the same perspective as the UP leader Clerides: where his concern was to avoid violent disruption of the meeting, theirs was to draw public attention to their opposition to him and all he stood for. One of the boys in the bus started to swear excitedly. 'I knew it. When he sang the national anthem at the end, did you notice, *he got it wrong*, he got the words wrong, he put *sword* where *sight* should have been.' This remark was greeted on all sides with the comment that this was just the sort of thing they expected from such a man. The other lively topic on the way back to the village was the Kalotes' reputation for toughness. One boy told how someone in the crowd had suggested doing something about the placards and his neighbour had replied, 'Don't do anything to *them*, they're Kalotes—they pull pistols on you.'

Later I asked the Kalo PF leader where the initiative for the demonstration had come from and he said from R. Tangos, Levendis's brother. He added that R. Tangos probably telephoned Sampson to discuss it, but that was all.[13] The next day Sampson's newspaper *Máchi* carried a description of the incident with an accurate wording of the eight posters. Clerides's newspaper *Agón* also carried a version of the incident, which managed to imply that the UP leader had in some way routed the placard bearers.

It also showed a big crowd listening to Clerides without the eight men carrying posters. As a photograph this was a considerable technical achievement; editorials masquerading as news coverage are commonplace in Cypriot newspapers.

It was clear from the comments a number of people made that they regarded the behaviour of the demonstrators as an insult to Clerides and a thoroughly wrong-headed approach to politics. I went to a number of election speeches in Cyprus and the one sentence in the town, 'You believe only in money,' was the *only* instance of heckling I heard. Otherwise all speakers were heard in complete silence. At a number of meetings when the speaker called for questions there were none at all from the audiences. It was also noticeable that most of the questions that were asked were asked by men in their late teens or early twenties, who were probably unmarried, and a 'new generation' in politics. Informants when asked to comment on this said that married men with family obligations might be unwilling to expose themselves to possible hazards by asking questions in public. Thus from several points of view the demonstration by the PF supporters was an innovation, and a daring one at that, for although the young men carrying placards were not family heads they were fairly deliberately exposing themselves as enemies of the UP whom they believed to have a near-monopoly of power in the island.

The next incident of the campaign was the speech by the United Party candidate Kefiros in Kalo on 2 July, three days before the election. He is from Kammari, a retired civil servant who is generally regarded as kindly, honest, and worthy of respect.

Like Vourros and Aglas he is a Nicosia resident, but also like them has local citrus orchards, and is a regular visitor to the district. He has been extremely active on behalf of his village, particularly over a long struggle with the government about water rights (pp. 202, 209 fn. 15).

Among the people who assembled before the speech in a show of support for the United Party was the *múktar* of Mastia, and the *múktar* of Parali. It was the latter who had received the involuntary haircut a few months previously, and when a week ago a PF group had visited his village with some Kalo supporters, the Kalo people had reported with some amusement that the *múktar* 'had not shown himself' during the meeting. His presence in Kalo was therefore overlaid with several additional meanings. His coffee was ordered by a man who had privately expressed to me the harshest condemnation of the UP's opportunism. The man who brought the coffee was one of the six men arrested for the haircut offence. The Mastia *múktar* was one of several who at the time of the incident had sent a telegram to the government asking them to take firm steps to deal with such lawlessness.

There was a good crowd, and Kefiros, like Clerides, had his table draped with a Greek flag. He spoke quietly and briefly. UP was open to and representing all Greek Cypriot nationalists. He stressed the trust the Greek Government and Makarios had in Clerides and his conduct of the talks. He clarified the position of the party on the Co-operative Movement—it was not true that they were against it—they were strongly with it but they did want to see it use its capital more efficiently, and its administration to be more democratic. After his short and conventional speech which I do not repeat here, he asked for questions.

The man who was to ask most of the questions was Lepini, a second cousin of Levendis, the man who a year ago had formally welcomed Sampson to Kalo. He is a heavy, slow-speaking farmer who spent several years in England. His first question essentially identified the UP with the Legislative Assembly, and asked why they had done so little in their ten years? Kefiros answered that the UP was a new party and could not be held responsible. The questions continued, and at one point Kefiros said he did not know the answer to something, to which Lepini said, 'But Mr. Kefiros you don't seem to know *anything*,' which in view of the educational and status differences between the two men would normally be seen as an extremely rude remark. Lepini then asked the question (p. 260) about Clerides saying Greek officers in Cyprus were illegal and that he was ashamed to be Greek. Kefiros tried to answer this by filling out the context: Clerides had said he was ashamed to be Greek when he had heard that officers from mainland Greece were punishing Cypriot soldiers extremely harshly, in spite of a mainland Greek law which forbade Greek soldiers to take part in the political affairs of a foreign country. As soon as the word *xénos* (foreign) left his mouth Lepini pounced on it to make the point that Kefiros did not appear to regard Cyprus as Greek, but Greece as 'foreign'!

Kefiros tried to develop his defence against the personal attacks on Clerides. He said that such attacks could not always be answered because otherwise the newspaper would be taken up with nothing else except Clerides's defence of himself, but more to the point the attacks were often baseless and absurd. For example was it conceivable that the Greek Government (which everybody knew to be an extremely strong supporter of the Orthodox Christian faith) would permit a Buddhist to conduct delicate negotiations with the Turks on the national question?

Lepini now turned his attack to the deceased Yorgadjis, by woodenly asking the question from the Market Town demonstration, in exactly the same words: 'Makarios condemned the moral instigator of the assassination attempt on him. To what party did he belong?'

Kefiros now switched from defence to attack. Was the questioner holding the UP responsible for the assassination attempt? This slightly alarmed Lepini who said well never mind that, and started to recite a list of names of fighters who had been killed after the end of the Struggle, and whose deaths were popularly attributed to the deceased Yorgadjis. Kefiros said he would not speak of the dead man who, whatever they might say, had been in his time a great fighter for the Greek-Cypriot cause; it would be a disrespect to his memory. Some of the cases referred to were in legal process and should not be prejudiced by public discussion. Besides, as he had said before he was not present as an apologist for the much-denounced 'ten years' but as the representative of a new party.

Lepini tried again to link Yorgadjis and his reputation to the UP and again Kefiros parried. So Lepini asked, 'All right, why didn't Makarios attend the funeral of Yorgadjis? Doesn't that prove that Makarios himself believed Yorgadjis to be the moral instigator of the attack against him?' Kefiros said he had not understood the question. Lepini then said in a forthright way, 'We believe that Yorgadjis's friends deliberately closed his mouth to stop him saying what he knew.' Now Kefiros countered, 'It's all very well saying "we believe"—but these matters are under investigation and speculation of this kind is simply irresponsible.'

It became increasingly clear as the debate went on that Lepini and Kefiros were not communicating with each other. The discussion was in two quite different idioms. That of Kefiros used the ideas of legal process, evidence, and the fact of Clerides's continued occupancy of the role of negotiator with the Turks, to justify his party's position, and never came near to giving an answer to the fundamental but unexpressed question—how could Clerides and the UP have teamed up with a man like Yorgadjis? Lepini used the 'facts' of known associations, assumed motives, personal ambitions to suggest a picture of intrigue and corruption. After the meeting the young PF supporters in the village insisted that Kefiros 'had not answered' any of Lepini's questions. This meant in fact that he had failed to dissociate the UP from the moral stigma of Yorgadjis, from its close association with the corruption of the elite, from its ambiguous position on *Enosis*. But the educated supporters of the UP afterwards complained that Lepini's questions were either illiterate, or meaningless, or both, and a serious insult to the age and position of a man like Kefiros. The two sides were shooting past each other, and with very different kinds of weapons.

Kefiros pointed out that as soon as there was the slightest rumour connecting Yorgadjis with the attempt on Makarios, he had resigned from the UP. Lepini did not take this point up but later others explained to me why it was 'no answer'. Since it had been Clerides who had passed the recent special Emergency Law in the absence of Makarios, and since in the event of the death of Makarios, Clerides as President of the Assembly automatically became the President of the Republic, and since Yorgadjis's men in the police force could be relied on under the Emergency Law to round up all opponents, then Clerides so obviously stood to gain by the assassination attempt that they insisted he *must have* been involved in it. The logic of the situation, and the respective self-interest of the parties involved, as well as the power structures they commanded, dictated the conclusion that Yorgadjis's resignation was just a blind, and meant nothing.

Lepini's next question was, 'When did Clerides ever speak for *Enosis*?' Kefiros either pretended to be (or genuinely was) taken aback by this question. Perhaps he suddenly realized the gulf between his way of thinking and that of Lepini. He replied, 'How can you ask how the man who was the chief defence lawyer of captured EOKA fighters during the Emergency ever spoke for *Enosis*? What do you think the whole struggle was about?'

Another young PF supporter in the crowd tried to argue that Clerides had not defended the fighters because he believed in the cause. 'Well why did he do it then?' 'Maybe he was trying to build up customers,' the boy answered. Kefiros now attacked strongly, by asking if the boy had ever been a fighter? The question was rhetorical for the boy was much too young to have been active in the period 1955–9. But even while Kefiros was attempting to deliver the *coup de grâce*, one of the Kalo buffoons, a butcher whose nickname is 'Chickenshit' with a loud very high-pitched rasping voice, renowned for the outrageous and slightly off-colour things he says, tried to get into the act. He started to

say in a somewhat incoherent way that during the struggle the
EOKA fighters had never gone around shouting for *Enosis*, at least
he had not heard them ... Everyone agreed afterwards that whatever the man's faults he had been trying to make some *other* point
and it had simply come out wrongly. But this was not to help
him. The Mastia *múktar*, an impressive man with a very large
fighter's moustache, and the reputation for having been one of
the main EOKA leaders in the district, made a sign to Kefiros
that he wished to use the microphone. He agreed and the *múktar*,
dark-suited and with lowering brows stood at the microphone.
'The fighters are insulted by such remarks, both the living and
the dead. I remind you all—since there are strangers here who
might easily get the wrong impression from some of the things
being said—that from start to finish our one and only purpose as
fighters was *Enosis*...' This and his other similar remarks
brought a strong round of applause, and rallied UP supporters. It
switched the tone from defence to attack. In a sense Kefiros had
been about to do something similar when he asked his last questioner if he had been a fighter. The point was for the UP to identify itself *directly* with the EOKA struggle, and this was what
the *múktar* had now managed to do. The moral was not lost on
Kefiros who now pulled out some of the remaining stops. He
made the brief point that George Grivas in his first pamphlet had
made it absolutely clear that the purpose of the struggle was
Enosis. Both the words Grivas and *Enosis* drew substantial
applause.

But the PF group were not put off balance. Why had Clerides
not answered the questions during the demonstration? Kefiros
replied: He had answered them—in Parali, and when had the UP
ever indulged in carrying placards attacking others?

Now the butcher jumped in again. 'Perhaps the other parties
don't have anything against them that United could carry posters
about...' Another PF man said, 'Clerides tried to fool us when he
said he'd answer our questions at Market Town and then didn't.'
Kefiros now repeated that the UP pursued peaceful, civilized
methods of campaigning and did not go around carrying posters
against people. A PF man said: 'But if we had been doing anything illegal the police would have stopped us.' Kefiros now said
he would accept any questions in good faith, but that he felt that
many of the questions which had been asked so far were more in
the spirit of provocation than anything else. He was all for civilized discussion, and so forth.

But it was not to end yet; why had Clerides asked for a salary increase to carry on the inter-communal talks, if he really cared about the future of Cyprus? Kefiros answered that Clerides was not a rich man, and that by taking on the additional burden of the inter-communal talks he was completely ruling out any chance of earning any money by the private practice of law. He sacrificed this to the national interest, and like most other people, he waits at the end of the month for his pay-cheque.

All right then, if he was so keen on the good of his country why did he publicly speak against his father? The relation between one point and another was tenuous. A little later Kefiros remembered the *múktar*'s lesson. 'I didn't want to speak about myself, but perhaps I ought to mention that there was an earlier phase of the Cyprus Struggle, that which ended in the Uprising of 1931 and for my part in that I went to prison.' This brought very loud applause.

The questions seemed to go on for a very long time. The issue of the baptism of Clerides' daughter was again raised. Kefiros always tried to keep his voice low, and to avoid heavy bombast, but he could not silence his questioners. His main tormentor, Lepini, chose one reply as an excuse to give a shrug which said, 'It's pointless going on with this,' turned his back on the speaker and walked slowly away from the meeting towards the PF coffee-shop. As finally the meeting started to break up, a man arrested for the Parali haircut, went over to the Parali *múktar* and gave him a handshake. Elsewhere groups of people went on talking politics for several hours. K. Karas the Kalo political client of the deceased Yorgadjis, had arrived from the capital, and was chatting quietly with best known of the deceased Levendis brothers. The two men had had a fight within the last year when K. Karas had accused him of trying to exploit the memory of his dead brother and had made reference to the Cretan arms trip (pp. 143–150) and the accounts problem. However, now they were talking on apparently friendly terms. The elections were only three days away, and one of the major opportunities for open conflict, the UP's meeting in Kalo, had passed without serious incident. But not without tension or novelty.

TENSIONS IN THE LAST DAYS: VILLAGE SOLIDARITY TESTED

One of the things which helped *reduce* tension on the evening of

the UP speech in Kalo was the unexpected arrival later on in the
village of a man called Mammas, an EDEK candidate who was
known to many of the villagers since he sells trucks and spare
parts. He gave an informal and extremely humorous analysis of
the elections, and soon had a crowd of fifty men around him all
in a very good mood. Some of the nationalists were saying that
EDEK was about to make a secret electoral pact with AKEL, to
cross-vote. Both parties denied this in the village, and AKEL
argued convincingly that a 'secret instruction' to its members
could not remain secret for long. Mammas, in his speech took it
for granted that the only issue was to belabour the AKEL supporters for not being with EDEK. So the bulk of the discussion
was between him and the AKEL supporters. Because he is naturally a funny man, the whole temper of this episode was light-
hearted, and must have helped reduce tension. Later a similar
episode occurred when an Independent candidate arrived in the
village whose main plank was to lend money without interest. In
his case the meeting was sheer buffoonery and the village enjoyed themselves wholeheartedly.

In the last few days before the elections certain of the activists
started to predict eleventh-hour alliances. D. Fanos for example
told me he had heard from reliable quarters that there would be
co-operation of several parties against the UP. The final event
of importance for the PF supporters in the region was the speech
in Market Town, on Friday, 3 July, of Odysseus Ioannides now
the head of their party since the merger. Most of them had
certainly never heard him speak in person before although they
had seen him on television in the coffee-shop. There was also a
good deal of interest to see whether he would have a bigger
crowd than Clerides had done. Throughout the election the
villagers put great weight on the size of crowds speakers drew,
and although people kept saying, 'Of course you can't be sure,
and maybe it doesn't mean anything,' they continued to show
great interest in estimates. People got angry with low estimates
of their own party's turn-out at meetings. To the villager the
strongest image of political organization is that which would be
expressed by an aerial photograph of a man on a low rostrum,
surrounded on all sides by followers. A man's following in
politics is a concrete and finite number of persons, who can be
called out to attend one of his meetings. 'Organization' in politics
suggests the ability to turn out these crowds.

Ioannides's meeting was held in a different part of Market

Town, so it was hard for anyone to judge objectively the size of his crowd. But PF supporters were jubilant, for they were sure it was much bigger than that of Clerides and that this was a sure sign that they would defeat the UP in the district. After the meeting they said to me, 'Did you see what a fine boss we've got?' Another said, more poetically, 'Ioannides seems to me to be a pure man.' He used the word *agnós* which in modern Greek means pure or chaste, and is the word used for the Lamb of God. Someone else commented, 'At the very least he isn't a killer.'

The evening was not to pass without tension however. After the Ioannides meeting people went back to Kalo and sat around the coffee-shops of the main square. Suddenly there were raised voices. Pavlos, the PF leader who for days had been keeping the younger, more hot-headed supporters quiet was now himself furious, and was directing his remarks to T. Krikou, a thin, very intense man with a reputation for being quick to anger and quick to fight. He is the brother of L. Krikou, one of the two key UP organizers in Kalo. They are first cousins of the powerful Mastia *múktar* (pp. 69, 266).

The burden of Pavlos's remarks was that some unknown UP supporter had reported to Koshis and Clerides the recent brawl in Kalo between P. Karas and his sister's husband (p. 258). The UP leaders had called young Karas in and said, 'What's all this about some PF people trying to stop UP posters being put up, and beating up our supporters and calling Clerides foul names?' P. Karas had denied all knowledge of the incident whereupon the UP leaders had got angry and said, 'We know this for a fact. Now tell us all about it.' Pavlos kept repeating that some UP *póushtis* had gone and reported an incident between *gambrós* and *kounyiádos* (sister's husband and wife's brother) and that this was a very bad thing to have done. 'Up till now we have held back, we of PF. For instance when I heard about the punch-up between P. Karas and my *koumpáros* Pyrgos, I told my *koumpáros* Pyrgos that it was wrong of him to get into it. He insisted that the whole thing had started out of a joke, but then P. Karas had said "your poove of a boss is *better*?" and naturally he got annoyed and there was a brawl. I told him he should have kept his temper. But now I can see it's no good holding back on our part because the other side doesn't play fair. Well, we know a lot of things, many many things and *once we start* I'm telling you for a fact *we* shall write things which will *never be rubbed out . . .*'

There was some confused interchange now between Pavlos and T. Krikou who whether he liked it or not by his very presence was put in the position of a UP spokesman. Someone made a remark, which drew from Pavlos the reply, 'If any one punches me I'll shoot him by morning.' T. Krikou said, 'You want to hit me?' Pavlos said, 'I'm not hitting anyone . . .'

Things were now extremely tense, with people speaking of shooting and brawling. One UP supporter said that everyone was thoroughly against the report to Koshis and Clerides, and that everyone condemned it. This was a frank admission that someone on his side was in the wrong and was meant to reduce the tension. D. Fanos, a strong PF man, a close friend of Pavlos and a specialist in mediation added, 'Our village has this one special good point; we can have an argument and we don't fall out over it.' Pavlos went on muttering dark threats about what his side would do once they started, and D. Fanos kept on condemning the report. The UP supporters kept on joining him in condemnation and the end of the incident was for Pavlos and T. Krikou, who had once seemed on the point of blows, to go off practically arm-in-arm.

Ten minutes later the biggest, toughest of the unmarried PF supporters (a first cousin of the deceased Levendis) got to his feet to hit someone, in the coffee-shop across the way, and was instantly seized by a number of people who made him sit down quietly. Another incident had been averted.

Saturday was a day on which all political activity was in effect banned by law, and no alcohol was to be sold, as was the case for election day, Sunday. The only event of any interest was the arrival of an AKEL representative in the village to inform the left leaders that there had been an eleventh-hour electoral pact between AKEL and EDEK to cross-vote. AKEL only had two candidates in the Nicosia district, so this gave them ten 'extra' votes. The agreement was that they should vote for the head of EDEK, Vassos Lyssarides, and the last five men on his slate. The reason given in the village by the AKEL representative and passed on by village leaders was that the AKEL leaders had been informed that attempts were being made to get an anti-Makarios bloc of M.P.s into the House, mixed up among the various parties. The EDEK candidates to be voted for by AKEL members were those who were guaranteed to be loyal to Makarios. The AKEL man also explained that in another electoral district the party was co-operating with PF in a similar deal for similar

FIGURE 3

Relationships affected by a political dispute, 1970

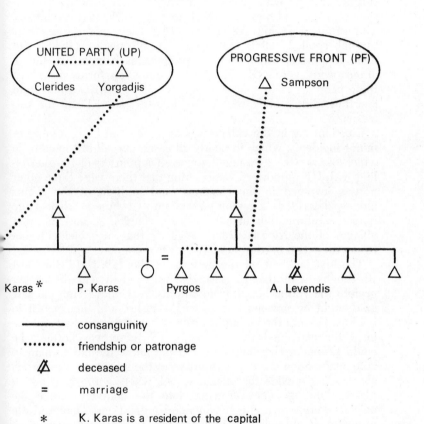

consanguinity

friendship or patronage

deceased

= marriage

* K. Karas is a resident of the capital

K

reasons. There was to be no co-operation with UP because they were the heart of the anti-Makarios group.

As events were to turn out the cross-voting procedure was to prove extremely difficult to operate, and the returns showed that the commonest tactic adopted by the AKEL group was to tell only their most reliable and sophisticated supporters the full details, and with others to greatly simplify it, so that for instance they voted both for AKEL and *all* the EDEK candidates. The problem facing AKEL was that they might lose votes through spoiled ballots if too many people made mistakes. But their supporters often saw the problem as 'supposing enough of our people vote EDEK, but EDEK don't vote for us back, then their people get in and ours don't?' Some AKEL voters told me they didn't obey the instruction to vote EDEK for this reason.

Election day in the village was to be marked by a number of minor incidents, which in nearly all cases, and all of the cases in which blows were exchanged, involved supporters of PF quarrelling with UP supporters. Considering that there were three other parties involved in the elections (and in light of the events already described), it cannot be thought that these incidents were random. Information about how the election passed in other villages of the Nicosia district suggests that such incidents between these two parties' supporters were common.[14]

The first incident set the pattern for the day: the PF activist R. Tangos (a brother of Levendis) watched his elderly mother go into the voting booth, from an outside window. He then saw or thought he saw her fail to mark her slip, and then pop it in the box. He told the voting inspector what had happened and the inspector explained that unfortunately there was nothing he could do under the law. He could not allow the old woman to vote again. Soon there were a dozen of the noisier PF supporters all standing outside the village school, where voting was taking place, shouting. They crowded into the doorway where the officials were, bawling comments and suggestions. They said the inspector should help the old people vote in the way they wanted, and that it was a crime to conduct the elections this way, and that undoubtedly this was happening because the inspector was a UP supporter. The senior policeman in charge, after trying to get them to move away quietly, had a word with an older, wiser Tangos brother, and after a while the crowd dispersed; but not before they had been threatened with a suspension of voting.

They went off down the road cursing and complaining, back towards their own booths.

On the way back, Oligos, a PF supporter in his forties in passing the UP table asked them what sort of dirty work they thought they were up to, rigging things like this? A wealthy young man at the table called out, 'Shut up you traitor.' This proved to be an unfortunate choice of words, and in the context an inexplicable one. Oligos leaped at him and it took several PF supporters to drag him away. The explanation for his extreme rage was uniform on all sides: Oligos had been a leading EOKA activist in the village and had been interned by the British. In prison-camp he was beaten up and suffered permanent damage to one leg. He walks with a pronounced limp and is not capable of full agricultural labour. His applications to the post-colonial government for compensation in any form had all been turned down. For a while he had a low-paid government job but towards the end of 1968 he was laid off and failed to get it back in spite of appeals. His brother Patris was a PF activist not because of any loyalty to Sampson, but because of his connections with PEK and PEK's boss, Azinas. But when Sampson spoke about those ex-fighters who had been denied compensation (p. 250) he was speaking about people like Oligos. Everyone in the village regarded Oligos's case as an injustice, regardless of party views, so when the young man used the word 'traitor' he could hardly have picked a more cruel or inflammatory expression.

Although no one suggested it to me I was aware that close relatives of these two men had been in a fight about six years earlier. Oligos's brother Patris had beaten up the young man's first cousin for saying things to his daughter. But I do not think this played any part in the incident between the two men, which was a flare-up directly related to relations between their two parties, the incident which had just taken place at the voting booth, and the choice of the word 'traitor' to the older man. Persons to whom I suggested this 'past' dispute between the two groups of kin were sure it played no role in the recent one, and were even amused at the suggestion.

Outside the house[15] being used as a PF centre a crowd of people collected who soon heard the details of Oligos's outburst. Since they were now physically separated by twenty yards from the UP table, there were two potentially hostile groups facing each other. Little side arguments were going on between people who had got involved, but after ten minutes the whole thing died down again.

There was no doubt but that PF were conducting the most vigorous campaign all day. Their cars went up and down the road with prolonged honking of horns bringing voters, which no one else did. Moreover they pursued people who were known to be supporters of other parties to the doors of the voting places trying to persuade them. People were literally dragged by the arm (though gently) from the table of one party to PF's table. This caused a good deal of hard feelings among the other party activists and there was much grumbling but no one was inclined to take the matter up.

There were several more incidents during the day between UP and PF representatives, and usually to do with the inspector and the voting system. Otherwise people in the other parties seemed to be on good terms with each other, and not inclined to take the whole thing too seriously.

The Minister of the Interior, Komodromos saw fit when the polls had closed to make an announcement over the radio and television in which he congratulated the Cypriot people on their coolheadedness, peacefulness and level of political maturity. This was explicitly because the elections passed off without major disturbances. Someone in Kalo who heard this announcement over the television commented, 'I wonder what he'd have said if he'd been in Kalo today?'

When the Kalo results came through (pp. 242–5) there was real joy among the PF supporters. A cheer went up which could be heard all over the village. But when the results for Nicosia district were finally clear, the PF were downcast for several days, and lay around outside 'their' coffee-shop in the evenings drinking and brooding. They started to collect and retail stories of the partiality of the electoral inspectors in the towns and how UP supporters in all sorts of branches of government had used their positions to disadvantage PF. My own belief is that these stories are very greatly exaggerated when it comes to the actual voting process, although I am quite sure that before the election the UP used all the government patronage powers at its disposal to persuade people to support it. The important point here is that many PF supporters were developing a set of views in which the UP gained its sixteen seats in the Assembly by illegitimate means. But they also said things which suggested how far this was a rationalization. For instance Pavlos said to me: 'If they had worked in other districts for PF as we did in Kalo, the result would have been very different.'

VOTING: IDEOLOGY AND OBLIGATION

Old men recalling the elections to the Assembly 1920–30 made it clear that vote-buying was common, though even then there were villagers with views they wished to express freely. In the 1940s at the municipal elections in Market Town voters were abducted to stop them going to the polls. In 1970 I heard of no vote-buying or abduction, but several villagers echoed the words of this informant: 'Don't expect much ideology in the village. People here are stubborn and oppose each other wilfully. I can be left, and you right, but I'll support capitalism, the opposite of my true beliefs, just because you are opposing it. Pure personal stubbornness.' In the next pages there will be examples of this kind of behaviour, but the comment needs examining. The man is saying two things at the same time: He points out that villagers have personal relationships which may dominate or swamp other values; but he is also saying that some villagers *do* have other values, not in themselves derived from the village. He is really cautioning us against expecting *much* village behaviour to be primarily (or simply) ideological.

The voting system made it possible for villagers to use their votes in a variety of ways. Since the district elected twelve representatives to the Assembly, each voter had twelve votes, to use as he wished. He could use one, several, or all twelve, for any combination of parties or candidates he chose. The ballot paper consisted of two parties (UP and PF) with twelve candidates each, one (EDEK) with ten, one (DEK) with six and one (AKEL) with two. Some village leaders and activists told me they voted for their own party only; but many other informants told me they had voted for candidates in several parties. Sometimes they did this because they liked or felt obliged to individual candidates while not caring for their parties; sometimes this was a response to cross-pressures from friends and relatives; sometimes they felt a party or person 'deserved' some support although the voter's main loyalty lay elsewhere; and sometimes (AKEL and EDEK) the voter had been told by his party leaders to cross-vote in a certain way.

The informal canvass by PF activists (p. 255) worked through the 740 registered Kalo voters, and marked down 400 as *adiáphori*

K*

indifferent. This did not simply represent women voters, since during the canvass a large number of women were assigned positions, due to the known positions of their husbands, or some other close relative. During this canvass, the principles which the activists used to reach their conclusions were these: old people, the very poor, the illiterate were assumed to be directly influenced by their closest kin, particularly their sons. If there were several sons with different loyalties, it was worth trying to persuade such voters to use a few of their votes for each of the parties their sons supported. Secondly, anyone holding a government job was thought likely to support the UP, unless a powerful man of some other party had got him the job, or his department head or man responsible for his promotion was known to be aligned with some other party than UP. It was argued that since the government and civil servants contain numbers of men who are not the political clients, friends or supporters of Yorgadjis and Clerides, there was always the chance that a person would be working for one such man, and thus have dual loyalties. Thirdly, party leaders, or those who were the close friends, or *koumpári*, of powerful politicians, were assumed to vote exclusively for their own party. During this canvass it was clear that certain individuals were regarded as totally committed to a party, others to be hiding their positions but secretly committed, others to be vacillating, others to be open to persuasion. Since most people I asked said they believed the ballot to be secret, there was clearly scope for people to say one thing and do another. But against this, the voting system made this almost unnecessary in many cases, except where a man was promising all the votes of his kin to someone, when he knew that in fact he would vote otherwise.

Villagers told me that they felt an obligation to vote for a kinsman or co-villager who was a candidate, even if they did not particularly like his party. This was apparent in the 1970 election, where a candidate from the village, Aglas, polled 396 out of 740 votes, 100 more than party average, 55 more than his own nationally known party leader. In Kammari village, next door, he was at least 100 votes ahead of most other PF candidates, and this is probably because apart from being local, he had been active in the Dam campaign (ch. 8). In Kammari the UP candidate Kefiros, born in Kammari, polled 426 votes, 150 more than his party leader Clerides, a nationally known figure.

When village leaders complain that villagers are politically backward, that ideology does not count for much, they are partly right, but partly their complaint is about their own inability to control would-be supporters. Village political culture stresses reciprocity, and village definitions of friendship require mutual help. A man who once helped one's son get a job is a friend, who must be supported when he needs help; if he is an activist, he will be able to call in at least some of the twelve available votes because of his past friendship, if he is a candidate, perhaps more. Also, villagers may give their votes in anticipation of future help, but this like much else, is made uncertain by the secrecy of the ballot, and the ease with which a man can say, 'I voted for you . . .' when perhaps he didn't. The electoral system even took the sting out of the possible conflict of loyalties that would face a man with two patrons, or whose kin put him under heavy cross-pressures.

Sophisticated Kalotes do not readily admit to using their votes for anything else but 'purely ideological' reasons; they have some idea of the rationalizations offered in a democratic system for voting. For some of them, the vote is (among other things) an expression of ideas about how the island should be governed. But I have argued earlier (pp. 122–3) that there is no necessary opposition between ideology and reciprocity, in Cypriot political culture or more generally.

WHAT DID THE ELECTION MEAN?

The elections have been shown to have intensified and defined certain cleavages in village social relations. There were a number of cases where it was clear that the elections forced certain individuals to rethink their alignments, and to demonstrate their positions.

On 1 March 1969 the Sampson newspaper *Máchi* carried lists of names of supporters in the village and other villages who had signed a letter of support to Sampson. There were certain oddities about some names—some were set down two or three times, others were of known leftists, and so forth, Masonos, a leftist with several younger brothers also thought to be leftists had signed. Hearing someone describe him as *dhiploprósopos*, two-faced, I asked the left leader, Sklyros, who said it meant nothing, it was a joke and would confuse the rightists. Little more than a year later there were clear signs that Masonos was now aligned with the PF group in the village—he sat around in their coffee-shop, attended their planning meetings, and in conversation supported their line. Sklyros again said, 'No', he was sure that 'Masonos is an idealist and so stable'; but he added that he and his family are two-faced and since his brother's daughter was married to a younger brother of the deceased Levendis and Masonos was renting a shop next door to this young man's coffee-shop, he was probably pretending to support them to improve his family and business connections. But Sklyros changed his mind three months later when during the elections he saw Masonos energetically working for the PF, trying to rally votes. He told me that clearly his change was not simulated, it was a real change, because he was actually *working* for them. 'He wasn't stable in his support,' Sklyros said regretfully; but this was condemnation, not explanation.

The left also lost the support of Hamilos, to the UP. Once again the final proof was that he was seen working hard for them. This seemed to rule out any notion of feigned support. Both these changes came as a surprise to the leftist leadership. But in other cases the election was merely the formal seal on a situation which had been well known to a number of people for a long time. For instance the position of D. Fanos had started to change as early as 1966 (p. 156). He was then in a state of real conflict, since he was an admirer of Vassos Lyssarides, but saw his career as squarely in the hands of his boss in the Co-operative Department, Andreas Azinas. By the middle of 1967 he had made up his mind in favour of the latter, but did not really get a chance to show this in public until the formation of the political parties in February 1968. The elections were for Fanos a good chance to convince Azinas and the village of the reality of his change of heart. Many people commented that he too, was 'two-faced' and this implies that they have some developed notion of what it means to be one-faced.

For other people in the village the elections were a chance to repay past favours. The fact that ten years had gone by without elections to the Legislative Assembly meant that people had had a long time to find out which political patrons were to be trusted, and which not. I mentioned earlier the case of indecent assault in which a *múktar* was seen to be intervening successfully (p. 69). In June 1970 the two brothers who had applied to him for help for their sister were to be seen working hard for the UP in Kalo, and the *múktar* himself put in a strong appearance at the Kalo UP speech by Kefiros.

Throughout this chapter the struggle between UP and PF has been the dominant issue, as it was in the elections themselves. Both at national and local levels, this struggle must be seen as having two aspects. One is that the PF supporters believe they are 'true Greeks' and true *Enosists*, and that the UP support for *Enosis* is hypocritical. The other is that PF supporters believe UP is well on the way to monopolizing patronage power in the island.

It is important to recognize the ease with which one kind of reason may be expressed in terms of the other, and the logic of the fit here. For if it is true that Makarios's closest advisors—some of whom lead the UP—believe they and only they have the proper approach to obtaining *Enosis*, then it is natural that they should attempt to exclude from power those they believe are irresponsible in their pursuit of *Enosis*. Those who have been excluded readily come to believe that they have been excluded because of their dedication to the ideal, and not because of doubts about their technical skills in pursuing it. Such a situation means that each side must condemn the other in the strongest terms, must suggest the others are hypocrites, traitors in the pay of foreign powers, fanatics and so forth. Because both groups are trying to occupy the same piece of ideological space—that is to monopolize the position of being the sole begetters of *Enosis* they must necessarily fight all the harder to distinguish themselves from each other.

The way in which the Levendis issue has factionalized Kalo (a local issue) expresses the relation of the theme of *Enosis* to the theme of the UP monopoly of power (local and national issues). The deceased Levendis is always mentioned by Sampson as a fallen *fighter* (*agonistís*) which stresses his contribution to the (national) struggle for *Enosis*; that his killer escaped unpunished is laid at the door of Yorgadjis, the former Interior Minister who in this version of events used his power to satisfy his personal whims. Thus the equation implicit in the manipulation of these symbols becomes (local) Levendis: (national) *Enosis* = selflessness and the sacrifice of personal to national interests. This is opposed to Yorgadjis (national office): betrayal of *Enosis* (antinational) = self-interestedness, the betrayal of the national interest for the personal/ local one. Such implications are then easily extended to the *parties* of the chief actors, so that Sampson, the PF leader who survived the death of his (virtuous) follower Levendis, must triumph morally over Clerides, UP leader who survived the death of his (contemptible) ally Yorgadjis.

Clearly, for Sampson to have available as a political resource the memory of a dead fighter is a rather special case. On his own estimate, some ten fighters were killed after 1960 in circumstances which he believes to be political. That is not a very broad base for electoral support. However, from a logical point of view death is only an extreme form of exclusion from power; Sampson has other examples of the United Party's abuse of power to deploy, which may not be as dramatic as a killing, but affect more people more of the time. This is the point of his stories about the families of ex-fighters being neglected. All over Cyprus are people who believe that they made an important contribution to the EOKA struggle which has gone unrecognized by those in power, who have rewarded instead unworthy people, people who 'did nothing' to further the patriotic struggle against the British. Such bitter views threaten to erode the legitimacy of government and civil service in the eyes of a small but vociferous section of the electorate.

Some votes in the village represented personal issues which had been amplified and distorted by the campaigns of national politicians. Others used their votes in the factionalist spirit of deliberately aligning with a party opposed to that of an enemy.[16] However, there were often several reasons for the way a person behaved, as the following case shows.

Kyrilis is an ex-fighter who is widely loved and respected in the village. He is in his mid-thirties, is the youngest of seven popular brothers, most of whom are leftists. I was at a PF planning meeting when people were estimating voting behaviour. When his name arose, someone suggested he would support PF. 'No one knows that for sure. He goes where he likes.' His closest friend, and baptismal *koumpáros*, Pavlos, was present and he did not see fit to contradict the remark, and if anyone could have influenced Kyrilis's vote it would have been Pavlos.

On election day, Kyrilis worked for the PF group. The most compelling reason for this is that he was a close friend of the deceased Levendis. He felt some obligation to support Sampson; but another compelling reason was his deep personal hatred for a certain wealthy villager, over a matter of sexual honour. Over the years this rich man became friendly with several government officials and politicians identified with the Yorgadjis faction. Since in the 1970 elections the UP represented that faction, everyone in Kalo expected the rich man to support UP, and several informed people predicted to me that he would do so and they were right. So his enemy Kyrilis had two reasons for supporting PF, (given that his more ideological views ruled out his support for the left parties AKEL and EDEK) and to this can be added the additional pleasure a man gets when his party and that of his enemy are already at loggerheads. Kyrilis told me that he actually believed the UP's Clerides to be a capable man, while his own PF leader Sampson lacked the qualities for high office. This belief must have taken the edge off what would otherwise have been a perfectly satisfying position.

Personal discontent can easily fit with an ideological attack—indeed, this is what at heart much ideology seems to be about. One of the commonest complaints among the PF group was that while he lived, Yorgadjis (UP) had filled the police force with his own men, that he ran it as he liked, and any friend of his got preferential treatment. During the 1970 elections I knew of at least three Kalo UP supporters who had been successful in getting police cases against them dropped, by working through 'friends of Yorgadjis'. When PF speakers were shouting about 'ten years of corruption', PF supporters in Kalo had some personal examples to bring the charge to life, for they were not 'friends of Yorgadjis', and they said that if the police charged them, they got convicted. To say that the PF supporters would have acted in the same way as UP supporters if they had had influence in the police force may be true, but that did not stop the PF's campaign being stated in terms of 'corruption', 'rule by the worthy' and 'change'.

So far I have been talking about the meaning of the elections in terms of changes of support, and the values involved in the rallying of support. But what did the elections mean for social relations in the village? Among other things they tested the norm of village solidarity, and since this solidarity survived the test, they may paradoxically have served to reinforce it (See Figure 4).

In his Kammari speech Sampson made a very strong attack on the UP. The anti-Clerides demonstration in Market Town which was mounted by Kalo PF supporters came close to starting fighting in the crowd, and at the very least caused Clerides to leave the meeting early. The UP speech in Kalo was again a very tense situation, and although there were no signs of fighting starting, the sense of relaxation and anti-climax after the meeting were some measure of the tension it produced. The incident in which the PF leader Pavlos was so publicly angry over the reporting of

FIGURE 4

Some links between Kalo political leaders and activists, June 1970

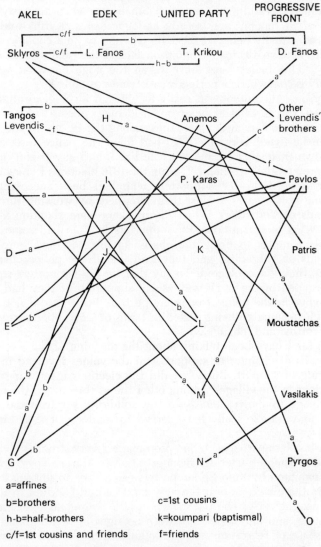

a=affines

b=brothers

c=1st cousins

h-b=half-brothers

k=koumpari (baptismal)

c/f=1st cousins and friends

f=friends

For the sake of clarity links within a party have been ignored;
nor are all the links shown between parties.

a pre-election scrap to Clerides was again an extremely tense one, in which UP supporters had to appear very conciliatory in order to keep him in check. Finally on election day itself, a number of small scuffles and incidents took place between supporters of the PF, and those of other parties, but particularly of the UP because the PF people believed that the electoral process was being manipulated in their enemies' favour. That they kept up this view after the election is important, for it is a possible indicator of the kind of issues which will be raised in future elections.

CONCLUSION

National elections have been rare in Cyprus (pp. 22–3) and in 1970 they put the norm of village solidarity to the test, as elections might do in any solidary community; but where in some communities such elections might leave permanent scars, in Kalo they were handled in a fashion likely to *increase* the future capacity of the village to control the divisive potential of national politics. To explain why the Kalo election results differed so markedly from those at the district level, it was necessary to consider both the *minutiae* of village social relations over a number of years, and also the use of salient issues by national level politicians. Those issues, in turn demanded an historical understanding of the wider Cypriot society.

Since many Kalo villagers strongly supported the PF, I examined the meaning of the PF ideological appeal (which is in essence a blend of populism and Greek nationalism) to understand how the local issue of Levendis's murder could be integrated into a more 'national' platform. Earlier (pp. 52–74) the need of villagers to provide for their children was discussed, and how far education was seen as a path to security; but recently in Cyprus villagers (and Kalo is no exception) had seen the spectre of graduate unemployment. The PF campaign continually stressed aspects of Greek education, and many writers have pointed to the primacy of education and language in support of nationalism.[17] The PF speakers often compared Greek and English university education. They insisted that many English and American universities were not second or third but *tenth*-rate, while those of Greece were 'internationally recognized' as being first rate. Why in that case, they asked, did those whose enthusiasm for Greek language and culture took them to Greece for study, find on return to Cyprus that their degrees could not get them civil service jobs, while those with degrees from inferior English universities, got them?

In fact, English is essential for the better civil service jobs in Cyprus, and English degrees do tend to get preference. But English university education is at least twice as expensive as that of Greece, and few village children (who in any case rarely know English well) can afford the difference. Elite children, who often have English lessons from an early age are normally sent to the U.K., if not for a first degree then for a second.

So having little money, being educated in Greek only, and then having poor job prospects are a pattern, which to those who have experienced it, fits neatly into a particularly appealing ideology.[18] This can be expressed as a syllogism:

True Greeks are excluded from power.
Those in power are not excluded from power.
Those in power are not true Greeks.

There are variants:

Those in power prefer English to Greek.
True Greeks do not prefer English to Greek.
Those in power are not true Greeks.

The same structural experiences do not always produce the same results, because there are competing ideologies. There is the left, offering an alternative critique of the distribution of power, but as has already been noted (pp. 127–30) there are dangers in each option, and these dangers change over time. To further complicate matters, many villagers support the UP not because they themselves have elite characteristics but because they are clients of members of the elite. Their client tie may be the nearest they come to a major stake in the *status quo*; here the logic is, if you must be a client, at least be the client of someone who is powerful in the elite, not someone who is marginal to it.

To explain why villagers act as they do in politics, involves consideration of a range of factors—social origins, wealth, education, job, patron-client ties, kinship and friendship bonds, and last but not always least, conscious ideological alignment. That is, the understanding of village political behaviour involves a range of factors in relatively complex patterns, and perhaps is therefore closer to the situation of more industrialized countries than might at first sight appear to be the case.

The elections showed the villagers, already seen to be both prospering and interdependent—seeking to control the increasing complex intrusions of national politics. The incidents, sometimes involving limited violence, and often involving a great deal of hostility short of violence, showed the political culture of the village in its most exposed state. The elections caused the re-thinking of alignments for many people, and some of the tension involved was undoubtedly because these alignments bear directly on access to key resources—jobs, scholarships, bureaucratic inter-ventions of all kinds. The villagers in seeking to ensure the pro-tection and prosperity of their dependants, face dilemmas of choice which involve calculations of risk, profit and loss of great uncertainty. Precisely because the business of national politics involves linkages and decisions which are far beyond the control of any villager, the decisions are so difficult, and the tensions so great.

Traditionally, villagers competed for scarce resources which were, in the main, in the hands of other villagers, and the rules of their competition were known, derived from the village itself. More recently, political competition has come to involve a set of ever-widening circles, and on their perimeters men make deci-sions of great moment. If the name of a villager is supplied to one of these distant men, placed on or crossed off a list, the villager may lose or gain some critical benefit, in Nicosia, Athens, Prague, Washington or elsewhere. The hostile action is invisible, and without appeal. For this reason, the villagers' hostility is so great to the carrying of tales or retailing of political informa-tion about co-villagers to these outside men. No 'reasonable' man would do such a thing, but not all men are reasonable. Some are 'fanatics' or 'ideologists'. That is why ordinary villagers say, 'Don't get mixed up in (political) parties.' The real crime in the village is not 'having ideology' for any man is entitled to his beliefs. The crime is to take either ideology or more naked forms of self-interest so far as to spoil the village for others.

The village has remained an important arena in so far as some men can be seen to align with national parties to hurt their village enemies, or at least, to express their opposition to or avoidance of them. This kind of behaviour has been widely re-ported, both for the Mediterranean area and for less developed societies. It is, perhaps, the final measure of the fact that in spite of the volume of transactions which flow across its boun-daries, the village preserves some inward moral character.

NOTES

1. The only useful work on these elections is still unpublished, that by P. Kitromilides (1972). The material in Adams (1971) is in addition to its obvious anti-AKEL bias, quite inaccurate, as Kitromilides points out.

2. For example, a government minister who resigned in 1970 to become a UP candidate, explained that at one point he and his associates had considered taking over the right-nationalist farmer's association PEK, but on closer examination had decided not to bother since they had found little or nothing to take over. (E. H. Hammonds, personal communication.)

3. In chapter 7, pp. 140–3, 150–8, Moustachas was again seen intervening in a similar way. This was one of the last occasions his authority went unchallenged, and perhaps contributed to its erosion.

4. Aglas had been a candidate for the Progressive *Front*, the party basically composed of an alliance between PEK and the Mayor of Nicosia. This party had merged, only a few days before, with Sampson's Progressive *Party*.

5. Later in this chapter I shall describe an incident on election day in which a Kalotis, Oligos, got into a brawl with a younger man who had called him a traitor. Oligos was injured by the British during the Emergency, and most Kalotes think he should have received compensation (p. 273).

6. Only Takis Evdokas, the leader of the extreme right-nationalist party DEK publicly attacked Makarios by name during the elections. He was the man who ran against Makarios for the Presidency in 1968, and failed to get more than 6 per cent of the popular vote.

7. Sampson, for example, continually stated that Clerides and Denktash kept no minutes of their conferences, and that the implied reason for this was because they wished to avoid Makarios knowing what they were discussing. In fact their talks are unofficial.

8. Lipset (1960, 1967) has written of the tendency for fierce ideological competition between small parties. 'This divisiveness encouraged by a multi-party system is perpetuated by the tendency of most parties to attack most virulently those with whom they have most in common and with whom they compete for a similar vote, thus magnifying the differences between them' Lipset, in (ed.) Macridis (1967: 65).

9. This comment by Pavlos also was a way of telling Sampson what his father had done, and at the same time, making it clear that his loyalty to PF went as far as persuading his father to change sides.

10. *Poúshtis* means a 'passive' homosexual partner, the recipient. *Poushtissima* is an adverbial form, which is not often used, and sounds to me at least, slightly absurd. Perhaps the best translation would be 'a buggered-up *Enosis*'.

11. A senior civil servant told me the following story, which shows what can happen when a man like Karas finds himself with a powerful patron. My informant on first starting work in the government office tried to get a cup of coffee. His colleagues explained that he could not because Karas, who had the coffee concession was a friend of Yorgadjis, and felt

it was too far to come. My informant called Karas in and asked him for coffee. Karas did not bring it and a row developed, during which he boasted of his friendship with the Minister, and his own readiness to use a gun. My informant's father had contributed large sums of money to EOKA and also has some very loyal employees, so he told Karas to bring his gun at any time, and see what happened. But although this made him feel better, he did not get any coffee. It is interesting to see how far the elite share the idiom of friends, supporters, guns and power; or even if they do not feel committed to the values implied, they need to use the idiom of men like Karas to deal with him. The man in question comes from one of the richest families in Cyprus and is a British university graduate.

12. It is worth mentioning that Pyrgos in fact eloped with Karas's sister, some years ago, and at the time, her brothers were extremely angry and would have done him violence had not mediators intervened. The matter was resolved, but it is possible that such a previous difference helped trigger the dispute in 1970. Pyrgos openly boasts that he has killed men. He is naturally feared in the village. He is a gambler. P. Karas is a gymnasium graduate, and a full-time farmer; although unmarried he works his own land, a very rare situation in the village.

13. In September 1970 Sampson told me that he had had no advance notice of the Market Town demonstration, and added that he had often stopped his Kalo supporters from doing various things, so that now they probably did not always tell him in advance what they were thinking of doing in case he stopped them. Yet in telling me this and other things, he made it clear that the toughness and readiness to do such things were characteristics he admired in young Kalotes. But in other ways Sampson has shown himself to be moderate (or cautious) in public. For instance in Kalo, 1969 he made a speech (p. 238) denouncing the murderers of Levendis Tangos. From the crowd a friend of Levendis called out, 'We'll shoot them.' 'No,' replied Sampson. 'Bring them to Justice.'

14. I do not mean to suggest that there were no violent disputes between other parties elsewhere. In fact there were a number of fights between AKEL supporters and right-nationalists, in various parts of the island. In the villages which surround Kalo I heard of no such incidents. It seems likely that disputes between right and left would be more likely in villages where the non-left were represented by one major party, instead of being distributed fairly evenly between several nationalist parties.

15. The house of the village priest. The use of this house was regarded by other groups as typical of PF cunning, since they argued the older women in the village would be unduly influenced into voting for the PF. In fairness the priest's house is very close to the school, and ideally located.

16. Similar behaviour is described by Stirling (1965: 280–2) Boissevain (1965: 128) and Cohen (1965: 146–73).

17. My argument here owes much to Gellner (1964: 147–78) and to Inglehart and Woodward (1967), particularly to their notion of the important relation between language dominance and blocked mobility. I have also received stimulation from Clive Kessler's work in Malaya.

18. Michael Attalides (personal communication) believes that I have taken the PF's definition of itself as a party of the under-privileged more seriously than it merits. He points out (i) that Sampson has patronage powers outside the government—e.g. in Army circles, and that (ii) since the death of Yorgadjis, the UP's hold on patronage was certainly weakened (iii) that O. Ioannides, an ex-mayor of Nicosia later became a Cabinet Minister. This is perhaps the difference in my village-based perspective, and that of someone in the capital. On points (i) and (ii) facts are scarce.

11
Conclusion

In one sense my book comes close to being a sociological confidence trick, for it has concentrated in unrelenting detail on issues
which in village life occur but rarely. Most villagers, most of
the time go about their lives with other things than politics on
their minds; they would be the first to point out that to stress
political discord is to stress the bizarre, the unwanted, the exotic.
They would approve of the analysis when it shows them successfully coping with the divisiveness of modern politics. But they
would have preferred a description of their everyday lives, in the
way they see them themselves as a community 'without politics'
in which apart from a few natural minor upsets over land boundaries and marriage arrangements, everyone gets on with everyone else. And this is all a casual visitor would see, on a normal
day.

But politics is not about the everyday, but rather about the
more basic questions of how in the long run men organize their
social world the better to deal with difficulties of daily life. It is
therefore about certain values and actions which may only become apparent in situations of crisis and discord. Hence the
paradox that in order to describe how villagers control political
disruption we are forced to dissect the rare occasions when they
almost failed to do so.

Two themes have dominated the book. One concerns the impact of modern political ideologies on village life, and the other
concerns the organizational tactics villagers employ to extract
benefits from the political and administrative sectors of the wider
society. The two themes obviously depend on each other; in
few words, modern politics offer certain benefits, but they are
uncertain, and to be had sometimes only at the cost of one man
being set at the throat of another. How can a man obtain the
greatest benefits for the least cost?

These themes are implicit in many recent books about politics in developing nations. It has become commonplace for village greybeards to recall an Arcadian state 'before politics came and spoiled things' and often the notion of politics is so odd that some variant on a European word is used. Not wishing here to prejudge the meaning of social change by using the idioms of political development I found myself asking some fairly bald questions about just how modern politics affected villagers. First, did the villagers get anything out of the new situation? Secondly, what did it cost them to get whatever they got? Thirdly, were there any particular new people who came to the fore, or did leadership remain unaltered? Fourthly, could one guess at how villagers perceived the new relationships that representative politics and modern government brought to them? Fifthly, could any overall changes for the village as a whole be detected? Sixthly, did new rules emerge to deal with new situations?

Cutting across these questions were other issues to do with the relation between private and public interests, between local and national community, between actions and forms, between long- and short-term advantages, between precise calculation and uncertainty.[1] Here it was not so much a matter of having specific questions to ask—for these issues are well worn—but rather of having a set of preoccupations which guided analysis.

SELF-INTEREST, SOLIDARITY AND UNCERTAINTY

The village has been increasingly affected by economic and political processes in the wider society, and much of the material in this book shows men trying to strike some balance or calculate where their advantage lies in weighing their commitment of resources (which include beliefs)[2] between the wider society's agencies, and those of the village. Most villagers do not have complete freedom of choice; they are constrained by their relative wealth, literacy, their special relationships with powerful people, their readiness to use force, their natural or learned abilities to speak persuasively. They readily perceive that certain things which they seek, such as land, and the good opinion of their fellow villagers in the marriage market, are not usually available through politics, in the sense of commitment to agencies outside the village. In the main hard work, thrift, and an honourable life are the most direct routes to these desirable goods. However, there may be short cuts, and here lies the element of greatest uncertainty.

Most villagers appeal to an ethic of *synféron*, self-interest, to express the belief that their first and greatest loyalty and guide-line in the allocation of scarce resources is to their immediate dependants. Yet self-interest can be hard to calculate. Jobs, scholarships, and various bureaucratic decisions can sometimes be secured by relations to politicians or political agencies, but it is very difficult to know when this commitment will deliver the goods, and when it will in fact make the applicant worse off.

This is because political commitment (the public support of a party or person by a villager) in some ways runs counter to an important village norm, the norm of village solidarity. The norm is a general one, but with important areas of imprecision. In one form it is the dogma that Kalo village is the best village in Cyprus; in another it is that Kalotes do not allow themselves to be divided by the fanaticism of party politics; in another it is that violence of all forms within the village should be prevented; in another it is that a man would be insane to quarrel with his relatives over politics; in another it is the injunction 'don't get mixed up with the parties'; in another form, it is the deliberate definition of areas of activity as 'non-political'; in another it is the statement that certain areas must not be coloured by party politics.

These varied normative statements are of course social actions of a substantive kind when they are made in everyday situations (as opposed to being made in response to an anthropologist's question). They are all ways of saying the same thing: the members of the village have certain obligations to each other which should not be weakened or threatened by commitments to out-siders. Party politics is the one 'outside' activity which offers a man *both* the prospect of concrete benefits *and* a set of values different from and in no way derived from village values; pre-cisely because these two powerful factors combine in politics, politics are seen as dangerous, a threat to important aspects of village social life. Villagers look on politics with a Wildean realism which says that men can resist everything except tempta-tion. The pull of politics is so great for some men that there must be control rules to limit political competition. The norms of solidarity just listed are precisely such control rules.

Rules for control do not always work, the existence of norms does not prevent deviation. Furthermore, they are not free-floating—the anthropologist must show cause why such rules exist. The notion of a compact village or face-to-face community *necessarily* producing such norms can be immediately dismissed, for there are enough examples of such villages which far from being face-to-face would be better characterized in Srinivas's words as back-to-back communities.³ Violent factionalism in Indian villages is commonplace. Mediterranean villages which are compact yet tolerate the feud. It is clear that the existence of cross-cutting ties is not enough to prevent violence within the compact community, although they may hasten mediation when tempers have cooled. We can be fairly sure that a unilineal descent principle, the existence of castes or clear-cut classes of haves and have-nots all provide excellent bases for continuous violent conflict *within* the compact small-scale community; and other predisposing factors may be found.

So if a village has an operating and efficient norm which states that violent conflict should be restrained, this norm needs a two-part explanation: why did it emerge, and why does it persist? My answers to these questions are simple but not I trust the less valuable for that. In Kalo the norm emerged and persists because most of the villagers see their futures as linked to that of the village as a whole. Most of them have a continuing stake in the village, and have seen things getting better for a long time. The village remains a key point of both moral and economic reference. It remains the place where they expect their main satisfactions, and they believe that certain kinds of actions are only likely to make things worse all round. They are here behaving like members of a corporation, and it is not unreasonable to see the village being valued in the same way as men might value their descent group in another society.

But the existence of norms, rules of thumb, do not tell men how to act in all circumstances, and their interpretation offers a good deal of leeway for manipulation and uncertainty. Consider the problem of those villagers with strong commitment to a political party. As a general principle, it is probably true that the stronger a man's proven commitment, the stronger the likelihood of his being rewarded. There are times in a man's life when certain benefits not available within the village are badly needed for the good of his dependants. These might be the times when he is tempted to forget or set aside the village solidarity rule, and involve himself politically in a way which will later invite criticism within the village. The villager who carries tales to his urban patron about the political views of his fellow villagers takes such a risk. If he is detected, his all-round acceptability in the village will be tarnished. If he gets away with it, his village status may be increased, for he may have succeeded in living up to other village norms, about the successful provision for one's dependants. The vital job, scholarship, or bureacratic decision may have been secured, and this is a 'success against the world', something which puts the recipient above his fellow villagers.

This then, is the dilemma for every villager, when faced with the political agencies of the wider society: how much will be asked of him, at what price? Once the left looked strong, later the right, today the centre. Who can be sure how long the political memories of the urban leaders will last? Perhaps the best thing is to have no opinions or commitments, keep all options endlessly open until the hour of greatest need. Then at least one can throw oneself on a great man's mercy and say, 'I have never belonged with anybody. There is nothing written against me in any book of the right or of the left. Now in my hour of need I have come to ask you a favour because you are the only person who can help me.'[4]

In general the more secure a man is economically the more he can afford public political alignment and take the consequences. The poorer he is the more such an action looks to him like a dangerous luxury, and the hedged bet looks the best bet of all.

SOLIDARITY AND STABILITY

It is worth asking what are the actual mechanics of preserving village solidarity? Here the implication is that village leaders are taking fairly conscious steps, to achieve a considered aim. They may have more personal, or more long-term aims than that of preserving the peace of the village; the point is that they imagine the future implementation of these aims as needing a peaceful village.[5]

Sheer repetition of the norm, particularly in crises, is one obvious device, particularly if this is accompanied by a deliberate separation of men who are fighting, with fierce injunctions to both sides. With such leadership activities goes the deliberate use of mediation between men who are violently angry with each other. In such situations, village leaders may invest much time and energy in delicate negotiations to ensure that neither man 'will be crazy enough to do anything to his enemy'. Successful mediation enhances a man's authority.

Another device is the deliberate avoidance of all-out contest over local administrative elections. The fact that right and left wings in the village have managed to do this is not strong evidence itself, for at the national level there have been continual appeals for unity among Greek political parties, and a degree of apathy in administrative elections is common. It is only when such behaviour is viewed within the villager's definitions of politics that it becomes decisive. For the villagers define the administration of the village as 'unrelated to politics', at the same time they adopt a principle that to avoid administration becoming political, the best solution is to allocate committee positions to both left and right, to avoid contested elections, and to get on with the job. The paradox is apparent: the definition of politics is a village device for *controlling* political conflict. Here it is worth remarking that certain fashionable structuralist approaches to linguistic categories appear to run the risk of setting language free of any important social action, in such a way that social change would be impossible to pin down. The definition of politics used by the villagers is required by critical social processes, and we can predict that if social relations change, the category 'politics' will change too; but the categories cannot be understood without prior analysis of social relations.[6]

The issue of village solidarity like any other norm can be the object of a political tug-of-war, and become a tactical weapon. This was apparent in the way the former EOKA leader in Kalo prevented a richer, much better educated man from founding a social club for secondary school graduates. Mass education and the economic changes in the larger society have brought into the village basic differences in skill, and in values. Traditional authority in the village went to men with the power to enforce their wishes, and the EOKA leader had been such a man. The 'new men' were men who believed in educational qualifications, bureaucratic criteria, and negotiation to get things done. A social club for secondary school graduates would have *institutionalized* (and so made symbolically explicit) a cleavage in village life which could otherwise perhaps be ignored. The EOKA leader was able to demonstrate traditional authority by simply saying he thought the club would become 'political'. His success showed that the 'new men' had not yet won the day. Some kinds of social change can be kept at bay by a vigorous denial of their existence. The EOKA leader was providing in a political action that the village 'had not changed', and his ability to apply the 'old' rules was proof of this.

The same two men met again over another issue which involved manipulation of the solidarity norm. Here, the volunteer

nil

militia was faced with a village hostility because of beliefs that funds raised by village-wide subscription had been misappropriated by militia members. The militia leaders accepted (or perhaps instigated) a co-ordinating committee to act as liaison between the militia and the rest of the village. On this committee the same 'new man' was again prominent in applying criteria of bureaucratic rationality to the problem. Furthermore, the committee explicitly included leftist leaders, in order to ensure that the entire village should be represented in the process of keeping the militia accountable, under the guise of 'liaison'.

Perhaps the final device involved in preserving village solidarity is best seen as the action of the self-fulfilling prophecy. Since the norm of solidarity is used in the tactical struggles for advantage of individuals, as well as in actual crises where a serious breach is threatened, the norm is continually on men's lips. Repetition in a climate of successful conflict control thus serves, in my view, to enhance the potency of the norm. That is, nothing succeeds like success: every time the villagers manage to turn away wrath by deploying the norm of solidarity, they increase the chance of being able to do so on the *next* occasion. Should they fail on a single occasion, this can be dismissed as an exception, because of all the times when the evidence went the other way. The importance of the norm lies in its continual invocation, and its *relative* success. That success is a matter of the villager's definitions and perceptions; for example, the Lyssarides affair (pp. 150–8) brought villagers very close to violence which would have involved political groups. In a village where the tradition was one of intransigence and violence, this dispute might have easily spilled over into bloodshed, or might have been defined as 'typical' rather than 'exceptional'.

This argument should *not* be taken to suggest that the villagers *will always succeed* in controlling conflict. It merely suggests why they are *relatively* likely to succeed in controlling the *next* threat of violence. A number of factors could alter the structural inducements to compromise: a higher rate of outsiders marrying into the village; an increasing number of relatively poor families emerging; an island-wide economic recession of some severity; the institutionalization of a rigid class system; an all-out war between left and right in the island, and so forth.

However, the argument about the self-fulfilling prophecy does raise a theoretical issue of some importance: Gluckman (1968b) has reviewed the issue of determining structural change and of

L

the use of the notion of equilibrium. He intends these concepts to be of use in analysing institutions and large-scale systems. But there are difficulties in deciding what the tendency is in a village, or indeed if a social system can be in Gluckman's sense abstracted from a village at all.

There are three logical possibilities. First, a tendency towards an increased solidarity—a success spiral would be an appropriate metaphor. Secondly, a continuation of the existing level of solidarity. Thirdly, a tendency towards increased cleavage. Whether the continuing appeal to a norm of solidarity is a case of the second or third seems to me beyond decision. It is easy to see what is happening at the extremes. Movement from some putative midpoint in one direction or the other is much more difficult to determine.

It is reasonable to suppose that a particular village moves in one direction or another largely as a result of a particular historical occurrence, which then becomes the basis for a norm. This does not rule out the importance of predisposing factors such as the strength of cross-cutting ties produced by economic, affinal or ritual interdependence; it suggests however, that structural factors alone will not determine the limitation of political conflict. The actions of particular individuals, and the consequent use of such actions by their incorporation into norms, will play an important role.

The settlement of the dispute between the two rival water companies (pp. 27–8, 42) was an historical incident which might have set the Kalotes off on the path of compromise, although in that case a decision was handed down. Clearly the traditional village was closer to what Durkheim meant by mechanical solidarity. We cannot know if conflict was more intense or more frequent than it is now, but clearly it was *different* for then it was essentially pre-ideological, that is, conflict within a common frame of values. The tantalizing question remains unresolved: have the rules villagers use to control conflict under present conditions of organic interdependence, emerged only recently? Or are they in fact traditional devices, now operating in a new environment?

This question requires a distruction between types of conflict in the village. To the villagers conflict between individuals, particularly between close kin is unfortunate but 'natural' if about property. Conflict over social reputation, or the arrangement of marriage is in the same class. These types of conflict are subject to informal rules, are open to mediation, and may be modified by those ceremonial opportunities which normally occur in family life—engagements, weddings, baptisms, funerals. These conflicts rarely involve those outside the close kin of the initial disputants, and are not seen as affecting the overall condition of the village.

Conflict over politics, whether between individuals or political groups, is regarded with profound disquiet by villagers, as something varying between the unnatural and the downright stupid. If it occurs it must be controlled. But the rules for its control although generally acceptable are not agreed by all, for it is in the nature of some political ideologies that genuine accommodation with an enemy is undesirable or impossible. Normal control rules do not restrain 'fanatics', hence the common village denunciation of 'fanaticism'.

POLITICAL CULTURE: REPRESENTATION AND DEPENDENCE

The villagers have had highly varied experiences of national politics over the last fifty years. They were granted rights to elect *múktars*, and Members of the Legislative Assembly by the British Government, but these were withdrawn after the 1931 Uprising. Fifteen years later, elections and parties were again allowed, but the 1955 EOKA insurrection again dramatically altered the development of representative politics. Since 1960 when representative institutions were again restored, there has been a continual situation of crisis government, which has hampered electoral experience. All this uncertainty and change it might be thought has done little to persuade villagers that they can direct the political life of their republic through the ballot box.

Given this background, what can be said of the way the villagers perceive and respond to the new resources of representative government? To answer this general question, I shall consider aspects of how villagers treat with government and politicians and their use of leaders.

The campaign of five villages to expediate the building of a dam would seem, at first sight, to be a classic example of political development, in which a regional interest group lobbies at the centre for its particular needs. This would be misleading, a consequence of seeing the form, a planned, orderly demonstration as a unit of action with the same meaning that it might have in a different culture. A demonstration can have many meanings. It can be a show of power, a serving of notice on a government to quit, a challenge to traditional authority, and so forth. In so far as it is possible to extract a key characteristic from a demonstration, the one described at the Presidential Palace was none of these things, but rather, a plea for attention to those in power. It was only secondarily, and for few of the participants, a calculated use of a new resource.

The other demonstration described was one in which certain young Kalotes first carried placards against a powerful politician, and later interrogated a candidate during his election speech. Since in 1970 it was still very uncommon for villagers to ask questions of political candidates, or to heckle them, these exhibitions of novel behaviour might again have struck an observer seeking 'political development' as steps towards Western parliamentary systems.

Yet an understanding of the particular events behind these acts would modify such a view. The young men involved were friends or relatives of a villager who had been murdered some years earlier. In Greek traditional culture, vengeance killing is preferably carried out by men who do not have wives and children to support. But the growing power of the modern state makes vengeance killing a costly luxury, and if powerful men can use the offices of state to protect murderers, it would be rash for a few villagers to confront their enemies head-on. Yet traditional values of honour and self-respect will not allow a man to do nothing in revenge. Thus, the actions of certain young villagers in national elections were to be understood by their attempts to redress the balance of blood debts. They supported the party leader who revered the memory of the dead man, and they attacked the party which was tainted with his blood; the fact that they used the devices of representative politics to do this should not obscure the local, particular and traditional objectives they held.

In talking about 'villagers' as if they were all the same, the issue of leadership retreats into the background. But as I have been at pains to show, the village has produced a variety of types of leaders, some pre-eminent in internal matters like agricultural administration, and others who are allowed to lead in matters of external relations. Here there is a key issue, that of literacy. The political framework introduced at Independence involving a constitution, universal suffrage and other rational bureaucratic procedures was of course an advanced form of certain tendencies encouraged by British colonial rule. However, although educated, sophisticated urban leaders were quick to exploit the changes brought by Independence, in the village these changes were less clearly understood. Suffrage does not automatically confer consciousness of citizenship rights and villagers do not learn overnight to distinguish the rules governing political roles among those in power. These remarks apply equally both to the way villagers behave during election campaigns, when they often fail to interrogate political speakers, and to the same actions at the A.G.M. of a citrus co-operative, for in both situations what is needed is a confidence in and understanding of one's rights and procedural rules. To many villagers an established civil servant and an elected representative are more alike than different—both are men with power, to be treated with extreme caution and deference. The best approach is retreat—avoid them altogether; the next best course is to approach them with the idioms of dependence, of clientage on one's lips, or to find another man who can speak up for you.

The villagers permit their own educated sons to lead them in the following situations: if leadership involves personal risk; if it involves matters of bureaucratic complexity; or if the interests of leaders and the other villagers are seen to be the same. Often several of these factors come together in a single situation when for example a villager needs to deal with a high-status government official. Shaky literacy, peasant speech and the insecurity of being responsible for a dependent family in a hostile unknowable world all make it hard for the villager to speak out. To criticize an official policy looks like a personal attack on the man who represents it. To question an official or politician is to risk becoming a marked man, or less serious to risk simply looking a fool for saying the 'wrong' thing. Public and private roles are not distinguished. Better by far to let a wealthy educated son of the village, who 'knows how to speak', take up matters.

In the absence of a recent feudal or latifundist tradition and with the knowledge that customary norms will work against the more blatant forms of betrayal, villagers can leave their affairs in the hands of the elite the village has produced, with a limited measure of trust. Contrary to Banfield's well-known speculations on 'amoral familism', the pursuit of self-interest, can permit relations of limited but effective co-operation, when the parties can agree that they have common interests, and when each is free to contract-out at will.

However, there are two conditions to be met for a man to become a prominent leader in external relations. One is that he is economically independent, and this includes not working in an organization where he might be subject to sanctions from above; the other is that he is properly literate. In structural terms relatively few men fulfil both criteria. Too many civil servants who have the competence in reading and writing, feel vulnerable to possible pressures from their superiors. Too many farmers, whose land might give them the economic security, are at sea with the language of bureaucracy and power. In the last analysis villagers are overly dependent on a few people. This is evident from the way in which the same man, Vourros, has featured in key positions throughout the political affairs of Kalo. It may be that in this instance the village was fortunate, but this must be something of a historical accident. Clearly I cannot say if a man with different views would have been given an equal amount of support, but the present political culture of the village suggests that it will be some time before less wealthy and independent villagers emerge who are ready to replace men like Vourros.

I have stressed the structural peculiarity of the village—the relatively even distribution of land, the absence of a rural aristocracy, the low rate of emigration etc.—because this community cannot be taken as typical of what is going on elsewhere in developing countries. Cyprus is so wealthy that Europe is a better standard of comparison than the third world; it is a small-scale republic with few communication problems, and Kalo village is one of its richer communities, in easy reach of the capital. Kalotes have had from the last half century a variety of experiences which lead them to be cautious about seeking too much from politics; in contrast, they have had in economic matters an experience of steady (and more recently, dramatic) improvement. I do not think they consciously relate economic prosperity and predictability to the growth of modern government, and they still set cautious limits to the use of national politics in village life. Their two contrasting experiences, and their choices may both be unusual. Elsewhere, in the many countries where rural peoples see their lives as getting harder and harder, it will not be surprising if they turn to politics for that certainty and security denied them in their economic life.

NOTES

1. For an excellent discussion of rationality and uncertainty in decision-making, see Ortiz, (1973).

2. Needham (1972) has examined problems in the notion of belief at length, It need hardly be said that political beliefs present almost intractable problems for analysis, hardly less severe than those related to religious beliefs.
3. Quoted in Bailey (1965).
4. For a fictional account of a similar action, see Puzo (1970: 27–32).
5. Cf., Spiro (1968).
6. Ardener (1971) has done his best to drive a wedge between what he insists are two incompatible approaches to analysis; but his short-sighted syntagmatic 'functionalist' is an obvious straw-man, and this seriously undermines the rest of his argument. By blowing the trumpet too loudly, he risks deafening his listeners, or simply driving them away.

Appendix 1

Method

The first point is a little unusual. I have a number of close kin in 'Kalo' because my father was born there. This made it possible for me to be classified as a *chorianós*, fellow-villager (although a rather odd one) by the Kalotes. I was however born in England and grew up there speaking only English and living entirely within English settings. I heard no Greek and my only knowledge of Greek culture came from taking Classical Greek at 'O' Level, G.C.E. My first visit to Cyprus was in 1966, where I failed to learn more than a few words of Greek in six weeks. Later, after discussions of the problem with Professor Raymond Firth I decided to try fieldwork in Kalo, being prepared to move to another village if the dual roles of kinsman and fieldworker proved incompatible, which they didn't.

The major period of fieldwork, my second visit to Cyprus, was from February 1968 to May 1969 which included two short breaks together lasting a month, in Israel. Two more visits to Cyprus were made in December 1969, returning January 1970, and from May to June in 1970. This last trip was made the more productive since I was able through the generosity of the Nuffield Foundation to bring with me a friend and colleague who is a political scientist, Edward Hammonds, and from his vantage point in the capital he gave me many helpful insights into the elections described here.

One day I hope to write something about the peculiarity of my situation as a fieldworker. For the moment it is enough to point out that when I reached Kalo in 1968 my spoken Greek was so halting and my cultural distance from the Kalotes so great that I was in the usual situation of the novice fieldworker. My great advantage was that there were a number of people in the village who felt a real obligation to help me in my work in so far as I made it clear to them what it was I wanted. Having heard from other fieldworkers of the difficulties of getting information from Greek villagers, I realize how very privileged I was. The most obvious disadvantage for my work was my tendency to overconform to the expectations of the Kalotes, but this seems to happen to many anthropologists.

My quantitative work included taking genealogies from some thirty of the oldest men and women; a small survey on aspects of citrus cultivation and marketing; and a sociological census of 200 male household heads. This was intended to cover all of the 318 households in Kalo, but I underestimated how long this would take and after ten weeks of the census, pressures of time prevented its completion. No formal sampling procedure was employed for the 200 selected, since I expected to cover the entire universe, but there is no reason to think the sample seriously misrepresentative. It covers aspects of kinship, marriage, land tenure, work, economics and politics. Lastly, from these 200 men I formally interviewed in depth a further 24 on kinship, economic co-operation, disputes, and patron-client relations.

The troubled years of Cyprus's Independence, and the military coup in mainland Greece (April 1967) made me cautious about seeking material on politics, and many Kalotes were equally cautious in providing it. I used no formal system for limiting the extent of my inquiries, but a rough-and-ready rule of thumb: not to seek interviews with politicians or civil servants, where there was any reason to think that by so doing I would draw undue attention either to the village itself or to my research. This may have been over-cautious, but it seemed at the time the sensible thing to do. It does point to an inevitable weakness in the material: it is too reliant on information derived from villagers (including those resident outside the village) and is thus to some extent a village-level view of events which must be incomplete. More information from national politicians, and senior civil servants would have been most useful.

However, I made frequent trips with villagers outside the village, particularly with village committees when they went to petition in the capital. I also had sophisticated contacts in the capital, including senior civil servants who were able to fill in some gaps, or correct my perspective.

Appendix 2

The Turks of Kalo

In this book I do not consider the Turkish community in Kalo, for several reasons. First, they were a tiny group, which during my fieldwork seemed to play little part in village life; secondly, since the political climate was delicate, it seemed to me not in the best interests of the Turks to single them out for special attention, or even to take too great an interest in their position. I collected information about them as it occurred in normal conversation and with certain trusted informants, sought more detailed information. I took genealogies from several Turkish men.

Nevertheless, some comment on them, however incomplete, is necessary. The most striking fact about the Kalo Turks is the decline in their numbers since 1891, in contrast to the gradual increase of the Greek population. In 1891 there was 1 Turk in Kalo for every 3 Greeks. In the 1960 Census, this ratio has dropped to 1 Turk for every 18 Greeks. During the same period, the national ratio of Turks to Greeks had changed from roughly 25 per cent:73 per cent (1881) to 18 per cent:80 per cent (1960) so the Kalo change is out of all proportion to the relative decline in the proportion of Turks to Greeks. Kalo Turks themselves explain the decline in terms of many of their numbers having married out. However, villagers also told me that numbers of younger Turks left Kalo during the intercommunal disturbances of 1964-5 and went to the Turkish enclaves in the towns. In 1968-70 there were almost no Turks in Kalo between the ages of fifteen and forty-five, with the exception of a school-teacher (an outsider), and one young man of dull intelligence. Although I did not carry out a census of the Turkish residents, I am reasonably sure that their numbers were lower than the 72 recorded in 1960. There were about twenty adults; in all cases they seemed to be rather poor. As might be expected, they took a very quiet, passive role in Kalo affairs, and at various points in the thesis, I mention incidents which involved them (see particularly, the first two cases in chapter eight).

The UN Police made patrols to the village roughly once a month to make sure the Turks were not in difficulties. Occasionally, Turks resident in the Turkish enclaves visited the village to see kin, tend to property and so forth, and I saw them cordially greeted by Greek villagers on a number of occasions. But as I mention in chapters one and eight, there have been episodes where individual Greeks attacked the persons or property of Kalo Turks and one factor which probably has contributed to the decline of the Kalo Turkish population has been a feeling of insecurity in face of the increasing and prospering Greek population.

Nevertheless, the Turks of Kalo seemed very much part of the Greeks' consciousness, and not always in a negative way. Numbers of older Kalo Greeks spoke some Turkish, and had had economic relations of all kinds with Turks both in and out of the village. During my fieldwork several Kalotes went to a Turkish wedding in a mixed village some fifteen miles away, and the leftist leaders in Kalo in particular did small favours for Kalo Turks, to show their goodwill.

The Greeks, however, also have a 'foundation myth' about how the current situation came about. It is roughly this:

> In the time of our great grandfathers Kalo was a Turkish village. The Turks owned all the land, but they were lazy. They had Christians working for them as labourers, a few at first, then more. The Turks would pay them by giving them a piece of land here, another piece there—poor land of course—but bit by bit the Christians saved up, and then brought in women, got married, worked hard and made their women work hard and bought more land. Eventually they bought up nearly all the land from the lazy Turks who neither worked themselves nor let their women work. And that's how things came to the point they are today . . .

Slender support for the view that Kalo was once a predominantly Turkish village (in spite of its Greek name) is supplied by Papadopoulos (1965) who published the *djizé* tax records for 1825–6. These show Kalo as having '27 + 2' payers of the *djizé* tax, paid by adult non-Muslims. Although it is not clear who qualified as an adult, and thus had to pay tax, the suggestion is that the Greek population was much smaller than 329 recorded in 1891. However, it gives no guide to the size of the Turkish population. The earliest school returns from the 1880s show more Turkish than Greek girls at the elementary school, and old people were firm in their insistence that Turkish women did not work in the fields when they were young (about 1920). They were working in the fields in 1968, however.

One other notable event must be mentioned. Old people remember that in 1914 three Kalo Greeks were sent to prison, one for ten years, for burning a Turkish coffee-shop in the village. This was apparently triggered, they say, by a speech made locally by a mainland Greek nationalist agitator, Katalanos, and followed the hostilities between Greece and Turkey in 1912–13. This does not seem to have been followed by any marked decline in numbers of Kalo Turks (1901: 104; 1911: 97; 1921:101). I have no information for what caused the decline to 68 by 1931.

Appendix 3

Land, Irrigation, Cultivation

In chapter two the importance of summer irrigation to the village was discussed. One result of the new irrigation, starting in the 1920s was that the villagers continually increased the area of village land under intensive cultivation. Even in 1968–9 men were still developing dry, rocky land (*kavkálla*) by trucking loads of rich earth to it, and then irrigating the new earth layer from underground water. Older men had used donkeys, and their own backs, in place of bulldozers and trucks.

Unfortunately, the actual extent of the increase cannot be gauged with great precision. The Report and General Abstracts of the Census, 1931 gives the following information: there were 3,231 *donums* of arable land—about 1,000 acres. The 169 *households*—three more than listed as complete in the 1931 census—had between them 118 oxen, 193 donkeys, 11 mules and 3 horses. Sixteen persons had less than 5 *donums* and 21 persons had no land at all, but I assume that by *persons*, married householders were meant. Thus, at very least 27 of the 169 households had less than enough land to live on. Some clue as to how at least 15 per cent of the households survived without enough land is given by Table 3, p. 30. If all persons who did not return 'farmer' as their occupation in the 1923–35 data are added, the total is 42 per cent. The listing of unskilled labourers (*ergátis*), shepherds, muleteers and artisans suggests how they lived. If the 3,231 *donums* had been divided equally between 169 households, this would have given each household nearly 20 *donums*. The 1931 data show that 15 per cent of the households fell a long way short of 20 *donums*, and it is a reasonable interference that the whole 42 per cent who were not farmers also fell short of 20 *donums* (a figure adequate for bare subsistence.)

The 3,231 *donums* in the report present a problem of interpretation, since what is meant by arable land is not explained. It might have been land irrigated in summer, but it might have been land used through winter rainfall only. Since very roughly one hour of water from the merged water company would have generously watered one *donum* every fifteen days, the conclusion is that there was roughly ten times more 'arable' land than available summer water; it is therefore more probable that the arable land refers to land put under cereals from winter rainfall.

By 1950, when Christodoulou (1959: 205–6, 216–17) included Kalo in his land-use study, the village ranked highest of 27 sample villages for the extent of its summer irrigation, with 81 per cent of its land so irrigated. The method cannot have been through powered pumps, for only 1·1 per cent of the agricultural land is listed as mechanically irrigated; the chain-of-wells method which had started the original water company in 1916 had been employed by several other companies to give some water to most village land. However, the crop figures suggest a strong continuity with traditional agriculture: wheat accounted for 24 per cent of land under cultivation; barley and oats another 19 per cent. The other main crops were: cumin and aniseed 13·3 per cent; food legumes 8·8 per cent; and potatoes 8·5 per cent. There were also about 2,000 olive trees on village land.

By 1969, when the village tax lists were consulted, the picture was this: 4,529 *donums* of irrigated land were taxed within the village boundaries, and all but 278 *donums* were owned by persons resident in the village. Village residents also paid irrigation tax on between 300 and 400 *donums* of land in the boundaries of some adjoining villages, bringing the total to nearly 5,000 *donums* of irrigated land. The total village land was reckoned to be 6,500 *donums* in all, within the tax boundaries of the village.

The 1931 and 1950 data do not make ⹂certain issues of boundaries and land categories clear, but the general picture suggests a great deal more land came under irrigation since 1931. The population of the village more than doubled between 1931 and 1960, but in this period the area of irrigated land increased by two-thirds of the 1931 figure. During the latter part of this period too the use of fertilizers, later of tractors, and of trucks to take produce to larger markets were altering the pattern of agriculture. Yet, as is shown by Table 3, the proportion of household heads employed as full-time farmers fell from 58 per cent to 41 per cent. In real numbers, with adjustments for population increase, the picture is different again. The 58 per cent of 166 household heads in 1931 would have yielded nearly 100 farmers. In 1969 there were 318 households, and extrapolating 40 per cent of these would give over 120 farmers. This brings some of the data into perspective, and can be restated thus: the larger population was cultivating more land in 1969, and although the *number* of farmers probably increased, the *proportion* of farmers was smaller.

Appendix 4

Land, Work, Family: Five Examples

When villagers describe a man's economic position, they usually express it in terms of his land holding, and the number of children he has. Since this in many ways is more helpful than simply saying that family X today has 5 *donums*, and family Y has 10 *donums*, I have tried approaching the problem of land holdings viewed over time, by the matrix in Table 17.

The matrix shows land holdings at maximum of 82 families married between 1931–50, expressed against the number of children in each family who will draw shares from the family holding. The effect of looking at land-holding data in this way is to estimate the future portion a child may expect to receive.

The matrix shows that some 27 families should be able to give each child more than 6½ *donums* at marriage; another 18 families should give from 4 *donums* to 6½ *donums*; and 37 families will have from 0 to 3 *donums* to give each child.

Such tendencies depend on a number of assumptions—that each child receives roughly the same amount as its siblings, that both sexes receive equal amounts of land, and that the family does not lose its holding through some unforeseen disaster. The point here is to approximate, in formal terms, the villagers' way of discussing wealth in land. In brief, and to avoid labouring the point further, they see it as relative to the number of dependants and future beneficiaries; and they see land holding in a context of time, rather than as a static fact: they are less concerned with or impressed by what a family has, than what its children will have at marriage.

The reader may now like to consider five examples of Kalo households. There are a few households worse off than (a) in that they have no land at all, or many more children. There is no household better off than (e) in Kalo; Vourros in Nicosia has half as much land, but three children. Note that (a) and (b) have not managed to buy more land, and this is common among land-poor families. (c) who is a farmer has bought more land, to add to his household's 30 *donums* at marriage, but (d) who has a full-

TABLE 17

Land at maximum and number of children of 82 households where first marriage of heads occurred between 1931 and 1950

Number of children

Land in donums	0	1	2	3	4	5	6	7	8	9	10	11
51+				E_2	E_2	E_2	E_1	E_3	M_1	M_1	M_1	
26–50			E_2	E_5	M_3	M_4	M_1	M_1	P_2			
16–25	E_1	E_1	E_7	M_1	M_1	P_5	P_3	P_4	P_2	P_1	P_2	
11–15	E_1		M_1	P_2	P_1	P_2	P_1	P_2	P_1	P_1		
6–10	E_1/M			P_1	P_1	P_1		P_1		P_1		P_1
1–15				P_1	P_1	P_1						
0								P_1				

E—Elite, more than 6½ donums=27
M—Middling, 4-6½ donums=16
P—Poor, under 4 donums=39

This diagram does not represent actual shares of land received, but rather, probabilities of approximate shares

time civil service job has not added to his 21 *donums*. At the moment (c)'s three children can each expect 15 *donums* at marriage, three times more than can each of (d)'s four. It is worth pointing out that with irrigated land valued in 1968 at £350 per *donum*, a man would need either a steady salary, or to mortgage land, before he could take on the large debts of long-term citrus cultivation.

(a)   MAKRIS, A POOR LABOURER (CENSUS NO. 125)

Makris is 64, his wife 58. They have five children, and some would say it is a good thing they don't have more, for Makris himself received from his own parents no land at marriage in 1936, his family being one of the poorest in Kalo, and his wife, who provided their home, had only three and a half *donums* of good, irrigated land, and five of poor, un-watered land.

Makris has never bought any land; he has worked as an un-skilled labourer all his life, he works as one today, and his income is irregular. His wife also works, doing paid agricultural labour. He says, 'What we get, we spend to eat.' In 1959 he married off his oldest girl, and managed to give her 6 *donums*, and a modest house.

In spite of this, in 1965 he planted 180 citrus trees, and by 1972 he can expect £90 a year from them; but the trees will in fact be a vital part of the dowries for his 25- and 23-year-old daughters, when grooms are found for them. The elder finished primary school only, and works as a wage labourer whenever she can, about the village. The younger finished secondary school and works in the Market Town office of a Kalo merchant; Makris's unmarried son is ill and cannot work.

Makris did manage to educate his oldest son who now has a salaried white collar job in Market Town, for he managed to get a technical degree. Makris hopes this son will help a bit towards the marriage of the girls, but this will have to be done discreetly, lest his son's affines protest. By the standards of men in the poorer mountain or plains villages, Makris would not be considered really poor, although in Kalo he is described as poor by most villagers.

(b)   PSYLOS, A SEMI-SKILLED WAGE WORKER (CENSUS NO. 88)

Psylos is 48; since his marriage in 1944 his wife has given him 7 children, of whom 5 are still unmarried. She also brought 10 *donums* of land to the marriage. He himself brought no land to the marriage, and has never managed to increase the land holding. He left school at 14, worked for two years as a kitchen boy in Nicosia, then for three years in the General Hospital as an assistant cook; later he had his own small café but in 1944 joined the Army, and worked until 1948 in the

Officers' Mess. At present he is a cook in the Mining Hospital on the coast, and this brings him a steady salary of nearly £1,000 a year. He gets a further income of £500 a year from 168 orange trees he planted in 1955, and from which in 1968–9 he cut 100,000 fruit. His debts at the moment are: £1,030 from expenses in marrying off his second daughter; £200 to the Agricultural Credit Society for farming costs; £25 to a villager for water; £16 to the truck co-operative in the village; £15 for fertilizer; plus a commitment of £10 a month school fees for his twelve-year-old daughter who is going to a private commercial school.

Psylos has married off two daughters, one aged 22, the other aged 18; he has given them a total of 6 *donums*, and is still building the house for the second; at home he has a 20-year-old son, who finished Technical School and works as a mechanic for the Mining Company; a 16-year-old son, who also finished the Technical, and works an an electrician; a 14-year-old son, still at the Technical; the 12-year-old daughter already mentioned; and a 10-year-old son at the primary school. Since he only has 4 *donums* of land left, which yields valuable income, he will not be in a position to give any land to the three oldest sons; it will probably go to the 12-year-old girl when she marries. The sons have their trades to help them find wives with a little land and at least are not unskilled labourers. Fortunately Technical School education is free; by most standards Psylos, thanks to his steady income from two sources, has been able to marry off his children reasonably well. His daughters have married young so his honour is intact. For a man who started life with so little land, he has managed to escape the major pitfalls. He cannot be called, in village terms, a very successful man; but nor can he be called a failure.

(c) KANDIS, A SOLID FULL-TIME FARMER (CENSUS NO. 30)

Kandis is 42; he got engaged at the relatively late age of twenty-seven, and married two years later, in 1956. From his parents he got 22 *donums*, and his wife got 8 from hers. This unusual ratio between his land and hers is partly explained by the fact that he has done a number of prison sentences, one of four years, usually for theft.

He settled down after marriage, added another 14 *donums* to his already substantial holding, by purchase. The 44 *donums* will be divided between only three children. The oldest, a girl of thirteen, at secondary school, has a younger sister of nine, and there is a baby of four months. Kandis does not plan to have any more children and the spacing of them is suggestive.

Although as a single man he did some labouring jobs, in the early 1940s, since marriage he has been fully occupied with his land holding. Like most farmers, he has debts, but is cheerful about them, and says, 'I can't sleep at night if I'm not in debt.' The £2,500 he owes is split into £300 to the village Credit Society, for fertilizers; £500 to the import agent for an irrigation pump; Kandis sells water from this pump at 10/- an hour; this debt is for repairs, since the pump was recently damaged; and £1,500 to the Co-operative Central Bank to fund his recent land purchases. In 1955, when he started to drill for the underground water he now enjoys, the debt was £3,000.

He planted 300 orange trees in 1955, another 300 in 1960, 220 in 1963, and in 1965 a massive 1,100. In 1968 he was receiving income from 600 of these trees, but was still cultivating 1,300 of them without income.

His land purchases have paralleled his citrus planting; 1955, 7 *donums* for £500; 1960, 3 *donums* for £900; 1968, 4 *donums* for £1,300. In each case these new plots joined other pieces of land he already owned, making their cultivation economically more efficient.

If Kandis buys no more land, each child will expect roughly 15 *donums*, putting them among the elite of Kalo. Kandis's outgoings will increase if he decides to give the children higher education. As things stand, they will be able to choose between education (keeping their land and having it worked by others) or being farmers. In spite of his material success, Kandis is a firm leftist.

(d)   PATTAS, A CIVIL SERVANT WITH GOOD CITRUS HOLDINGS
       (CENSUS NO. 143)

Pattas is 34; his wife brought 14 *donums* to their marriage, as well as the customary dowry house. Pattas, tall, well-built, personable and intelligent, himself received 7 *donums* at marriage, and his personal attributes more than make up for his smaller portion of land. He has put all 21 *donums* under citrus, in four plantings: 400 trees in 1958; 220 in 1961; 420 in 1962;

140 in 1968. His current debt stands at £2,500. But he grossed £2,000 from his citrus trees in 1968, so he is not concerned.

One reason he has done so well is that since 1955 he has had regular work as a prison officer; his salary of £650 in 1968 was about to rise to £850. This helped him finance the earlier planting of his land, and the situation is now economically independent. He can, if he chooses, expand his holdings. He has four children, and plans not to have more.

He drives a four-year-old English saloon that he bought second hand. His house cost £3,000 in contract labour and materials, and in it he has a radio, a refrigerator, a modern gas stove and a washing machine.

In 1961 he put down £500 towards a tractor, and his brother, a farmer, put £100. The brother then used the tractor to plough both their holdings, and also to plough those of other men, for profit. Pattas stated that the accounting system is informal: whenever the tractor needs repairs, each brother pays a half.

He has just bought two shares of £75 each in a new co-operative company which will sink a bore hole for underground water.

Pattas is typical of an emergent elite in the village, who have profitable land which handsomely subsidizes their other occupations. Other members tend to have more formal education than Pattas (to have finished the secondary school) but his wealth, life style, urban white-collar job and good political contacts make up for this deficit. His sister has married a veterinary doctor, he has a younger brother at university in Athens, and a younger sister who is finishing secondary school.

(e) PATRIS, A WEALTHY FARMER (CENSUS NO. 148)

Patris is 47, and typical of the old elite, except that he made an exceptionally fortunate marriage. He came from a well-off and respected family, and received 12 *donums* from his parents. The woman he married was the adopted daughter of a childless man who, though a farmer, had become rich in land through money-lending to other villagers. The girl had five years elementary schooling, and was then engaged to a pharmacist in Market Town. This would have been a most prestigious match in the early 1940s, when few daughters of the village had married men of such status. But the engagement was broken off by the man.

Patris was tall, handsome, strong, and had finished elementary school. The match was arranged, and the girl brought a massive 120 *donums* of land to the marriage. From her family's point of view, it was better to save face with a worthwhile young man from the village, than to wait for another high status outsider, and risk further humiliation. In 1946, when they married, tractors were rare in Cyprus, and the young couple would have more land than they could work anyway, so Patris's unequal portion of land did not matter.

Patris was one of the first men in the village to buy a tractor, which he did in 1947, 'by halves' with the brother of his wife's mother. Later he bought another 12 *donums* of land and he gives use of some land to relatives. There are 5,000 citrus trees which keep him and—since 1953—a full-time labourer completely busy.

His current debts are between £5,000 and £6,000 to several banks, and the Agricultural Credit Co-operative Society. In 1968 he received £4,000 gross from citrus, carrots and potatoes, of which he estimates some £2,000 as profit. In 1968 he was still increasing his citrus plantations, intending to plant 20 *donums* with seedlings.

The one cloud on his horizon is the fact that his seven children are all girls. The first one has married a young civil servant from the village, and Patris gave her 17 *donums*; her husband had no land. Patris was persuaded to take her away from secondary school to make the match, but plans to give the other girls more education. Two are studying in Greece, at universities, and their expenses are £900 a year; the four girls at secondary school need together a further £900 a year, he estimates. This estimate is on the high side, poorer families manage both types of education more cheaply.

Patris is one of the most prominent political figures in the village, being on several committees, and the local representative of PEK, the National Farmers Union.

Appendix 5

The Social Origins Of EOKA Militants

My source for this material is Papachrysostomou (1969). Although 229 persons are listed as having fallen, these are spread over six categories, of which I have here considered only (i) 68 persons 'killed in action' (ii) 9 persons 'hanged' (iii) 9 persons who 'died under torture'. I have ignored the 50 persons 'killed by Security Forces', the 79 'slaughtered by the Turks' and 15 persons who were accidental fatalities. My reason for this distinction was a concern to examine the backgrounds of persons who could be assumed to be EOKA militants and not merely victims of the emergency. Obviously there are further problems with such an approach, for example, the possibility that those militants killed were socially different from those not killed, on the lines of 'other ranks' and 'officers'.

Papachrysostomou gives certain social data for the 68 men 'killed in action'.

By occupation		by education		by age	
schoolboys	16	primary education	41	under	
craftsmen	12	secondary education	24	20	17
farmers	13	university graduates	2	20–30	39
clerical (*ipállili*)	7	illiterate	1	30–40	11
various occupations	13				
labourers	4				
scientist	1				
school teacher	1				
housewife	1				
	68		68		67

There are a number of difficulties here. The 24 men of secondary education might have contained a number who would have gone on to further education. The breakdown by occupation suggests that at least 16 of them were still attending gymnasium when they were killed.

Another problem is the meaning of the 13 persons *Epangel-matíai Diáphoroi*, which could mean either 'different occupations' or 'different professions'. My own analysis of the data Papa-chrysostomou provides in his short biographies of the dead men (1969: 10–30) suggests he has used the classification for a number of cases where no information was available.

There are difficulties in the interpretation of the origins of the men, in terms of an urban/rural classification. Six of the 86 (6·3 per cent) in the three classes I examined (68+9+9=86) were born in one of the six major towns of the island (Nicosia, Fama-gusta, Limassol, Larnaca, Kyrenia, Paphos). But Michael Attalides (personal communication) on a preliminary examination of some data he has collected, believes that throughout the century, a high proportion of urban residents have themselves been born in villages. And obviously place of birth is not in itself sufficient indication of elite or non-elite status. In 1946 77·4 per cent of the island's population lived outside the six major towns, though this figure had fallen to 63.6 per cent by 1960.

One final difficulty is that there are a number of intermediate communities, which can be regarded as country towns, or over-grown villages. They may have 5,000 or 10,000 residents and are referred to as *komópolis* in official publications. They some-times have municipal authorities, a doctor, a gymnasium and so forth. My own view is that in terms of elite status, residence in a *komópolis* counts for little.

The highly qualified picture which emerges, then, is that the EOKA militants killed were probably similar in general social characteristics to the general population. They do not seem to have been at all skewed in the direction of the urban elite; but very many of them were of rural origins, and becoming up-wardly mobile through secondary education.

Works Cited

ADAMS, T. W. *AKEL: The Communist Party of Cyprus*. California: Hoover Institute Press, 1971.

ALASTOS, D. *Cyprus in History*. London: Zeno, 1955.

ANDERSON, J. N. D. 'The Family Law of Turkish Cypriots', *Die Welt des Islams*, pp. 161–87. Leiden: N.S. Vol. V, nr 3–4, 1958.

ARDENER, E. 'The new anthropology and its critics', *Man*. N.S. Vol. 6, No. 3, pp. 449–67, 1971.

ATTALIDES, M. A. *An analysis of urbanism in Cyprus with special reference to Nicosia*. Nicosia: Department of Town Planning and Housing, 1970.

BANFIELD, E. C. *The Moral Basis of a Backward Society*. New York: Free Press, 1958.

BENEDICT, B. (ed.) *Problems of smaller territories*. London: Athlone Press, 1967.

BAILEY, F. G.
  (1) *Politics and Social Change*. Berkeley: California University Press, 1963.
  (2) 'Decision by consensus in Councils and Committees' in ASA 2 *Political Systems and the Distribution of Power* (ed.) Banton, M. 1965.
  '3) *Stratagems and Spoils*. Oxford: Basil Blackwell, 1969.
  (4) (ed.) *Gifts and Poison: the politics of reputation*. Oxford: Basil Blackwell, 1971.

BARTH, F. *Models of Social Organization*. United Kingdom: Royal Anthropological Institute, 1966.

BOISSEVAIN, J. *Saints and Fireworks: religion and politics in rural Malta*. London: Athlone Press, 1965.

BROWN, R. and GILMOUR, A. 'The pronouns of Power and Solidarity', in (ed.) Sebeok, T. A. *Style in Language*. Massachusetts: MIT Press, 1960.

BROWNING, R. *Medieval and Modern Greek*. London: Hutchinson, 1969.

CAMPBELL, J. K. *Honour, Family and Patronage*. Oxford: Clarendon Press, 1964.

CAMPBELL, J. K. and SHERRARD, P. *Modern Greece*. London: Benn, 1968.

COHEN, ABNER. *Arab Border-Villages in Israel.* Manchester, University Press, 1965.

CRICK, B. *In defence of politics.* London: Weidenfeld and Nicolson, 1962.

CHRISTODOULOU, D. *The evolution of the rural land use pattern in Cyprus.* London: World Land Use Survey, monograph 2, 1959.

CYPRUS BLUE BOOK. 1909–10.

CYPRUS GAZETTE. CO 456, 1881.

CYPRUS GAZETTE. 1883–4.

CUTILEIRO, J. *A Portuguese Rural Society.* Oxford: Clarendon Press, 1971.

DAHRENDORF, R. *Class and Class Conflict in an industrial society.* London: Routledge and Kegan Paul, 1959.

DAVIS, J.
    (1) 'Honour and politics in Pisticci'. United Kingdom: Proceedings of the Royal Anthropological Institute, 1969.
    (2) *Land and Family in Pisticci.* London: Athlone Press, 1973.

EPSTEIN, A. L. *Matupit: land, politics and change among the Tolai of New Britain.* Canberra: ANU Press, 1969.

FIRTH, R. *Essays on Social Organisation and Values.* London: Athlone Press, 1964.

FOLEY, C. *Legacy of Strife: Cyprus from rebellion to Civil War.* Harmondsworth, Middlesex: Penguin, 1964.

FRANKENBERG, R. *Village on the Border.* London: Cohen and West, 1957.

GELLNER, E. *Thought and Change.* London: Weidenfeld and Nicolson, 1964.

GLUCKMAN, M. 'The utility of the equilibrium model in the study of social change', *Am. Anth.* Vol. 70, pp. 219–37, 1968.

GRIVAS, GEORGE. (ed.) Foley, C. *Memoirs.* London: Longmans, 1964.

GRIVAS-DIGHENIS, GENERAL GEORGE. *Guerilla warfare and EOKA's struggle* (translated by A. A. Pallis). London: Longmans, 1964.

HARBOTTLE, M. *The Impartial Soldier.* London: Oxford University Press, 1970.

HENDERSON, R. N. *The King in Every Man.* New Haven: Yale University Press, 1972.

HILL, SIR GEORGE. *A history of Cyprus:* Vol. 4. Cambridge University Press, 1952.

INGLEHART, R. and WOODWARD, M. 'Language conflicts and the

political community', *Comp. Stud. Soc. Hist.* Vol. X, pp. 27–45, 1967.

JENNESS, D. *The Economics of Cyprus.* Montreal: McGill University Press, 1962.

KENNA, MARGARET E. *Property and ritual relationships on a Greek Island.* (Ph.D. thesis, University of Kent) 1971.

KITROMILIDES, P. *Patterns of politics in Cyprus.* (B.A. thesis, Wesleyan University, U.S.A.) 1972.

KYRIAKIDES, S. *Cyprus: Constitutionalism and crisis government.* Philadelphia: University of Pennsylvania Press, 1968.

LEGG, K. R. *Politics in Modern Greece.* Stanford: Stanford University Press, 1969.

LEYS, C. (ed.). *Politics and change in developing countries.* Cambridge University Press, 1969.

LIPSET, S. M. 'Party systems and the representation of social groups' in (ed.) Macridis, R. G. *Political Parties: contemporary trends and ideas.* New York: Harper, 1967.

LISON-TOLOSANA, C. *Belmonte de los Caballeros: a sociological study of a Spanish town.* Oxford: Clarendon Press, 1966.

LOUDON, J. B. 'Teasing and Socialisation in Tristan da Cunha' in (ed.) Mayer, P. *Socialisation: the approach from Social Anthropology.* ASA 9. London: Tavistock Publications, 1970.

MAYER, A. C. 'The significance of quasi-groups in the study of complex societies' in (ed.) Banton, M. *The Social Anthropology of Complex Societies.* London: Tavistock Publications, 1966.

MARKIDES, KYRIACOS. 'Colonialism, Modernisation and Revolt in Cyprus'. (unpublished paper).

MORIN, E. *The Red and the White.* New York: Pantheon, 1970.

NEEDHAM, R. *Belief, Language and Experience.* Oxford: Blackwell, 1972.

ORITZ, SUTTI. *Uncertainty in Peasant Farming.* London: Athlone Press, 1973.

PAINE, R. 'In search of friendship: an exploratory analysis of "Middle-class" culture'. *Man.* Vol. 4, pp. 505–24, 1969.

PAPACHRYSOSTOMOU, CHR. *Archeion Pesonton.* Nicosia, 1969.

PAPADOPOULLOS, TH. *Social and Historical Data on Population, 1570–1881.* Nicosia: Cyprus Research Centre, 1965.

PERISTIANY, J. G. (ed.).
(1) *Honour and Shame: the values of Mediterranean society.* London: Weidenfeld and Nicolson, 1965.
(2) 'Introduction to a Cyprus Highland Village' in *Contribu-*

tions to Mediterranean Sociology. Paris—The Hague: Mouton, 1968.

PITT-RIVERS, J. A. *The people of the Sierra.* London: Weidenfeld and Nicolson, 1954.

PUZO, M. *The Godfather.* London: Pan, 1970.

Report and General Abstracts of the Census of 1931. Nicosia, 1931.

RUEL, M. *Leopards and Leaders: constitutional politics among a Cross River people.* London: Tavistock Publications, 1969.

SHENIS, J. *Provincial and local administration in Cyprus in comparative and historical perspective.* (New York University, Ph.D. thesis), 1962.

SPIRO, M. E. 'Factionalism and politics in village Burma' in (ed.) Swartz, M. J. *Local-Level Politics.* 1968.

STEPHENS, R. *Cyprus: a place of arms.* London: Pall Mall, 1966.

STIRLING, P.
  (1) 'The domestic cycle and the distribution of power in Turkish villages' in (ed.) Pitt-Rivers, J. *Mediterranean Countrymen.* Paris: Mouton, 1963.
  (2) *Turkish Village.* London: Weidenfeld and Nicolson, 1965.

STORRS, R. *Orientations.* London: Weidenfeld and Nicolson, 1939.

SURRIDGE, B. J. *A Survey of Rural Life in Cyprus.* Nicosia: Government Printing Office, 1930.

SWARTZ, M. J. *Local-Level Politics.* Chicago: Aldine, 1968.

TARROW, S. G. *Peasant Communism in Southern Italy.* New Haven: Yale University Press, 1967.

TSOUCALAS, C. *The Greek Tragedy.* Harmondsworth, Middlesex: Penguin, 1969.

VINCENT, JOAN. 'Anthropology and political development' in (ed.) Leys, C. *Politics and change in developing countries.* Cambridge University Press, 1969.

WATERBURY, J. *The Commander of the Faithful: The Moroccan political elite.* London: Weidenfeld and Nicolson, 1970.

XYDIS, A. G. 'The Military Regime's Foreign Policy' in (eds.) Clogg, R. and Yannopoulos, G. *Greece under Military Rule,* Secker & Warburg, 1972.

Index

Adams, T. W., 286
affinity, 63–84, 166–9, 217; affinal co-operation, 74–6
Aglas, xvi, 176–209, 223–4, 244
agriculture, 6, 25–31, 41–2, 44–62, 145–6, 178; mechanization and village solidarity, 102
AKEL (communist party of Cyprus), 13, 15, 18, 20, 119, 122–33, 150, 235, 238; compared with other parties, 239
AKRITAS plan, 174 n.4.
Alastos, D., 23
Anderson, J. N. D., 24
Ardener, E., 301
Attalides, M., xi, 203, 288
azádes, 105–6, 149
Azinas, Andreas, xvi, 157, 158–62, 167, 210–33

Bailey, F. G., xi, 11, 103, 104, 138, 175, 230, 301
Banfield, E. C., 299; see also self-interest, *synféron*
Barth, F., 5, 85, 99
Benedict, B., 209
Boissevain, J., 138, 287
Brown and Gilman, 86
Browning, R., 138

Campbell, J. K., xi, 18, 23, 55, 62, 63, 65, 74, 86, 102, 138, 175; and Sherrard, 18, 23
capital, agricultural, 45–51, 56–61, 310–16
change, 25–41, 41–2, 289–300
Christianity, see Church
Christodoulou, D., 43
Church, 15, 36–42, 87, 124, 130; opposed to left, 36–42; – Committee, 37–8, 106–7
CITCOP, 101, 177–8, 208, 210–233
citrus, 6, 25, 28, 56–61, 101, 211, 210–33, 310–16; see also CITCOP

Civil Service, 18, 113, 185–90, 231, 276, 283–4, 297–300; EOKA's influence in, 17
Clerides, Glafkos, xvii, 20, 21, 174, 199, 237, 235–88; election speech in Market Town, 259–62; role in 1970 elections, 235–88
clientage, 8, 44–6, 85–94, 156–7, 167, 258, 267, 276; see also patronage, friendship
Cohen, A., 11, 103, 287
Colonial Government, 13, 14, 23, 35
Committee, Advisory, 177, 190–209, 215, 231
Committee, Carrot and Potato Association, 104–15, 158–62, 169–174
Committee, Co-operative Store, 104–115, 131
Committee, Co-ordinating, 145–50
Committee, Credit Co-operative, 104–15, 131, 166–74
Committee, Irrigation, 104–15, 169–174; and dam campaign, 176–209; elections for, 169–74; of Market Town, 176
Communist party, see AKEL, left-wing
cousins, 66–70
Crick, B., 6, 11
Cutileiro, J., 2

dam, 9, 176–209
Dahrendorf, R., 208
Davis, J., xi, 54, 62, 138, 208
debt and credit, 27, 28, 32, 56–61
DEK, 238, 286; compared with other parties, 239
Denktash, Raouf, 20, 251
Dhaskalos, xv, 135, 140–50, 150–8, 192, 195, 196, 211, 214
domestic group, 63–84; developmental cycle of, 70–4, 310–11
Durkheim, E., 296